Dear Barbara —
All my best!

PRAISE FOR *ONE SIZE NEVER FITS ALL* AND ARIN REEVES

"Dr. Reeves has proven herself as a pioneer on advancing women in the workplace. She has shifted the conversation beyond recruiting and retaining women to focus on understanding how the one-model-fits-all approach to business development should change to help drive gender equality in professional services firms. I see her book as a blueprint for women (and men) to better understand, define and create new business development strategies for themselves and their organizations. *One Size Never Fits All* is a must-read for women in advertising, an industry that is a traditionally a one size fits all, competitive model."

—*Debbi Vandeven,*
Global Chief Creative Officer, VML

"Warren Buffet has partly attributed his success to the fact that he was only competing with half the population. It's time for us to pull the other half of the population in so that we can all reach higher heights. Arin Reeves has provided a compelling tactical guide on how to do this—a guide for women in business to compete effectively. She has dug deep into the behaviors and business systems that hold women back in professional services businesses, and she offers a brand-new way of thinking about the problems faced by women in firms. She challenges the 'one size fits all' prescriptions for successful rainmaking and offers research and case studies for alternative approaches that individuals and firms can employ to diversify their business development approaches. This book offers women and companies the first practical guide of its kind to bringing talent off the sidelines, and its lessons on team approaches to business development extend well beyond women and professional services."

—*Anita Antenucci,*
Senior Managing Director, Houlihan Lokey

"Can women be successful rainmakers? Reeves says 'yes,' and clearly explains how through her research, the science of gender differences pertinent to business development, concrete strategies—and her basketball shoes. This is the book for firms that want to develop more business. This is the book for women who are frustrated and tired of wearing someone else's shoes as they try to develop business. And, this is the book for men who want to understand why the women who read this book and implement the strategies are climbing to the top of the compensation and leadership positions (i.e., money and power)."

—*Catherine Lamboley,*
General Counsel, Shell Oil Company (retired) and
Leader-in Residence, Center for Women in Law,
University of Texas Law School

"*One Size Never Fits All is* the best business book I've read all year. It goes straight to the heart of one of the most complex and seemingly intractable issues derailing women on their climb to the top. The stories and new research are compelling, making this a go-to resource for leaders and companies who want to win."

—*Terry A. Barclay, President and CEO, Inforum*

"Dr. Reeves artfully balances intuition, empirical data, and pragmatism to make a compelling case for the need of today's leaders to embrace a radically different mindset and approach to leading through inclusion and by seeking many different perspectives in search of all the right answers and solutions to a problem and not simply selecting one 'right answer' to solve the problem. This is exactly the type of mindset needed within DuPont to maximize the growth opportunities that exist in the 'developing markets' throughout the world."

—*Thomas L. Sager,*
Senior Vice President and General Counsel,
DuPont Legal

"Dr. Arin Reeves's new book, *One Size Never Fits All*, may be the most important analytical and strategic consideration of one of the thorniest issues facing professional services firms in the 21st century—how to facilitate effective business development by all of its partners or principals, especially women. With this book, Dr. Reeves continues to cement her reputation as one of the most data-driven and avant-garde strategists of our times. She has transcended her long-held role as a premier researcher and consultant on traditional talent management issues, progressing first into the realm of visionary, inclusive leadership with her book *The Next IQ,* and now into business development—the backbone of financial success. Dr. Reeves's focus is how professional services organizations can effectively create and support business development practices that may be outside of the box, but more suitable and effective for women (and some men). In tackling that challenge, organizations can augment their future growth, ensure their financial stability, and open the door for more robust leadership by female professionals. For women, this book is affirming and encouraging. For firm leadership, it provides a blueprint to address a significant challenge. As Dr. Reeves herself stresses, 'data as a tool for change is empowering.' Through her well-grounded use of empirical data and her pragmatic strategy, Dr. Reeves empowers both women and men to go beyond historical vehicles for business development, and challenges them to look at new and more universally effective paradigms. This book is an absolute 'must read' for both the leadership and partners/principals of professional services firms."

—*Sandy Chamblee,*
Chief Diversity Partner, Steptoe & Johnson, LLP

"Dr. Arin Reeves is someone whom I have long considered the leading mind addressing issues of diversity and inclusion in the legal profession. But...Dr. Reeves has transcended the legal profession to squarely establish herself among today's foremost executive management and international business thought leaders. And she does so with great stories and practical exercises to put the ideas into action."

—*Veta T. Richardson,*
President & CEO, Association of
Corporate Counsel

"In her new book, Dr. Reeves brings great clarity and depth to the challenges that exist for women in developing business for professional services firms. She has introduced a solid road map for navigating these obstacles for female (and male) professionals, and she introduces a new way of thinking for firm leadership. Firms that employ these new ideas can create cultures that attract the best talent and create platforms for different profiles to be successful in developing new business. Her book is a must read for any professional tasked with creating new revenue for his or her firm."

—Lori Stanovich Tucker,
Senior Manager, Business Development, Deloitte
Financial Advisory Services

"Generalities no longer suffice when it comes to diversity and inclusion initiatives in professional service firms. Firm leaders, firm members and diversity professionals need specific, concrete, focused research that can support game-changing initiatives. Arin Reeves's new book provides just that — on a topic of critical importance. Arin dissects firms' failure to create inclusive conditions for women's business development and leadership with humor, common sense, and illuminating original research. Her affirmative contributions to changing the face and practices of modern professional service firms are truly valuable and much appreciated!"

—Sally Olson,
Chief Diversity Officer, Sidley Austin LLP

ONE SIZE NEVER FITS ALL

BUSINESS DEVELOPMENT STRATEGIES
TAILORED FOR WOMEN (AND MOST MEN)

ONE SIZE NEVER FITS ALL

DR. ARIN N. REEVES

Printed in the United States of America.

18 17 16 15 14   5 4 3 2 1

Cataloging-in-Publication data is on file with the Library of Congress.

ISBN: 978-1-62722-489-5

Discounts are available for books ordered in bulk. Special consideration is given to state bars, CLE programs, and other bar-related organizations. Inquire at Book Publishing, ABA Publishing, American Bar Association, 321 N. Clark Street, Chicago, Illinois 60654-7598.

www.ShopABA.org

DEDICATED TO

eric
caelan
miles

IN REMEMBRANCE OF

loved ones whose legacies live on
through each of us

CONTENTS

ABOUT THE AUTHOR

Arin studied business at DePaul University's College of Commerce, attended law school at University of Southern California and received her Ph.D. in Sociology from Northwestern University. As a researcher, a writer, an "attorney in recovery," and an advisor to many organizations on various aspects of gender equality, Arin has traveled many paths in the journey of advocating for women to be valued for who they are and the amazing gifts they contribute in workplaces of all types. Her first book, The Next IQ: The Next Level of Leadership for 21st Century Leaders, focused on cognitive biases in the workplace and how organizations can identify and interrupt these individual and institutional cognitive biases in order to maximize the potential of all talent in the workplace.

Arin is the President of Nextions, a new way of seeing and doing leadership and inclusion. Prior to her work in consulting, Arin practiced law and served as an Adjunct Professor at Northwestern University for several years where she taught classes on law and society. She has led research studies on women in leadership, gender differences in work-life balance expectations/experiences, generational differences between women in workplaces, and many aspects of women's equality, empowerment and collective success. Arin has been featured on NPR for her work on gender in workplaces and is cited often in online and traditional media as an expert in leadership and inclusion in workplaces. Her column "Diversity in Practice" was recognized by the Herman Kogan Media Awards for excellence in journalism. She also serves on the Boards of Directors of several civic and not-for-profit organizations.

Arin lives in Chicago with a husband who is as funny as he is cute and two children who teach as much as they learn on a daily basis. She is an avid amateur photographer and has been "outed" in the *Wall Street Journal* as a professional addict of all things politics.

INTRODUCTION

"IT'S GOTTA BE THE SHOES"

I played basketball in junior high school. I was not the best on my team, but I played well enough to be a starter, and I consistently put up at least a few points during every game. In eighth grade, at the last home game of the season, I went to my locker to suit up when I realized that my shoes were gone. I looked everywhere for them as did several other players, and the shoes were nowhere to be found. Maybe it was a prank. Maybe my shoes had been stolen. Maybe I had misplaced them. As all of these various alternatives raced through my mind, I realized that the important issue I needed to focus on—pranks, thieves, and absentmindedness aside—is that I did not have shoes for the game.

My coach asked the other players if anyone had an extra pair of shoes with her. A couple of players did—one girl with size 6 shoes and another with size 7.5 shoes. I was a solid size 9. No one was available to bring me another pair of shoes from home, so trying to get a different pair of my own shoes was not a viable option. I could either try to play in the 7.5 shoes or sit the game out. I chose to play in the 7.5 shoes. (I did ask if I could play barefoot, but that was not an option according to the rules!)

I put on the size 7.5 shoes and was initially surprised that they didn't hurt that badly . . . if I curled my toes in just a little. I walked out with my teammates and even warmed up for a few minutes with relatively little pain. My coach asked if I was okay to start. I said yes. She looked at me skeptically, but she let me make the decision.

Approximately four minutes into the game, I fell—hard!—as I was dribbling the ball down the court. Approximately five minutes into the game, I fell again. Although I continued to try and shake it off, the coach made the call about six minutes into the game—I was sitting this game out. As I sat down on the bench and gingerly began peeling the 7.5 shoes off my size 9 feet, I heard someone behind the bench (not someone I knew) mutter something like "who let the klutz start." I wanted to scream that I was a good player, not a klutz, but in reality, in *that game* and with *those shoes*, I had been a klutz.

A few years later, Nike launched an ad for Air Jordans in which Spike Lee asks Michael Jordan what makes him "the best player in the universe." After asking Jordan if it's his long shorts, bald head, short socks, and the like, Spike Lee concludes, "It's gotta be the shoes!" It was a great ad, but every time I saw it, I was reminded how shoes can indeed change how a player plays the game . . . for good and bad.

In the ad, whenever Spike Lee asks Michael Jordan if it's the shoes that make him great, Jordan tells him no over and over again. While Jordan is denying that it's the shoes that make him great, a message from Nike flashes on the screen: "Mr. Jordan's opinions do not necessarily reflect those of Nike, Inc." It's a great tongue-in-cheek ad because without great talent, great shoes won't make a difference, but Spike Lee (and Nike) concludes that "it's gotta be the shoes" anyway. What I remember taking away from the ad is that of course, Spike Lee would never be able to play like Michael Jordan regardless of the shoes he wears, but *Michael Jordan would not play like Michael Jordan either if he were wearing shoes that did not fit his feet.* (Of course, that wasn't the message that Nike intended, but it's the message that stuck with me.)

I think back often to how frustrated I was in the game when I couldn't play like I knew I was able to because the shoes I was wearing didn't fit. Unlike other childhood memories that have faded with time, this memory is as sharp in my mind today as the pain I felt in my feet on that day. I especially remember how the smaller shoes did not initially hurt if I contorted my feet a little and how it did not seem like a big deal (for a little while) to contort my feet to fit the shoes, and the pain is indeed tolerable in the beginning when you put on the wrong shoes. I remember initially feeling like the pain was not a big deal, and once the pain increased, I felt that I had to tolerate it because I committed to wearing these shoes. I remember the conflict I felt in admitting that it hurt because I would be out of the game if I said that. I remember getting pulled out anyway because I was falling down every other minute. I also remember feeling the need to explain to people afterward that it was the shoes, not me, that had failed.

When I started researching gender inequities in workplaces many years ago, these memories kept returning to me as metaphors for helping me understand how certain frameworks of work and success can make talented people look like klutzes if those frameworks don't fit their talents. In many workplaces, these frameworks have evolved over years based on who has primarily been in those workplaces—men. Although the frameworks may not be inherently flawed, they are indeed flawed for people—women—whose feet weren't represented when the organizational shoe size was being determined.

These people, a majority of women (and many men too, as we learned), feel the same urgency that I did when I realized that wearing my own shoes was not an option, but not playing was not an option either. These people contort who they are and squeeze themselves into ways of working that initially don't hurt much, and when it really does hurt, they struggle with admitting the extent of the pain because they don't want to be taken out of the game. They are doing their best in shoes that don't fit, and they live under the constant threat of hearing "who let the klutz start" because their true talents are hidden under the stumbles caused by the bad fit.

The "it's gotta be the shoes" metaphor is not about the right fit as an alternative to great talent. It is about the right fit being necessary to express the great talent that already exists but looks klutzy when squeezed into a bad fit.

Let's apply this concept directly to workplaces with a quick game of hopscotch.

A few years ago, I was asked to speak on gender dynamics in leadership at a seminar for professional service firm leaders. There were about fifty leaders in attendance at this seminar, and not surprisingly (we will get into plenty of statistics later!), there were fewer than ten women in the group.

I created a makeshift hopscotch grid on the floor and went over the general rules of how the leaders were supposed to hop and jump through the grid and back. I asked for ten volunteers—five men and five women—to take off their shoes and traverse the grid as fast as they could in their socks/stockings. If they stepped out of the lines, they had to redo their turns until they completed the grid correctly. I recorded their times from the fastest to the slowest of the volunteers, and the women ranked 1, 2, 4, 7, and 8. The men ranked 3, 5, 6, 9, and 10.

Then, I asked the volunteers to do the exercise again with their shoes on. The women who had originally ranked 4 and 7 dropped in rank because they had to go slower due to the heels they were wearing, but they were still able to complete the grid, albeit slower. This time, the women ranked 1, 2, 5, 8, and 9 while the men ranked 3, 4, 6, 7, and 10.

The men at this point started grumbling sarcastically that this was an unfair exercise because men did not play hopscotch as much as women did when they were younger. The women who had on heels were complaining that it wasn't fair that their scores had lowered because of heels, and they asked that the scores they received when they had their shoes on should not count more than the scores they got with socked/stockinged feet.

I assured all of them that their complaints were valid and that they only had one last exercise to endure. For the last exercise, I split the volunteers into five pairs with each pair having one man and one woman. I then asked the pairs to exchange their shoes with each other—the man was asked to put on the woman's pair of shoes and vice versa. The complaints exploded! From "I don't want his feet stretching out my shoes" to "I just don't wear other people's shoes" to "no way am I getting my feet into those small shoes," the volunteers' reactions ranged from absolute refusal to engage in the exercise to laughter at the absurdity of the exercise.

After the shock had subsided, there were six volunteers who committed to continuing with the exercise. As each of these six leaders fit their feet into shoes that did not at all fit, the laughter from the remainder of the group was combined with sincerely enthusiastic support. These six volunteers were supposed to traverse the hopscotch grid as they did before, but not a single one was able to complete the grid. Between shoes falling off when someone was hopping to people tripping when they tried to jump, the sheer inability to control one's body with ill-fitting shoes on became abundantly clear.

In the group discussion that followed, we talked about how inherent talents have the opportunity to fully manifest when people's shoes fit their feet and how much talent can be missed when people are expected to perform in shoes that don't fit their feet. Further, participants dug into how highly talented people can often look inept if they are asked to work in ways that don't fit their working styles and how harmful these perceptions can be if they are applied not just to individuals but to groups. People brought up examples of what happened to racial/ethnic minorities, gays and lesbians, people with disabilities, and women. All of the women, in fact, talked about how this exercise truly captured how they felt when they were the only one in a room full of men who were consciously aware that there was only one woman in the room.

The leaders then talked in small groups about what the "shoes" were in each of their organizations—policies, programs, protocols, feedback loops, advancement criteria, leadership models, and so on—and who they felt these shoes were designed to fit. Once the individuals in the group identified each of their organizations' metaphoric shoes, all of the women and several men quietly acknowledged that the shoes they had described did not, in fact, fit their own feet . . . that it hurt every day to do what it took to succeed, and it hurt even more because the pain could not be vocalized or discussed because it would be seen as weakness, ineptitude, cowardice, and/or failure. They also talked about good pain and bad pain. Good pain was described as the kind that comes from really trying to achieve something you want, but it was the pain of working really hard in shoes that fit your feet. Bad pain, on the other hand, is a frustrating type of pain where you work really hard but know that your shoes don't fit your feet, and you are hurting and not being given a chance to show what you can really do.

One male leader quietly said, "My organization's shoes fit my feet . . . they fit really well. . . . It never occurred to me that I loved my firm's culture because it fit who I already was." A few other male leaders agreed with him, and we closed the session with the understanding that we don't want to take away the shoes from people whom the shoes fit; we want to make additional sizes available so that different ways of working, succeeding, and leading can also feel like the culture fits well and works.

IN A NUTSHELL

Women (and many men) in professional service firms are wearing business development shoes that do not fit their feet, and their efforts to succeed in these shoes are hurting them, their firms, and the future generations of men and women whose talent is not captured to everyone's benefit. More sizes benefit everyone, and if the intent and will are there to create new sizes, it's not very difficult to do so.

This book offers a comprehensive and candid analysis of how women and men develop business in professional service firms differently and what they and the firms in which they work can do to create models for success that recognize these differences and allow equal opportunities for women to thrive. The integrated data from professional service partners/principals and associates, business development coaches who work with women and men in this area, and firm leaders who grapple with what all of this means take you on a journey behind the rhetoric to give you a better view of how the "one size fits all" model is not working for women (or most men). This book is for you if you are

- A woman in a professional service firm or other similar setting and you want to better understand and develop your own business development skills;
- A leader in a professional service firm or other similar setting and you want to better understand and reduce the differentials in business development between the women and men in your firm;
- A woman or man who cares about the overall advancement of women in workplaces and you want to better understand how to make workplaces work well for women and men equally;
- A student or young professional who is planning to enter a professional service firm and you want to better understand these workplaces and the realities of business development in these workplaces;
- A curious person and you just want an interesting read that will capture your attention and provoke interesting thoughts and ideas.

Business development is what stands between women and their rise into leadership in professional service firms. Women are not developing/generating business at the same rates as many of their male colleagues, and getting business these days is the prerequisite to getting ahead and getting into leadership. Women are literally hitting glass ceilings en masse at the point in professional service firms where business generation becomes as (if not more) important as being good at what you do. And the women who watch this happen to women ahead of them make plans to get out before they also become casualties.

The way that business development is done, recognized, measured, and rewarded in firms today is not working for women (and many men), but you don't have to be limited by the one size that is dominant in these firms. By better understanding the shape of the one size, you can change that size, introduce new sizes, or at least ensure that your shoes fit you well.

Throughout this journey, you will see that women and men do indeed think differently, plan differently, and execute differently when it comes to business development, but only one way of developing business is currently being recognized and rewarded. If we want to see women truly succeed in any of these firms, the current size for business development needs to be altered significantly to fit these differences. These differences, however, do not mean that men and women differ in what they can accomplish; they simply differ in how they can accomplish the same things. Women can cover the same (or greater) distance in the same (or less) amount of time but only if they can wear shoes that fit their feet. (The data also reveals that there are many men whom the current size doesn't fit, and a business development model that comes in different sizes will benefit many men as well.)

This journey is neither simple nor logically linear because it requires us to navigate neurobehavioral gender differences, the nature versus nurture debate on whether men and women are born different or raised to be different, and the structure versus agency push and pull of how we may or may not adhere to the gender stereotypes to which we are encouraged (or required!) to adhere.

John Dewey, a preeminent psychologist and education reformer, once said that "a problem well put is half solved." A large part of this journey is about using data to guide us to a "problem well put," but I recognize that leaves the problem only half solved. In order to move the dial on the solution process, I complement our problem-defining journey with experiments that alter the one-size model and demonstrate some promising strategies on how to expand the number of sizes that work successfully in firms.

These strategies move us beyond the half-solved point of better framing and understanding the problem. However, to get even further requires action: your action. The actions you choose to take upon reading this book will make the gender inequities in professional service firms ultimately solvable.

Moreover, the actions also make sense from a business perspective. In a world where no firm can afford to ignore the assets contained in more than half the population, adding more sizes to business development models is not only an exercise in competitive survival, but it is also necessary for competitive excellence. Business development strategies that work for how women (and men) actually work is a good investment for professional service firms and the women (and men) who work in them.

THE RESEARCH AND METHODOLOGY

The research for this book grew out of the stories I heard as I worked on gender initiatives in professional firms of different sizes in various industries. The insistent buzz of "women don't develop business as well as the men" seemed to transcend industries and firm size. The firms were articulating the problem in a way that made women's performance inferior to that of men instead of different from that of men. Thus, firms were more inclined to ask women to do better instead of questioning the ways in which they were recognizing and rewarding business development.

Professional service firms are losing women at a shockingly rapid rate (and women of color at an even more shocking rate), but it's equally shocking how accepting we all have been of the firms' explanations of why this is happening. The firms say that it's mostly work-life balance and personal lifestyle choices. Our research tells a different story. While work-life balance and personal lifestyle choices play *a* role in the attrition of women from professional service firms, there is one lever that is most responsible for keeping women from succeeding at the highest levels—business development. When really pushed on the issue, firms do admit that business development has had the greatest impact on the progress of women toward parity in firm partnerships.[1]

The business development shoes in firms today do not fit women, and women are growing tired of being told to fit into shoes that hurt their feet and make them look like klutzes, so they leave. These departures should not be considered personal lifestyle choices—they should be calculated as a tremendous loss of talent that wanted to stay but refused to remain in pain. That is the core finding from our survey and interview data, and this research is a candid and comprehensive exploration of that finding and what we can do to turn the tide on these unacceptable losses.

This book is the product of many people's experiences, perspectives, and insights. These experiences, perspectives, and insights were gathered via survey responses, formal interviews, informal interviews, extensive e-mail exchanges when interviews were not possible, and countless conversations in which discussing "shoe size" took on a particularly serious and applicable undertone. Based on the perspectives and voices of these professionals, this book is specifically about business development differences between men and women in professional service firms, but the broader implications of the research, stories, and working strategies are relevant for any workplaces where success comes in only one size and there are people for whom that size just doesn't work.

Given the sensitive and confidential nature of much of the information shared with us, all aspects of our research were designed to collect perspectives without direct attribution. Each individual who participated in this study was ensured the highest degree of confidentiality, and many of the respondents told us candidly that without this protection, they would not have participated. Although some individuals' stories are highlighted throughout the book, the individuals' names and other identifying information have been altered to protect their identities. The data is reported in the aggregate to the greatest extent possible with individual narratives integrated to provide texture and nuance to the aggregate perspectives.

There is no adequate way for me to fully express the gratitude I feel for the hundreds of people who contributed their stories and insights to this book. While many of their perspectives are reported in the aggregate, my gratitude for the investment of time and effort is offered to each person individually. If you are one of the people who contributed to this book, please know how grateful my team and I are for everything you gave and shared!

QUANTITATIVE SURVEY

The research team at Nextions developed and distributed a comprehensive survey that was shared with approximately 500 individuals in professional service firms and networks through a snowball strategy. We identified professionals in various professional service industries and asked them to distribute the electronic survey to applicable people in their networks and let us know generally how many people were sent surveys. While we have extensive demographic information on the people who completed the surveys, we do not have the same level of data on the full universe of people to whom the survey was distributed. Of these approximately 500 individuals, we received 250 completed surveys.

The survey respondents represented a diverse array of personal and professional backgrounds from professional service firms of various sizes and industries. Although the numbers of men and women in the study were roughly equal, the number of women is more reflective of our targeted outreach to ensure high levels of female participation than it is of their representation in their firms.

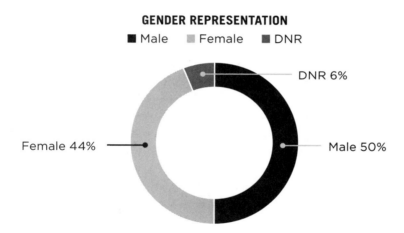

GENDER REPRESENTATION
■ Male   ■ Female   ■ DNR

DNR 6%

Female 44%

Male 50%

We were equally deliberate in trying to reach racial/ethnic minorities who were in partnership-type positions in professional service firms, and we were astounded by the incredibly small numbers of people of color in these positions. While this paucity demands a book of its own, we were able to get a respectable representation of racial/ethnic minorities with an even split between men and women. This representation, while proportionate to their participation in partnership-type positions in professional service firms, was not significant enough to warrant an isolated analysis of race/ethnicity in these firms. However, where appropriate, I apply insights from other research studies we have conducted in these areas to nuance the findings through the perspectives of women and/or men of color.[2]

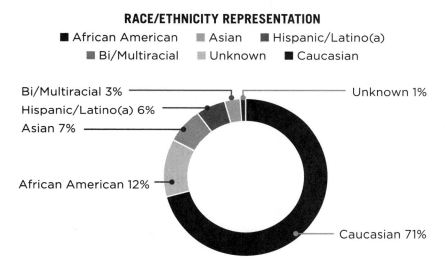

RACE/ETHNICITY REPRESENTATION

■ African American   ▥ Asian   ■ Hispanic/Latino(a)
■ Bi/Multiracial   ▦ Unknown   ■ Caucasian

Bi/Multiracial 3% —
Hispanic/Latino(a) 6% —
Asian 7% —
African American 12% —
Unknown 1%
Caucasian 71%

We did inquire about sexual orientation, and, not surprisingly, we had very few people identify as gay/lesbian/bisexual/transgender. While the numbers were indeed too small to create analyses of any kind, we did hear stories of how their sexual orientation informed some women's experiences of their gender, and those stories are woven in to highlight the relevant experiences.

The generational representation, although well spread out across the major generations in today's workplaces, indicated a slightly lower representation of the older segment of baby boomers (over age 55) than is currently represented in professional service firm partnerships. This segment, however, comprised the overwhelming majority of our sample of leaders who were interviewed. Where certain trends may be impacted by generational influences, I parse out—to the greatest extent possible—gender differences within generational contexts and generational differences within each gender.

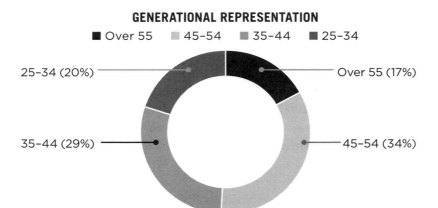

GENERATIONAL REPRESENTATION

■ Over 55   ■ 45–54   ■ 35–44   ■ 25–34

25–34 (20%)

Over 55 (17%)

35–44 (29%)

45–54 (34%)

One area where we saw a strong generational influence was the length of time the survey respondents reported being at their current firm. About 66 percent of the respondents had been at their firms less than ten years. Partially due to their ages and length of time in their professional generally and partially due to individual choice to make lateral moves between organizations, professionals between the ages of 25 and 34 and between 35 and 44 had a proportionately shorter tenure in their current organizations than did those who were older than 45. Of all the respondents, 61 percent have worked in two to four firms over the course of their careers, while 26 percent have been at only one firm; about 12 percent have worked at five or more firms.

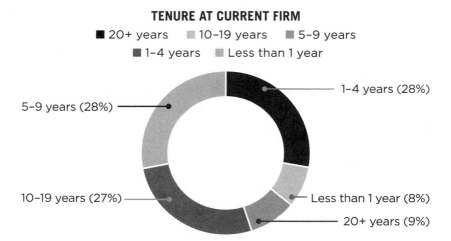

TENURE AT CURRENT FIRM

■ 20+ years   ■ 10–19 years   ■ 5–9 years
■ 1–4 years   ■ Less than 1 year

5–9 years (28%)

1–4 years (28%)

10–19 years (27%)

Less than 1 year (8%)

20+ years (9%)

Of the respondents, 40 percent worked in large firms (more than $100 million in annual revenue), 34 percent worked in midsize firms ($5 million to $100 million in annual revenues), and about 20 percent worked in small firms (less than $5 million in annual revenues). Of these firms, 28 percent had one to two locations, 14 percent were regional firms, 22 percent were national firms, and 33 percent were international firms. The respondents represented firms from the following industries:

Given that addressing the work-family conflict issue is necessary in dealing with any issue in the workplace, we asked our survey respondents for information about their marital status and their caregiving responsibilities at home. Consistent with the larger scale demographical analyses done by the Pew Research Center and others, the men (91%) in our study were far more likely to be married than were the women (70%). While men of color were as likely to be married as their white male counterparts, women of color were less likely to be married than their white female counterparts, making the gap between men of color and women of color greater than the gap between white men and white women.

GENDER COMPARISON IN MARITAL STATUS FOR SURVEY RESPONDENTS

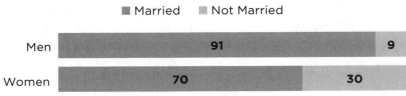

Of the people who were married, 79 percent of women were married to spouses who worked full-time in comparison to only 56 percent of men. There were no significant differences based on race/ethnicity. Both men and women indicated that having the support of a spouse who did not have an active career was essential to juggling the demands of practicing and developing business simultaneously. Men overwhelmingly reported having this type of support at home while women overwhelmingly reported struggling with the challenge of trying to develop business while doing the yeoman's work at home. Women who had spouses who did not work outside the home reported far higher levels of responsibilities within the home than did men who had spouses who did not work outside the home.

GENDER COMPARISON FOR HAVING A SPOUSE WHO WORKS OUTSIDE THE HOME

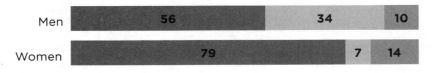

QUALITATIVE INTERVIEWS

Although many studies have been done on business development in professional service firms, the majority of them have relied solely on quantitative data. The few studies that have been based on qualitative data (interviews, focus groups, etc.) have not been combined with quantitative data to provide both a macro and a micro lens through which the issue can be analyzed and understood.

This study is the first of which we are aware that combines quantitative and qualitative tools to understand gender differences in business development behaviors and outcomes in professional service firms.

Our qualitative component was comprised of interviews with 113 professionals (61 men including 19 men of color and 52 women including 21 women of color) who are partners/principals or the equivalent thereof (all of whom have some responsibility for developing business in their respective firms) in professional service firms in the various industries represented by the survey respondents.

In addition to the partners/principals in the professional service firms, we interviewed 21 business development coaches (14 men and 7 women—3 were people of color) who are engaged by individuals or firms to specifically assist someone in meeting and/or increasing her or his business development outputs and accomplishments. Of these 21 interviews, 8 were formal interviews and 13 were informal interviews.

Finally, we interviewed 72 leaders of professional service firms (61 men including 12 men of color and 11 women including 4 women of color). For the purposes of this study, we defined a "leader" in professional service firms as being one of the top five to seven individuals involved in firm governance, including but not limited to Chair/CEO, Vice-Chair, Managing Partner/Director, Officer, Senior Director/Partner/Officer, Creative Director, Client Executive, and other members of the highest level leadership teams in the firm.

While no research study can fully capture all of the perspectives and nuances of a particular topic, the multifaceted aspects of this study give us a very comprehensive understanding of the dominant "one size" of business development in professional service firms. The data also illustrates how people (many women and some men) contort themselves to fit this size and eventually resolve to be in pain, be viewed as klutzes, or get out of the game altogether.

That's the bad news. The good news is that once we recognize that there is only one size and it never fits all, we can design frameworks that fit other sizes.

GENDER IN THE WORKPLACE: A QUICK PRIMER

"Why are you studying problems faced by privileged women when there are real inequalities, life and death type of inequalities for women that need attention?" That was the candid and emotional reaction from a good friend and colleague when I told her about this book. My immediate reaction to her question was that gender inequality was something worth researching no matter where it was occurring or the demographic background of the women to whom it was happening. My friend pushed back. "True. But, why this subject at this time?"

In retrospect, getting questioned (and challenged!) on this "why" was a critical turning point in how I understood and contextualized this book and the research contained in it. Yes, inequality of any kind in any place is worth studying, but something had driven me to prioritize gender inequality in business development in professional service firms as the site of inequality that I wanted to explore. Understanding that impetus was important, not just important for me personally but for the clarity needed to explore this research to its fullest.

As a researcher, my philosophy has always been to study problems not just to understand them but to solve them. Years of exploring gender inequalities in workplaces has narrowed my focus to the top of the workplace pyramid because decisions are being made at these elite levels that affect hundreds of thousands of women globally. The very few women who are in these arenas or poised to enter these arenas do make a lot of money and do enjoy many privileges that are not available to the majority of the world and do not include many women of color, but their presence and participation at these levels change how the world works for all women.

For example, let's take the connection between these women and politics. In the 2012 political/election cycle, "28 percent of all disclosed [required for donations over $250.00] political contributions came from just 31,385 people . . . these donors represent the 1% of the 1%, an elite class that increasingly serves as the gatekeepers of public office in the United States."[3] The overwhelming majority of these top 1 percent of the top 1 percent donors were employed by financial, legal, and lobbying firms,[4] and women were barely—if at all—represented among these 31,385 "gatekeepers of public office," a fact that greatly affects the participation of women in politics and the election of women to political office.[5] The people driving politics in this country are primarily coming from an elite economic apex where women are severely underrepresented, and political decision making has reflected this lack of representation often.

In September 2013, the Center for American Progress released a study on how women were faring in each of the 50 states in the United States, and researchers found a very strong correlation among women's economic conditions, women's participation in public and private leadership, and women's overall health.[6] When women achieve higher levels of economic success (not just income parity with men but generation of wealth), they become leaders in the public and private spheres at greater rates. When women's participation in leadership increases, the overall health of women rises significantly. Other studies have found similar correlations between women in leadership positions and the benefit to women on a more global scale: in health care policies,[7] in health care rights such as reconstructive breast surgery and extended maternity stays in hospitals,[8] in criminal justice policies,[9] in overall political engagement for women and girls,[10] and in women's rights in general from pay equity to sexual assault prevention to rights for working mothers.

WE HAVEN'T REALLY COME A LONG WAY, BABY

Before we dive into the details, I acknowledge that this book's foundational proposition is that achieving gender equity in our workplaces is critical not only for the success of our workplaces but for the overall health of our economy and society. This book is not written for anyone who disagrees with the need for gender equity in workplaces. There are other resources that would be far more interesting and useful for someone seeking to debate this point.[11]

In 1968, Virginia Slims entered the market as cigarettes made specifically for the sophisticated (and sort of working) woman with the tagline, *You've come a long way, baby*. I don't quite know what the company meant by a *"long way,"* but when it comes to women in today's workplaces, the tagline should read, *"We have a long way to go, baby!"* In doing the research for this book, I was asked by several leaders of firms something along the lines of *"Aren't we done with this gender thing yet?"* This primer is a quick read to familiarize you with the research on gender in the workplace. (If you consider yourself adequately familiar, please feel free to skip ahead to Chapter 1.)

"Aren't we done with this gender thing yet?" Globally, this question has been asked and answered so many times that the third goal of the United Nations' eight Millennium Development Goals is to "[P]romote gender equality and empower women."[12] At the most macro level, the United Nations' Gender Inequality Index (GII) begins with this stark but unsurprising foundation: "There is no country with perfect gender equality—hence all countries suffer some loss in their HDI [Human Development Index] achievement when gender inequality is taken into account, through use of the GII [Gender Inequality Index] metric."[13] The GII impacts the overall Human Development Index by showing the percentage loss to overall human development in a country that is linked to gender inequality. The global average on the GII is 46.3 percent—we are losing 46.3 percent of our human development potential globally because of gender inequality. The averages range from 28 percent in Europe to 57.7 percent in sub-Saharan Africa, and the United States ranks 42nd in the world with a 25.6 percent score.[14]

Gender inequalities in the workplace, one of the key factors in the GII, have extensive and very real economic and social implications for societies. For example, gender inequality in labor force participation perpetuates poverty,[15] and creating equity between men and women in the labor force could raise the GDP (Gross Domestic Product) in the United States by as much as 5 percent.[16] Five percent of our current GDP ($16.6 trillion) would be an addition of approximately $830 billion to our economy.

Further, since the majority of developed countries now have women who are getting higher levels of education at an equal or even greater rate than men, the overall ability to increase the quality and productivity of a country's workforce is dependent on integrating women effectively. Not only would we add a significant amount to the economy by creating gender equity in the labor market, but without effective integration of women, we cannot sustain the economy we currently have.

When we narrow the focus to professional workplaces, especially in the developed countries, increasing the equal participation of women would allow companies to expand and grow in ways that they cannot do right now.[17] Not only would companies expand and grow with more equal participation of women, but these companies would expand and grow in ways that yielded greater levels of higher performance than if the companies expanded and grew without gender equity.[18]

Gender equity throughout organizations definitely improves an organization's overall performance, but several studies by McKinsey, Catalyst, and Credit Suisse Foundation have all found that gender equity at the leadership levels has even greater potential to enhance an organization's performance. Studies in 2008, 2010, and 2012 by McKinsey all demonstrate that companies with three or more women on their senior management teams score higher on all nine organizational performance dimensions and the three dimensions—leadership, work environment and values (culture), and coordination and control—that directly impact higher financial performance. A study by Catalyst in 2005 found a direct correlation between women in management/leadership and increased value to shareholders. A Credit Suisse Foundation 2012 study found that companies with women on their boards outperformed similar organizations with all-male boards by 26 percent through higher increases in equity, lower incidents of risky investments, and faster reductions in debt liabilities. The higher levels of performance were especially enhanced during financially challenging times such as the economic downturn in 2008. A Thomson Reuters report in 2012 found that companies with greater gender diversity in their leadership ranks perform better, especially in harsh market conditions.[19]

The few studies summarized above represent only a small percentage of the dizzying volume of research that now unequivocally demonstrates that gender diversity at all levels of an organization leads to higher financial and organizational performance, with gender diversity at the leadership levels being most impactful in increasing the organization's performance and value.

Yet, even with all of this data, the lack of progress in advancing women into these leadership positions is quite startling. The 2013 data from Catalyst's analysis shows that approximately 16.9 percent of Fortune 500 board seats are held by women, including a very anemic 3.2 percent of women of color. Moreover, the increase in women on these boards is only about 3 percent in the last ten years.[20] In these same companies, women also comprise only 14.3 percent of executive officers, the primary pool of talent from which future board members are selected.[21]

There was no change in this data between 2012 and 2013. While there has been some progress in those numbers over the past two decades, it is important to note that women have held the majority (51 percent) of management, professional, and related positions in companies for the same past two decades.[22] So the pipeline of women available to be advanced is approximately three times the number of women actually advanced.

So, according to research, *we need gender equity to survive and thrive as individual organizations, aggregate industries, and a global economy*.

This research-derived conclusion has led to fervent articulations by organizations that they are passionately and actively committed to change the inequity into sustainable equity. Yet, in spite of this increasing body of knowledge and loudly voiced intention to change, the pace of change has been lethargic at best. Using Catalyst's research, if the pace of change over the last ten years (approximately 3 percent) is sustained at its current rate, women on boards in Fortune 500 companies will reach parity with women in the managerial/professional pipelines in workplaces in about 120 years. That would occur circa 2133. It would take even longer than that to reach gender parity in the executive ranks within Fortune 500 companies.

While the overall pace of change with gender equity is torturously slow, some industries are doing better than others, and still other industries are doing particularly badly. Knowing the common challenges across all industries is helpful, but digging deeply into specific industries gives us the ability to not just understand the data but actually work to change the outcomes in the future.

Exploring these issues in professional service firms is especially fascinating because these firms are insulated from change in ways in which other industries and workplaces are not. Change eventually finds professional service firms like it finds all organizations, but they definitely are among the last to be found.

◢ PATRICIA

Patricia is a principal in an advertising/marketing firm, and the first thing she wanted to talk about in my interview with her was the 3% Conference (http://3percentconf.com/). The title of the organization/conference refers to the fact that only 3 percent of Creative Directors in advertising agencies are women. These are the people in the highest level leadership and the people who get the credit for bringing in and keeping the clients.

"There are so many reasons that women aren't making it to the CD [Creative Director] level, and Kat Gordon [the founder of The 3% Conference] is doing a lot to educate and agitate the industry and make sure that women and men are paying attention to this terrible stat. But, that's not what upsets me the most . . . it's that the women in America who consume the crap that these CDs put out aren't raising a stink. Partly, it's because they don't know, and partly it's because we are taught to be unquestioning consumers."

Unlike many gender initiatives whose mission statements focus on the women in a particular field, The 3% Conference's mission statement is about all of us as consumers, our children, and the customers served by the agencies:

Our mission is to support more female creative leadership in advertising agencies because:

- Female consumers deserve to be marketed to from a place of understanding.
- Brands deserve to not have their marketing budgets wasted in a 97% testro-fest.
- Everyone—especially children—deserve a healthier media diet in the 3,000 ads they consume daily.[23]

"There has not been a single year in the over 10 years that I've been working in this field when the public and the media don't go nuts about the sexism in ads on the Monday after the Super Bowl. In the last few years, it's like the top story the day after the Super Bowl because the ads, in general, get more attention than the game, especially if it isn't an exciting game. I have these conversations with my mom, my sister and my friends, and I ask them why they are surprised at how sexist the ads are when there are no women who are the creative leads behind the ads."

The Institute for Diversity and Ethics in Sport (TIDES) conducts research on the people behind the ads aired during the Super Bowl. According to TIDES, the lack of women and people of color in the agencies that create the ads for the Super Bowl greatly influences the types of ads that are produced for our consumption.[24] With only 7 percent people of color and 6 percent women as the creative leads behind Super Bowl ads, it's not particularly surprising that sexism in these ads is a cause of major consternation among female and male consumers on the Monday after Super Bowl Sunday.

"It's like a horrible hangover that people have on that Monday after consuming really bad ads on Sunday except if we asked more questions about who was serving up these ads, we would know to demand change."

Ad agencies are professional service firms that most of us will never have the need or opportunity to buy from or work in directly, but Patricia's story reminds us that we are still explicitly affected by both the gender equity of the leaders in these firms and the decisions they make.

A NOTE ON GENERALIZATIONS

A thorny paradox undergirds the core of all work on inclusion and equity—you have to separate people into groups in order to bring them together as individuals. You have to generalize based on group identity in order to create equity and parity for individuals in that group while recognizing that it is the group identity that created the inequities that you are now trying to resolve. This paradox constantly serves as my conscience as I delve into any research project because I know that if my research does not account for this paradox, I will reify the very biases that I have committed to breaking in workplaces.

It is with this paradox in mind that I offer this note on delineating the differences between generalizations and stereotypes. Any research that explores the intricacies of social groups and social identities relies on understanding the culturally shaped and shared norms, values, beliefs, attitudes, and behaviors that inform and influence who we are and what we do. Generalizations, in this context, are the patterns or tendencies that people in a particular group express or exhibit in regard to norms, values, beliefs, attitudes, and behaviors. Generalizations help us better understand how social groups and social identities are formed and how they impact who we are as individuals even if we did not actively enroll in the groups by which we are identified.

Stereotypes are overgeneralizations. Where generalizations create probabilities for certain realities or outcomes, stereotypes assume these realities and outcomes. Where generalizations provide insights for consideration, stereotypes rely on prejudgments to reach conclusions without any consideration.

This research uses generalizations to create insights, and these generalizations are about gender differences, not sex differences. Gender refers to how men and women act at the intersection of biology and socialization; sex differences are purely about biology. The generalizations in this research are rooted in mutable gender differences, not immutable sex differences.

Sometimes these generalizations can feel like stereotypes because I talk about women in comparison to men, but the research was conducted and is reported from the perspective that not all women fit the generalizations about women and not all men fit the generalizations about men.

This research also uses generalizations in order to offer strategies for change. While there are many similarities between firms that allow us to craft practical solutions that are workable in firms from different industries, geographical locations, and organizational structures, each firm is a unique organism, and strategies will need to be tailored to those considerations. Every accounting firm is not like every other accounting firm. Every large firm is not like every other large firm. Every firm in Manhattan is not like every other firm in Manhattan. Every law firm partnership is not like every other law firm partnership. The generalizations help us craft solutions that many of you will find helpful for your organizations, but we would never stereotype and assume that every solution will work for you as it is presented in this book. Please take the solutions, change them, apply them, revise them, and make them work for the unique ways in which you work.

As a woman who has often been explicitly told how I am the exception to many generalizations about women, I take this distinction between generalizations and stereotypes very seriously. I also always keep in mind Albert Einstein's warning that "[a]ll generalizations are false, including this one."

PART 1

THE
FOOTPRINT
OF THE
ONE SIZE

CHAPTER 1

THE LAST
6.2 MILES

A friend of mine who runs marathons once told me that a marathon is a 6.2-mile race that has a 20-mile warm-up period. Skill and training will get you through the first 20 miles; the last 6.2 miles require true grit and the will to finish. In professional service firms, the first 20 miles in the marathon for gender equality have been about recruiting and retaining women; the last 6.2 miles are about ensuring that women have equal and unfettered ability to thrive as partners in and leaders of these firms. That equal and unfettered ability for women to thrive as partners and leaders requires firms to change the shape of their core engine of power: business development.

I wrote this book for the women who want to and are trying to run these last 6.2 miles because these women are skilled runners with incredible stamina who have the grit and will to finish but are being asked to run these last 6.2 miles in shoes that don't fit their feet. They are leaving professional service firms in droves, which hurts them, their firms, their professions, and future generations of all of these because firms don't want to offer different sizes of shoes in which women (and many men) can better run the last 6.2 miles.

This book is also for current leaders of professional service firms who realize that changing the shape of business development isn't about helping women; it's about survival and success in a business environment where the status quo is no longer working.

Part 1 digs deeper into the evolution of business development in professional service firms, why the shape of business development looks the way it does, and why the right fit is so critical for business development success. Part 2 explores how this shape fits or doesn't fit men and women, especially when it comes to significant differences in how men and women view competition versus collaboration, business development versus sales, and self-promotion as a business development tool. Part 3 offers strategies and ideals to tackle the challenges and create new sizes for yourself, your firm, and/or workplaces in general.

We interviewed many women who talked about how the ability to develop business the way their firms wanted them to had either almost derailed their abilities to make partner or filled their lives as partners with insecurity, conflict, and dissatisfaction. One female partner in an architectural firm told me, *"It's hard not to feel like you have failed when you have given everything you have to get here, and you are good at what you do, and you are looked down on because you don't have business in the same way that guys do. Your previous successes are almost like erased because of the game as they have defined it. Especially because you know you can do it if were just done differently, without the meanness and fighting. If it weren't so ugly, maybe more women would want to be a part of this profession."*

This partner's perspective offers a personal insight into the statistic that although 49 percent of architecture students and 39 percent of interns are women, only 17 percent of principals and partners in architecture firms are women.[25] Architecture firms, unfortunately, are quite representative of how poorly professional service firms are generally performing in advancing women. Women have comprised about 50 percent of prerequisite education programs and 50 percent of entry-level professional hires in firms for over 20 years. Yet, they only comprise: 21 percent of partners/principals in accounting firms,[26] 20 percent of partners/principals in law firms,[27] 17 percent of partners/principals in consulting firms,[28] 11 percent of venture capital firm executives,[29] 10 percent of mutual fund managers,[30] 3 percent of hedge fund managers,[31] and 3 percent of creative directors in advertising firms.[32]

The statistics are stark, but even the starkest of numbers don't tell the full story of the frustration, anger, and pain endured by women as they see no choice for themselves other than to leave. Moreover, when highly talented women leave for business development reasons, their departures impact realities far beyond their own lives or the firms they are leaving behind, realities such as the gender wage gap that is such a hot topic in the media today.

According to the U.S. Department of Labor, women are consistently overrepresented in the lowest earners category and extremely underrepresented in the highest earners category.[33] This contributes more to the gender gap in wages than do the differentials between men and women in the middle earners categories—so, it's not that all women earn about 80 percent of what men earn, it's that there are too many women earning next to nothing and very few women earning the kind of money that impacts the shape of the economy, the players in our political system, our national priorities, and so forth. Of the few women who are in the highest earners category, the majority work in knowledge-based fields, and many of them work in professional services such as business, finance, and law.[34]

Beyond the gender wage gap, having more women in leadership positions in these firms translates into an increase in female talent for leadership positions in many industries and a decrease in the gender leadership gap, another issue that has dominated the news lately. Executives in corporations from all industries recruit many executives from professional service firms—Chief Financial Officers from accounting firms, Chief Legal Officers from law firms, Chief Marketing Officers from marketing/advertising firms, and so on. Even many executives in niche industries such as health care, transportation, and others recruit executives from professional service firms that serve these industries. The lack of women at the highest levels of these professional firms greatly impacts the ability for women to be recruited and hired into executive leadership roles in organizations across industries and functions.

◢ ELIZABETH

Elizabeth used to work at a midsize firm where she began her career and eventually made partner. She was highly respected and sought out for her professional expertise in a field where women are severely underrepresented, but her life as a partner was nothing like she thought it would be.

"Partnership was that ultimate goal. I worked so hard to get it, and when I got it, it was nothing like what I expected. I was told to develop business, but I was

given absolutely no help. No mentoring. No support. No casual words of wisdom from anyone. In the third year after I made partner, I was put on a complex and crazy deal that had me working 18-hour days for weeks on end when I was in town, and I also had to travel extensively. I barely saw my husband and kids. I missed a lot of things for the kids that I should have been there for. I was sad all the time, but I was determined to surpass the client's expectations, and I did. The client was ecstatic with our work. The work wound down just a couple of weeks before Thanksgiving, so I went to the head of my department and asked if I could take a couple of weeks off so that I could reconnect with my family and just get myself together. He told me that I deserved it and should take it.

"While I was gone, I checked in by e-mail pretty frequently, and I made sure to be on calls when it was necessary. When I returned to work in early December, my department head told me that he wanted to give me a heads up that my compensation might take a hit that year because I had not brought in much business. I told him that I should get some credit for the client project that I had led and given so much to. He told me that he had already tried arguing for me, but the partner who was getting credit for the deal was not budging."

Elizabeth was furious and frustrated, and, in a moment of furious frustration, she confronted the partner who had received credit for this particular deal. The partner told Elizabeth to *"stop whining"* and to *"get real."* She talked to a few other partners about what was going on, and many offered sympathies, but no one offered any tangible support. While she was processing all of this, she found out that the partner who had gotten credit had signed up two additional clients who had contacted the firm because of the results she had achieved in the transaction.

"I'm not the confrontational type so it was definitely out of character for me to be aggressive about getting credit for a client project. I found out from another female partner that the guy I had confronted was telling people that I was hysterical and emotional, and it must be because the project was too much for me. He was making it sound like I was weak when he was just a bully. I thought that the other male partners would stand up to him, but no one really did."

Elizabeth got her compensation letter just before the holidays in December, and her overall compensation had been reduced by about 10 percent. *"I read this letter at my desk, and I went home and cried for hours. I literally was not able to get out of bed for two days. I cried and slept and cried and slept. My husband told me to quit, but I told him it wasn't that easy. Getting out of a partnership is not like quitting a job."*

Elizabeth started the new calendar year feeling "off." She was alternating between anger and depression every time she went to work, and she constantly beat herself up for not having thicker skin and for letting the whole situation get to her. *"This was just not me. I'm competitive. I'm tough. I'm not a crier. I wanted to be stronger, and I tried to be stronger, but it felt like something had broken inside me."*

Elizabeth contacted a friend of hers who was an executive recruiter and told her that she wanted to know what her options were. She polished up her résumé per her friend's suggestion, and she officially put herself "on the market."

"I didn't want to leave the firm. I loved what I did and the variety of clients that I worked with. When I put myself out there, I was very nervous about it getting back to the partners in my firm because I had not told anyone that I was considering leaving. Then I got a call from a woman who used to be partner here who had just been hired to lead a major client of ours. She asked me to come work with her and told me that she wanted to be upfront that I would be in a great environment and have high levels of responsibility, but the compensation would be much lower than what I made at the firm. I told her, kind of but not really kidding, that I would come work with her if I could fire this firm on my first day. She said yes, and I accepted. I figured that my compensation would continue to tank at the firm, and I wanted to be respected for what I did instead of being made into a hysterical emotional caricature because I stood up for myself."

Elizabeth left the firm shortly thereafter.

"The firm had a farewell lunch for me. I know they would not have done that if I had not been going to a client. The head of the firm toasted me and said how proud the firm was that an 'alum of the firm' was going to a client. That has always stuck with me. You become an alum after you graduate. I don't consider myself an alum of the firm. I don't feel like I graduated. I feel like I dropped out."

Elizabeth did slowly transition business away from the firm. An even bigger hit was delivered to the firm when the two new clients that had signed up with the firm based on Elizabeth's work left because she was no longer there.

Elizabeth's story is a powerful illustration of what is happening in firms today, but it is, by no means, unique or infrequent.

PUTTING WORK-LIFE BALANCE IN PERSPECTIVE

Most marathon training programs only train you to run a 20-mile distance because there is really no way to train people to run the last 6.2 miles. Theoretically, anyone who runs 20 miles can run 26.2 miles, but you learn to run the first 20 miles through programs. You run the last 6.2 miles because you won't let anything stop you from finishing, and that isn't anything that can be programmed, coached, or trained.

If we break the first 20 miles of gender equality in professional service firms down into smaller chunks, the first few miles were about basic equal rights under the law (suffrage, civil rights, etc.), the next few were about equitable access into and treatment in workplaces (protections against gender discrimination, sexual harassment, pregnancy discrimination, pay inequities, etc.), then we ran the miles of creating business cases for women in the workplace, and the last leg of the first 20 miles involved creating inclusive workplaces that allowed for greater work-life balance, flexibility, and recognition for ways in which women and men are differently but equally capable. These 20 miles have been challenging, frustrating, and exhausting, but they were the easy miles.

Many firms are still stuck in that last leg of the first 20 miles—balance, flexibility, and the creation of better cultures for women. The majority of research into why women are not advancing into partnership and leadership positions in firms has focused on the topic of work-life balance. Galanter and Henderson, in their comprehensive analysis of law firms, accurately commented that the "economic pressures of the elastic tournament [competing and succeeding in professional service firms like law firms] . . . create significant headwinds for female lawyers . . . [female associates] report a lower likelihood of receiving coveted work assignments and training . . . this trend is often attributable to disproportionate family responsibilities."[35]

They further assessed that "firm managers lack the leverage to impose a top-down policy for the benefit of female lawyers with children."[36] Galanter and Henderson, along with other researchers of professional service firms, found that professional service firms develop and tout work-life balance policies including part-time, flex-time, and other opportunities for working moms; however, the research indicates that these opportunities most often exist only in theory for recruitment, branding, and reputation purposes.[37]

Women do not avail themselves of these opportunities because doing so would slowly dismantle their careers.

The research has been clear that women are not advancing into partnerships and leaderships of professional service firms, at least partially, because of work-life balance, and the processes put in place by professional service firms to address the problem seem to not be smart career moves for anyone who actually wants to advance into partnership and leadership. When you combine this data with the survey responses in this study demonstrating that of the professionals who were married, 79 percent of women were married to spouses who worked full-time in comparison to only 56 percent of men, the importance of work-life balance begins to emerge as critical for women's success. This is especially critical given how many women in our study reported that they continued to bear the overwhelming share of housework, child rearing, and home management duties.

It seems logical and necessary to vote for women's work-life balance needs as the primary culprit to neutralize in order to retain and advance women in professional service firms, but recent research by McKinsey is starting to chip away at our dependence on work-life balance as the primary (often only) reason for women not advancing in the workplace. In January 2014, McKinsey released a study that found that *"female executives are ambitious and sure of their own abilities to become top managers, though they are less confident that their companies' cultures can support their rise."*[38] Women are getting more frustrated with the barriers in the way of their ambitions and their capabilities. Women's focus over the past two decades has gone from *"I don't know if I can do this"* to *"I don't know if I want to do this"* to *"I want to do it and I know I can do it and you are in my way."*

The McKinsey study found that men and women had equal ambitions to advance and they were equally likely to say that *"they are willing to sacrifice part of their personal lives to reach a top-management position."*[39] However, 40 percent of these ambitious women also felt that their leadership styles didn't fit with the culture of their organizations and that their gender was an impediment in realizing their ambitions. Not surprisingly, men did not agree that women faced any problems because of gender, and men saw less value than women did in initiatives that sought to correct gender inequities.[40]

Our research revealed that women share the sentiment that gender inequalities in their firms are being unfairly attributed to work-life balance choices made by women. A female partner/principal who led the women's initiatives in her firm said, *"Every time we have a women's anything, the conversation turns to work-life balance. It's the safe topic to discuss when it comes to women, but you peel back that curtain, and much of what is really holding women back has nothing to do with work-life balance. It has to do with unequal opportunity to access power. Women are uncomfortable talking about that because they know that the men could not even begin to have that conversation."* Fewer women are leaving firms for work-life balance reasons than we think and more men are leaving firms for work-life balance than we think, and neither explains the extent of the differentials between men's and women's success in firms.

In our study, women definitely reported having greater responsibilities for child rearing: 62 percent of women compared to 41 percent of men said that they had primary or shared responsibility for children under 18. This 21 percent differential is tremendous, and it is what draws highly warranted attention. That said, the 41 percent of men who have primary or shared responsibility for children under 18 should not be ignored because many of these men are also leaving professional service firms for work-life balance reasons . . . they are just not saying that as they exit.

In workplace assessments that we conducted in two large professional service firms, our research found that for professionals under 45 years of age, men were leaving firms for work-life balance in rates almost equal to those of women. However, they were not giving that reason as they walked out of the door because they did not feel that it was in the best long-term interest of their careers for them to do so. One junior shareholder at a large professional service firm told me that *"I knew I was leaving for the same reasons that many of the women were leaving . . . I want to spend more time with my children . . . I want to have greater control over my time . . . but do you have any idea how I would be looked at if I stated that explicitly? No, absolutely not. I say that I'm leaving because I have a better opportunity . . . no one bothers to ask why this other job is a better opportunity than working at the firm, and that works just fine for me."* So, women may be leaving to achieve greater work-life balance, but men are doing so as well.[41]

Work-life balance may be *a* reason, but it is not *the* only reason why women (and many men) are not advancing into leadership in professional service firms. Our research clearly illustrates that the most pernicious factor keeping women out of partnership and leadership in professional service firms is not work-life balance but underperformance in business development.

Our study, for example, found that women with no children or dependents in professional service firms still do not achieve the same levels of success as men with or without children or dependents. *"Even when we control for individual choices in examining work-life balance desires, we still find that among men and women in these firms, women are consistently underrepresented in the rainmaker ranks, both in and out of the partnership. In almost all of the firms, women were three to four times more likely than men to be in the lowest quartile of the business-generation rankings."*[42]

Further, women were more likely than men to report not having the time to do professional development activities. However, men were far more likely than women to report that they enjoyed the business development activities that they or their firms organized. For women, there was no discernible overlap between what they personally enjoyed doing and what they listed as accepted business development activities. For men, on average, there was about a 50 percent overlap between what they personally enjoyed doing and what they listed as accepted business development activities. Attending athletic events and participating in golf activities were two of the highest value activities for men in both their personal and business development interest arenas. Women also ranked these two activities as high in what they felt they needed to do for business development reasons, but these were rarely mentioned in women's lists of personally enjoyable activities.

When the data is overwhelmingly clear about the need to address differentials in business development, why do we continue to focus on work-life balance? Honestly, we focus on balance because it is easier to talk about children and family than it is to talk about power and money. And, that is what business development is at its most elemental level—power and money.

In our interviews with professional service firm leaders, many talked about the exceptional success stories of women who were equity partners/principals in the firm but worked reduced hours or a flexible work schedule. These women were small in number, but the primary thing that all of them—across different firms, different industries, and different age ranges—had in common was that *they all had business of their own*. The business development path leads more directly and effectively to work-life balance than do policies, programs, or initiatives.

One firm leader commented that *"having your own clients is currency in firms . . . you can use the currency to buy yourself a part-time schedule, a telecommuting arrangement or anything else you want . . . having a program that makes part-time equity partners will be resented by the rest of the partners, but a partner with her own clients will get enthusiastic nods when she tells everyone she is going to be part time."*

Addressing business development in professional service firms is indeed like running the last 6.2 miles of a marathon. It's the distance left after everything that is relatively easy has been done. As marathoners like to say, you run the first 20 with your feet, and you run the last 6.2 with your guts. Business development is where professional service firms meet their guts, and it is not always a pleasant encounter.

SHIFTING THE FOCUS TO BUSINESS DEVELOPMENT

So, what exactly is business development, and why does it warrant such a vaunting metaphor as being the last 6.2 miles in a marathon? Basically, it's sales. We don't like to call it that, but that is what it is. As opposed to the selling of a product or even a general service, business development is the selling of you, your brain power, and your time by you. Selling your firm overall or your team in general is called marketing, public relations, or even branding and is measured in overall organizational financials, but business development is an individual statistic—how much business did you bring in as an individual by selling yourself as the key professional or the leader of a team that will service a client?

That question—how much business did you bring in as an individual— is the question that drives the majority of decisions in professional service firms. From advancement into partnership to selection of leaders, all other qualifications and credentials are evaluated after assessing the answer to the business development question even if firms are stating otherwise.

This is the one issue that had unanimous agreement across the 72 professional service firm leaders who participated in our study. Business development trumps everything . . . even the commitment to gender equity unless the women are thriving in the business development arena.

That sounds like a criterion that is "equal" in the way that it works—men or women who bring in business thrive—but that's also where the "one size never fits all" lens comes into play. It's only "equal" if the business development framework works in a way that works equally well for men and women. Right now, it doesn't work that way, and we see that play out in firm after firm where women are consistently in the lowest quartile of the firm's business developers.

One senior partner/principal of an accounting firm told me that *"asking why business development is important for firms is like asking why the number of burgers sold is important to McDonald's . . . business development should be the focal point of your study . . . really, it should be the only point of your study."*

With all of the effort, resources, and attention on retaining and advancing women in professional services firms, business development (the achievement versus the avoidance of it, the success versus the failure of it, etc.) accounts for a large part of the gap between the 50 percent of women who enter as professionals and the less than 20 percent of the women who remain as partners/principals.

There are two major reasons for honing in on business development as the issue through which to catalyze change in professional service firms and beyond:

- First, it was the top issue mentioned by every single one of the 72 firm leaders I interviewed as the greatest obstacle to neutralizing gender inequalities in their firms. We can argue whether this should be the case, but we cannot argue that this is the case right now.
- Second, the hypercompetitive environment in professional service firms has created a situation where "the 'firm' itself has remarkably little autonomy to pursue noneconomic objectives, such as racial and gender diversity or the training and mentoring of the next generation."[43] Firms cannot rely on people who are extremely successful leaders in their ranks to radically change the model through which they became extremely successful. Given the increasing competition for and within these firms, change in "noneconomic objectives" like gender equity is going to come not from eradicating the current model (the one size) but adding to the current model (more sizes).

Although the coverage of women "opting out" or "leaning in" has captured our attention in the last couple of years, even if women leaned in with all their might and shunned every opportunity to opt out, business development is the particularly tough but essentially the only portal into partnership, highest levels of compensation, and upper echelons of leadership in professional service firms. This portal called business development currently only comes in one size, and while some women do fit comfortably into this size, not enough do to expect gender parity to happen without additional sizes.

The American Bar Association's publication *Closing the Gap: A Road Map for Achieving Gender Pay Equity in Law Firm Partner Compensation*[44] focuses on neutralizing the gender pay gaps among male and female partners in law firms primarily through the lens of business development. With many tips for firms ranging from increasing transparency in the compensation process to diversifying compensation committees as well as pitch teams to involving clients more thoroughly in business development and succession planning processes, this publication is a good resource for those who want to better understand the links between compensation, business development, and gender equity in firms.

Closing the Gap rightly zooms in on business development as the critical way through which to negate the gender bias in compensation. The strategies, however, are fixes that aim to reduce the pain of playing in shoes that don't fit instead of demonstrating why women need new shoes altogether. For example, greater transparency in the compensation process allows women to better navigate the compensation process, but it doesn't change what is actually compensated. Similarly, more diversity on compensation committees will greatly improve the current process but won't change the process itself. While mitigation of unfairness is better than not doing anything, mitigation of unfairness should not be seen as the creation of fairness.

If you recall the Hopscotch in Heels™ exercise discussed in the Introduction, mitigation of unfairness is the equivalent of teaching people how to navigate the grid in shoes that don't fit. Fairness is ensuring that everyone has the most optimal type of shoes, in her or his individual size, to best demonstrate each person's hopscotch skills.

In the next chapter, you will meet Caroline and hear her story about being a trailblazer in her firm. The business development model in her firm did not fit who she was or how she developed relationships; her success in this area grew when she stepped away from the firm's model and created her own model, one that actually fit her. Although she had the experiences, insights, and internal resources to do something very different, she was also a trailblazer. Firms often try to replicate the success of a female trailblazer as the blueprint to achieve gender equity, and it is truly folly to use a trailblazer's actions as the model for how larger groups of women can succeed.

Trailblazers, by their nature, are exceptions to the rule, and gender equity in organizations cannot depend on waiting for the exceptions to the rule to blaze their own trails every time while men travel clearly marked trails that are landscaped regularly by the firms. Women like Caroline will always blaze their own trails, but if institutions don't adopt these and other newly blazed trails as part of the organization's business development infrastructure, it will be difficult, if not impossible, to achieve gender equity in all the areas where business development is a prerequisite for entry.

Business development, also referred to as client development, rainmaking, and building a book of business, is a portal through which women don't fit as well as their male counterparts. Over the next few chapters, we will delve into an empirical, narrative, and practical exploration of why this happens, what individual women can do to sustainably walk through the portal with greater ease, and how the firms they work in can be supportive of this journey while changing the shape of the portal. It is an exploration of the "one size" that firms are utilizing and how that size can be altered to fit others instead of requiring women to alter themselves to fit the unyielding size.

The last 20 miles have been exhilarating even while they have been exhausting. That said, the focus moving forward has to be on the last 6.2 miles and the unique efforts it will take to finish this run. Basically, what got us here won't get us the rest of the way, and our only choices today are to keep going or . . . to keep going.

CHAPTER 2

THE EVOLUTION OF THE ONE SIZE IN BUSINESS DEVELOPMENT

Professional service firms were traditionally founded and grown as places of knowledge and skill transference from experts to novices until the novices became the experts and could train novices of their own. The guild model of apprenticing under masters was the most common way of becoming a master in accounting, law, architecture, and the like before education became more professionalized and professions became more regulated through entrance exams.

Under this guild model (roughly through the late 1800s), young apprentices were selected by masters to learn the art and craft of a specialty. The apprentices did not expect to be paid very much, but they expected to learn a lot from people who were recognized as knowing a lot. The journeymen were accomplished apprentices who were not yet accomplished enough to be masters. Journeymen continued to fine-tune their skills while they mentored the apprentices and executed some of the more complex tasks that the masters would not feel comfortable passing through to the apprentices. The masters fully expected complete dedication and loyalty from their apprentices and journeymen, and they, in return, promised that successful apprentices and journeymen would become masters of their own one day.

Because the masters were recognized for their mastery of a particular skill, the clients came because there was greater demand for the services of masters in esteemed professions such as law, accounting, architecture. and so forth than there were masters to fill that demand. The apprentices, understanding this supply-and-demand relationship, focused almost exclusively on honing their skills and building their reputations because they knew they would be in equally high demand when they achieved their own mastery levels.

This guild model began to break down in the early 1900s as the number of masters grew and the professional competition between those who had mastered certain knowledge bases and skills intensified. The apprentices-journeymen-masters model slowly eroded, and a new model emerged: the grinders-minders-finders model, a radical departure from the apprentice-to-master process.

The grinders-minders-finders model reflected the shift in professional services from greater demand than supply to greater supply than demand. The professional guilds evolved into professional firms that were founded by professionals who were also entrepreneurial in how they thought about their profession. These firms now needed the grinders to crank out the work that needed to be done, the minders to teach and supervise the grinders, and the finders to find and keep the clients whose loyalty could no longer be taken for granted. Neither the grinders nor the minders have the assurances any longer that mastering skills will elevate them to finder status.

The grinders are at the bottom of the professional food chain. They do the work with their noses to the grindstone (hence their name). They are skilled, but they are replaceable. They have the potential to become minders and maybe even finders, but there aren't any tears shed when grinders leave because the supply of grinders is deep. Most professional service firms turn over about 20 percent to 25 percent of the grinders at the lower levels every year.

The minders basically mind the grinders. The minders act as the bridges between the grinders and the finders by teaching the grinders hard and soft skills, professional norms, and behavioral expectations. The minders are the critical glue in the professional service firm hierarchy because they literally hold the top and the bottom together, but they are vulnerable to economic realities where either the grinders are reduced in number or the finders are struggling to find new business opportunities. Minders are above the grinders, but their careers are vulnerable to changes both above and below them.

Finders are the masters of old, except they now are the ones who are the best in bringing in the clients, not necessarily the ones who are the best experts in the field. Of course, many finders may straddle both groups, but the finder status is based much more in the finding of clients, not in the mastering of the craft of a particular profession. Professional service firms invest much in keeping their finders happy because the finders are their sources of revenue, and the finders are their sources of work for the grinders and the minders.

This shift from the guild model to the grinder-minder-finder model is the shift from success in professional service firms being rooted in pure accumulation of skill and experience to success being rooted in business development. So, the finders find, and the finders lead. Unfortunately, the process of finding is defined very narrowly in many professional service firms, and most finders are able to become finders because they fit comfortably into that one narrowly defined size.

◢ TERRI

Terri is a senior member of a professional service firm that primarily serves government agencies in long-term and complex projects. Terri was recruited to the firm from one of the government agencies that the firm represented. She was recruited by the head of the firm at the time who "wanted to shake up the male and stale environment" in the firm.

Once she came into the firm, Terri discovered that several of its clients had been actively and vocally pressuring the firm to bring in more women and racial/ethnic minorities. She asked the head of the firm if he had recruited her because she was a woman. He responded by saying that he recruited her because she was good, and the fact that she was a woman definitely helped him make the case for her.

As soon as she started at the firm, Terri began to be invited to go on pitches to potential clients and current clients with new projects in the works. She decided to see this as an opportunity to get to know current and future clients, so she offered to prep some of the presentations and help in any other way she could. She realized soon enough that she was not necessarily being asked to work on the projects that were coming in as a result of the pitches in which she participated. She complained to the head of the firm, and he promised to talk to the senior leaders responsible for these projects.

Nothing changed. She was still being asked to *"tag along"* on the pitches, but now there were expectations that she would prepare and help put the pitch together even though she stopped offering to do so. As she advanced to a more senior role, she reached a point where she should have been included as a team member when it came to distributions of revenue generated. Not only was she excluded, she continued to be treated in much the same way she had been treated when she was much more junior.

As the numbers of women had increased in the firm, Terri and another senior woman put together an informal women's group that met periodically to discuss *"being a woman at the firm"* and other issues related to the workplace. Terri actively mentored a few of the younger women, especially the younger women who worked in her department.

One day, one of the young women she worked with in her department told Terri that she did not want to attend the women's group meetings anymore. She told Terri that she really did not enjoy the meetings because they were treated as an unfettered opportunity to complain and whine. When Terri asked the young woman what she would prefer to see in the meetings instead, the woman replied, *"Senior women with some power who were treated with respect."*

The woman left the firm shortly after this conversation, but Terri painfully recalls how the woman told her that she never wanted to be like Terri and tolerate being treated like a second-class citizen.

"The hard part is that she's right. I was recruited because I was a superstar in my previous position, and I still am at what I do, but it's not enough. It's not even important, it seems. It's been rough because I'm used to achieving big when I have given it my full effort. Here, I try, but it doesn't work. I don't like how I'm being treated, but I am also the main breadwinner for my family so I can't quit or start fights that will get me fired. She is right. She should not want to be like me. I don't want to be like me, but I'm stuck. I hope that she finds something better wherever she lands."

THE NEW ONE SIZE: THE GRINDER MINDERS

In professional service firms, the ideal distribution of grinders, minders, and finders is that professionals enter as grinders at the associate level, rise to minders as senior associates, managers, or directors, and eventually advance to finders as partners/principals, managing directors, and more senior leaders. Women and men enter firms as grinders at relatively equal rates, but the leakage of women begins as the promotion process begins, and the worst leakage occurs in that final advancement into partnership, that transition from being a minder to becoming a finder.

Much of the research in this book focuses specifically on that transition between being a minder and becoming a finder. The perspectives provided by men and women in professional service firms whose compensation and/or career advancement depends on developing their own clients offer some unique insights about how men and women diverge in their experiences.

Before we jump into the gender differences in this transition, it is crucial to note that the transition itself and its impact on men and women has been the subject of intense study and media attention since the recession. In the case of law firms, for example, *Fortune* ran an interview in November 2013 with Roberta (Robbie) Kaplan of Paul Weiss who commented on this shift through the lens of her own career: *"When I became partner at Paul Weiss, it had to do with the ability to be what's known as a first-chair lawyer. It had much less to do with one's ability to get business. It's a different world today, and I want to be able to develop business and bring clients into the firm."*[45] The struggle faced by partners/principals to become finders was also the focus of a January 2014 *New York Times* article in which the career of Gregory M. Owens is dissected from the perspective of this transition (or lack thereof) from minder to finder:

> Mr. Owens's situation is all too emblematic of pressures facing many partners at big law firms. After Dewey & LeBoeuf collapsed, Mr. Owens seemingly landed on his feet as a partner at White & Case. But he was a full equity partner at Dewey, Ballantine [one of the firms merged into Dewey & LeBoeuf] and Dewey & LeBoeuf. At White & Case, he was demoted to nonequity or "service" partner—a practice now so widespread it has a name, "de-equitization." Nonequity partners like Mr. Owens are not really partners, but employees, since they

do not share the risks and rewards of the firm's practice. Service partners typically have no clients they can claim as their own and depend on rainmakers to feed them.[46]

Mr. Owens's story illustrates how men and women in law firms are being impacted by the difficulties of this transition; however, in our study, women reported a significantly higher rate than men (23 percent to 9 percent) of being partner/principal without equity or ownership. This statistic was relatively consistent across all professional service firms that had some form of ownership and/or equity partnership. The group of partners/principals without equity described their work experiences to be a hybrid of grinders and minders in that they did have a lot of expertise and they trained the younger professionals. However, for all intents and purposes, they were treated and compensated like service partners or grinders among the partners/principals. Without ownership or equity, these partners/principals were partners/principals in name only with no representational profit sharing or voice in the firm's decision-making processes.

When the partners/principals with equity or ownership were asked how they compared to their peers in their firms' revenue generation scores, 42 percent of women in comparison to 25 percent of men reported being in the bottom half of the revenue generation range. For the women and men who did have business, only 41 percent of women in comparison to 61 percent of men reported that the majority of their client billings had been originated directly by them.

This reality has not changed much in the past 20 years. In 1995, a study of gender differences in law firms commissioned by the Association of the Bar of the City of New York entitled "Glass Ceilings and Open Doors" found that

[i]n the firms studied, women are known to be minders (or grinders). That is, with some exceptions, once they get the assignments from partners for particular clients they are good at keeping the business. However, a number of associates and partners of both sexes attribute women's lack of power in the firms as resulting from their dependency on male partners in these business relationships.

In most firms, there is clear stratification between the rainmaking partners and the partners who service these clients. . . . There is considerable ambivalence about whether women have an equal chance to develop into rainmakers through the channels that men have developed. . . . Of course, no man encounters the prejudice that his sex would be an impediment to his business-getting ability.[47]

The stories and comments from male and female partners in our study were eerily similar to the findings from this study conducted 20 years ago.

Whether they were stuck in the "partner/principal in name only" ranks or the bottom half of the compensation ranks regardless of equity or ownership, many of the women in our study described feeling like second-class partners/principals, a group we are referring to as the new "grinder minders." Members of this group have very little say and/or power in the firm in spite of their "partner/principal" titles, and they feel highly vulnerable in their positions within their firms.

One female partner talked extensively about how exposed she felt knowing that she was one of the lowest revenue generators in the firm and dependent on the others for the billings that she did have. *"It's not just me. Almost every senior woman at the firm is in a similar situation. We don't have original billings, but we are the ones who work on the projects. We are the ones that the clients want to work with, so we get partial credit. But, we don't have a voice, and if any major changes occur, I know I can't protect myself. I don't know when it became so much more important to bring in a client than to do the work that actually kept the client here."*

Another female partner/principal commented on her lack of ability to speak up when she did not feel that business development credit was allocated equally based on who actually brought the client in if two or more people were involved. *"I hate having to ask for the credit I deserve. I hate the fighting. I wish we could celebrate together and get to the work of serving the client. And, it's definitely an old boys club. I have to be careful when I fight, even when I'm right, because the leaders in the firm take the men's side almost always."*

When asked about these issues, women had significantly more conflicts about "who should get credit," and women were significantly less likely to be satisfied with how these conflicts were resolved. This feeling of not being able to effectively fight for yourself is a feeling very much associated with this emerging group of "grinder minders."

In our study, 55 percent of women in comparison to only 32 percent of men reported having conflicts around origination in their firms. When asked about their satisfaction levels with how the conflicts were resolved, 4 percent of women in comparison to 19 percent of men said that they were *very* satisfied with the resolution, and 11 percent of women and 21 percent of men said that they were satisfied. When the "very satisfied" and "satisfied" statistics are taken together, only 15 percent of women reported some level of satisfaction in comparison to 40 percent of men. Conversely, only 8 percent of men reported high levels of dissatisfaction with the resolution in comparison to 20 percent of women.

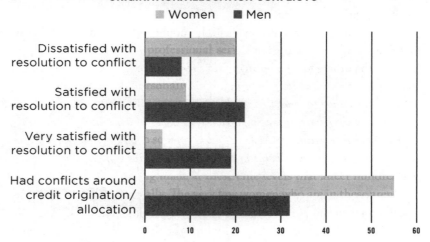

GENDER DIFFERENCES IN SATISFACTION WITH CREDIT ORIGINATION/ALLOCATION CONFLICTS

In answering questions about the conflicts in this area, men responded with comments like "resolved through senior leadership," "not happy with the result but this stuff balances out in long run," and "didn't like the compromise but that's what a compromise is . . . no one wins." The women, on the other hand, responded with comments like "bully won, no compromise," "people in competition with each other creates bad behavior," "too much to relive," "leader told me I was getting too emotional," and "backed off after realizing my career would suffer if I kept fighting."

The evolution of this new group of "grinder minders" illustrates a clear divergence in how men's and women's career paths generally progress in firms. After reaching the minders stage, men are treated more like journeymen who are ready to become masters, and women are looped back into being grinders, albeit at a higher level than the entry-level grinders.

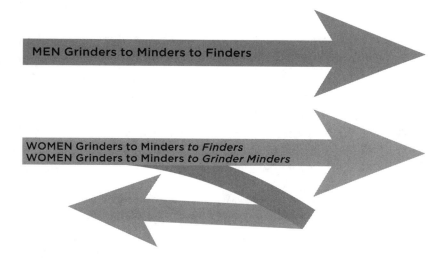

This new group of "grinder minders" includes men, but the overwhelming likelihood is that if you are in this class, you are a woman. This is not only demoralizing to women, but it repels younger female professionals who see women's career paths strewn with interrupted advancement and nasty conflict. Because men are adequately if not overly represented at the highest levels of these firms, young men are not repelled in the same way that young women are.

By default, if not by explicit intention, firms are clearly articulating the size into which a professional must fit if that professional wants to rise into leadership or even to have a greater voice in the trajectory of her own career. Younger women are watching senior women contort themselves into this business development model, and they are choosing to not try and fit in ways they know they can't. This choice—to not contort to fit a size that may never fit in spite of the willingness to accept the pain caused by the contortion—is seen by many firms as "women opting out." Moreover, it's not just the younger women who are choosing to not try and fit when they know they can't. In comparison to men born before 1964 (the baby boomers), men in the Gen X and Gen Y generations (born between 1964 and 2000) are more likely to agree with the women in their own generations than they do with older men. The distaste with contorting oneself to fit an unyielding model of success is becoming less gendered and more generational even though it still informs women's decision making far more than it does men's decision making.

When I listened to professional service firm leaders talk about how much they wanted to retain their women but how difficult it was to keep them when they had so many options including that of not working at all, I remembered how hard and often I fell when I had on the size 7.5 shoes. The argument that women are opting out as opposed to being driven out by a model of success that does not fit them would be like my coach saying that all players had to wear size 7.5 shoes in the game, and those who chose to not play because their size 9 feet hurt in those 7.5 shoes were opting out because they had "so many other options."

Some women may be leaving because they want to make different career or personal choices, but attrition rates suggest that women are making decisions that go beyond just personal or family-related choices. Perhaps attrition rates are at least partially explained by looking not at the choices women are making but at the the choices actually available to women when they are forced to wear "shoes" that don't fit their "feet."

Terri's story is a personal reflection on being a "grinder minder." She thought the term was quite appropriate for how she felt the firm saw her. She saw how the younger women she mentored assessed their career decisions given how the more senior women were perceived and treated in her firm. Terri's experiences were consistent with those of many female partners/principals in professional service firms, regardless of industry or location.

CHAPTER 3

THE ONE SIZE VS. THE RIGHT SIZE

"Business development is sales," some will say, concisely. "Business development is partnerships," others will say, vaguely. "Business development is hustling," the startup folks will say, evasively.[48]

Scott Pollack, a writer for *Forbes*, starts his article entitled "What, Exactly, Is Business Development?" somewhat facetiously with the preceding three statements, but he goes on to articulate a definition that is clearer than any other that I have seen thus far: *"Business development is the creation of long-term value for an organization from customers [clients], markets and relationships."*[49]

In this new age of grinders, minders, grinder minders, and finders, a holistic understanding of business development is necessary before we delve into gender differences in how business development is executed successfully or otherwise.

In our research, we found that business development was indeed sales, partnerships, and hustling to create economic value for firms from their clients and the overall market. We also found that women (and many men) felt that there were very specific ways of doing all of these activities that were recognized and rewarded by their firms. *"I am really good at getting additional business from clients we serve,"* said one female principal in a technology consulting firm, *"but that doesn't count in the same way as bringing a brand new client in the door. So, I'm seen as less valuable even though what I do actually may have higher profitability for the firm. They [the firm] say it's about business development, but it's really about business development in their way on their terms."*

ONE SIZE NEVER FITS ALL

ONE SIZE NEVER FITS ALL. It's a simple enough concept to understand when we talk about shoes or even guns (as you will read in the following pages), but it is a slightly more complex concept when applied to how people are expected to work, succeed, and lead in many of our workplaces. That complexity makes the application of the concept to workplaces more difficult. However, it is in this complexity where elusive answers to tough questions about gender equality in certain contexts can be found.

The focus on fit is especially relevant in professional service firms. A recent study by Lauren A. Rivera at Northwestern University found that professional service firms "described fit as being one of the three most important criteria they used to assess candidates . . . more than half reported it was the most important criterion at the job interview stage, rating fit over analytical thinking and communication."[50] The right fit is important at every stage of success in a professional service firm—from getting hired to advancing into partnership and eventually into firm leadership.

Looking for fit would not be a bad thing if firms offered several sizes into which one could fit, but as Rivera found in her research, evaluators at firms sought people "who were not only competent but also culturally similar to themselves in terms of leisure pursuits, experiences, and self-presentation styles."[51] Considering that partnerships in these firms are on average about 80 percent male (and over 90 percent Caucasian), the size that fits the "similarity" shoe rarely fits anyone who is not male and Caucasian. It is important to note that identity alone does not cause or perpetuate this similarity. It is the focus on similarity in "leisure pursuits, experiences, and self-presentation styles" that theoretically are gender neutral but in reality "have a stereotypically gendered nature"[52] that can make the difference.

"One size never fits all" is a powerful concept in understanding why women in the higher levels of professional service firms consistently underperform in business development in comparison to their male counterparts.

Not only do women generally underperform men in this area, but they consistently fall into the lowest quadrant in the compensation range among partners/principals in these firms. As one leader of a professional service firm commented, "[T]his lowest quadrant is like hospice for careers . . . in today's economy, if you are in this quadrant, your career is dying. *Yes, that is where the majority of our women are.*"

In today's market, the only ticket to get out of this career hospice is business development—having your own clients—and the surefire way into this hospice is to not have any clients of your own. But if the path into and out of this professionally deadly quadrant is a "one size fits all" path that only has one way of defining, evaluating, and rewarding success, this quadrant may have many incredibly talented business developers who look like klutzes and eventually fail because the shoes don't fit.

Considering Rivera's research on fit, would women have better outcomes in their careers if they matched their preferences and behaviors to men's? According to our data, the answer is a resounding no. More effort cannot make a wrong fit right—it only makes the person who doesn't fit frustrated and tired.

Of course, one size never fits all, but when only one size is available, those who walk comfortably into business development successes in professional service firms do not always realize that while their ambitions and capabilities do in fact make them successful, their natural fit into the only size available allows them to succeed in ways that others cannot. Although most professional service firms are not explicitly or deliberately forcing everyone to fit into one mold, most of these firms today are in fact using a single model of business development into which all must fit . . . or fail.

This model, initially constructed when women were not present in these firms, is patterned on predominantly male communication styles, relationship-building patterns, and behavioral norms. So, the metaphoric business development shoes in professional service firms primarily fit men, but the ability to walk is evaluated for everyone as if the shoes fit all equally. And, when some people (mostly women but some men as well) stumble, they are deemed klutzes who cannot compete at the highest levels. When they stop walking altogether because the bad fit is too uncomfortable to make the journey worthwhile, the decision to stop walking is attributed to a personal choice to "opt out" of the journey and is often perceived to be unrelated to what is actually going on in the workplace.

Most firms do not deliberately adhere to only one model of business development to intentionally exclude anyone, but the model inevitably does not include people whose styles, patterns, and preferences are not consistent with the "one size" mold. So, while women (and most men) are not actively being excluded, they are also not being given a fair chance to succeed.

It is important to note that what we are talking about is *not* differences in talents and abilities, but, rather, differences in how talents and abilities are expressed and manifested. When borrowed shoes did not fit my feet, my natural basketball talent (as average as it may have been) did not change, but my ability to express that talent changed. I could not express my talents and abilities fully in shoes that did not fit my feet.

If Terri's story reveals a glimpse into the journey of not fitting into the one size that is supposed to fit all, Caroline's story illustrates what it looks like to create a new size altogether that fits well. Through the stories and perspectives I heard in the research I did for this book, I recognized how extensive the vocabulary around "fit" actually is, and I learned the extent to which perceptions about fit may influence experiences and constrain opportunities for success in professional service firms.

Fit. Misfit. Unfit. Fitting in. Refusing to fit in. Lack of fit. And so on. The ironic reality in Western culture is that we actually idolize rebels who don't fit in . . . as long as they don't fit in an acceptable way. One female partner/principal framed it this way: *"Good rebellion is fitting in before you stand out . . . bad rebellion is if you stand out before you ever fit in."* A male partner/principal provided another framework for thinking about this powerful irony: *"People may like rebels, but they don't like rebellions . . . rebels are interesting people, but rebellions are not interesting, especially if you are in power . . . the women's issues in our firm have always felt like a brewing rebellion . . . I like the rebels, and I've mentored many of them, but the conversation about how it's not working for women always feels like it's teetering on the edge of changing everything."*

Caroline did not fit into the business development model in her firm. Her attempts to fit in only made her feel more like a misfit until she drew on a lesson from her adolescence: because having the right fit is so critical, it is essential that you start with the right size.

↗CAROLINE

Caroline, a senior shareholder in a large global professional service firm, is one of the top 20 most prolific business developers in her firm. She is the first woman in the firm to break into this elite level of firm shareholders, and she is the only woman in this group of business generators, individuals from whom the firm selects many of its leaders. With her slight build and soft-spoken style, Caroline does not physically stand out as the trailblazer that she is, but it is exactly this physical incongruity that taught her how to blaze these trails.

Caroline, the youngest of four children, grew up with three older brothers. Her father and brothers were all gun enthusiasts who enjoyed spending hours upon hours at the shooting range. While she enjoyed spending time at the shooting range with her brothers, she was constantly frustrated by the lack of improvement in her shooting accuracy and the lack of strength in her shooting hand. Her head also often ached from straining her eyes on the target while her shooting hand tired easily and cramped often. Given her intensely competitive nature, not getting better at something that she was working hard at was especially frustrating for her.

When Caroline was in her first year of high school, her brothers gently tried nudging her to give up shooting and take up a different activity. She ignored them and continued to go to the range with them, put up with their frequent ribbing about how she *"couldn't hit water if she fell out of a boat,"* and continued to ice her hand and wrist after every outing without complaining.

A few weeks into her first year of high school, she was shooting at the range with her brothers when a man walked up to her and asked her who had selected the gun that she was using. She pointed to her brothers and told the man that she was using one of their older guns. He introduced himself as one of the new coaches for the local high school's rifle team and told her that while she looked like she had great form, she would never get any better using a gun that didn't fit her hand. He showed her how her hand was stretched too tight over the grip of the gun, causing her trigger finger to angle downward instead of curling in a level way. He explained to her how painful shooting this gun would be to her hand and how difficult it would be for her to aim well when her hand was not in control of the gun.

After switching out her pistol for a rifle, he gave her some additional pointers and watched as she adjusted her form and style to the new gun. He told her that working so hard with the wrong gun had strengthened her hand muscles to the point where she would be unstoppable with the right gun. He told her that he would reconnect with her in a few weeks to see how she was doing, and he suggested that she think about trying out for the rifle team at school. Caroline tried out for the team (partially to spite her brothers), and she not only made the team, but she went on to win several high school competitions before becoming a ranked rifle shooter at the collegiate level.

"Women are actually better shots than men!" she stresses emphatically. *"But, the majority of guns are made for men's hands, big men's hands. So, if women try to shoot with guns that don't fit their hands, they will look like they can't shoot, but you get the right gun in their hands, and they will outshoot the men more often than not. That's why I keep a picture of Margaret Murdock on my desk."*

In the 1976 Olympics in Montreal, Canada, Margaret Murdock competed alongside men in the shooting contests. Shooting was one of the few Olympic sports that was not segregated by gender. Men and women were on national teams together as teammates and competed against each other without a great focus on gender—until Margaret Murdock. In the 1976 Olympics, Margaret Murdock tied for the gold medal with her teammate, Larry Bassham. The judges examined the targets with great scrutiny and awarded Larry Bassham the gold and gave Margaret Murdock the silver. Two notable things happened next:

1. Larry Bassham pulled Margaret Murdock up onto the gold medal block with him as "The Star-Spangled Banner" began to play.
2. The shooting competition was segregated thereafter, ensuring that, since 1976, men only compete against other men and women only compete against other women.

Margaret Murdock's story inspired Caroline to question and rethink what is assumed to be or is accepted as reality. Although shooting is a gender-segregated sport today, it wasn't always that way. More importantly, it became segregated not because women were not able to compete with men but because they were able to compete a little too well. In 2010, Texas Christian University's rifle team—all women because of a Title IX requirement at the university—won the championship against gender-integrated teams from across the country, including the team from Alaska-Fairbanks (mostly men), which had won 9 out of the previous 13 championships.

Women win in shooting by shooting better, and they shoot better by shooting very differently than men. Men shoot using their upper bodies to steady the gun while women use their hips to create the balance they need. Men shoot using guns that fit into larger hands with stronger fingers while women shoot using guns made for smaller hands with slimmer fingers. Men use their legs to absorb the recoil while women use their core abdominal muscles to absorb the recoil. Men have dominated the sport of shooting for so long that the weapons that fit them have become the standard weapons, but the weapons are standard for men, not women. So, even in a sport like shooting that is dominated by men, women can win . . . if they use guns that fit their hands. Women cannot win if they use guns made with men's hands as a reference point.

When Caroline was promoted to shareholder, one of her colleagues told her that he was excited to have her along on business development pitches because *"there hasn't been any good eye candy on the pitches for a long time."* Another colleague offered to take over one of Caroline's presentations to a potential client because he did not think Caroline would be taken seriously because of her *"girlie voice."*

Caroline ignored the comments as much as she could and tried to utilize the resources available in the firm to develop clients. She asked her colleagues to include her on client pitches. She met with firm leaders to get suggestions on how to expand her networks. Even though she did not enjoy them, she attended the sporting events, golf tournaments, cocktail receptions, fund-raisers, and anything else that would allow her to penetrate the client development networks inside and outside the firm.

After two years of high levels of activity and very low levels of results, Caroline had an epiphany. *"It's the gun, not my shooting."*

She stopped asking her colleagues to invite her to client pitches, and she stopped attending events that she did not find enjoyable. Instead, Caroline made a list of 20 people she wanted to develop as clients, had each one over to her home with his or her significant other, and cooked them dinner. She and her husband loved to cook, and they loved to entertain informally in their home, so she used that to develop clients. She learned about her clients' interests, families, ambitions, and she began to invite them to her home to introduce them to other people in her network that they would benefit from knowing. She had one client who was stressed out about getting his daughter into a particular high school; Caroline knew one of the senior administrators at the school and had a small dinner party to introduce the client and his wife to the administrator and her husband.

Not only was she getting more business, she was enjoying herself tremendously. Yet, the firm did not consider her client development efforts to be reimbursable by the firm. In spite of her success, her expenses, unlike those of her colleagues who took potential clients to sporting events and golf games, have never been approved for reimbursement. She was even told that if her dinners were catered, the reimbursement would be easier to justify, but reimbursing the ingredients for cooking a meal at home just *"did not feel right."*

"I had to do it my way to succeed at this game. But even though the success is evident, the message to me is clear that my way is just not quite the 'right' way even though it works."

Caroline's journey from grinder to minder to grinder minder to finder is one that she traveled one step at a time because she had to blaze the trail while she traveled it. As we have already discussed, the journeys of trailblazers help us see what is possible, but their journeys are not easily replicated. There are lessons to be learned from Caroline's story, however, that can be replicated. Caroline carved out her own size, but there is no reason that the firm cannot take the size she created and make it available to everyone as another option of how to develop clients. Perhaps, the firm can even start this process by reimbursing her grocery expenses instead of telling her to get a caterer.

CHAPTER 4

A FULL MEASURE OF THE ONE SIZE

One of the firm leaders in our study adamantly iterated how important it was for business development in firms to be contextualized appropriately: *"It's not just business development. It's business development in professional [service] firms. You have to understand how firms work if you want to understand how business development works in firms."* Business development is indeed different in professional service firms than it is in other arenas because professional service firms significantly differ from other workplaces.

Andrew von Nordenflycht, a scholar who has studied professional service firms extensively, states that "a significant obstacle to progress in understanding professional service firms is the ambiguity of the central term: what is a PSF?"[53] Integrating his research with other recent scholarship on professional service firms, Von Nordenflycht has crafted a definition of professional service firms that is framed by the following characteristics: high knowledge/human capital intensity, low capital intensity, and a highly professionalized workforce.[54] Professional service firms are workplaces where people get paid to think and solve problems with thought. There are no products exchanging hands, and the services provided are high-knowledge services, which means that they cannot be replicated easily or purchased/consumed en masse.

Business development in professional service firms is the ability to convince clients that your intellectual and creative abilities are better than those of your competitors. The process is both highly competitive and deeply personal, a combination that resonates in a particularly complicated way for women as we will explore in the second section of this book. The following unique attributes of professional service firms highlight why they are particularly vulnerable to inefficiencies in regard to gender equity and less open to changing the status quo.

1. Assessing value in professional services is much more subjective and difficult than assessing products or even easily replicable services. Evaluating a person's intellectual capacity and potential creates much greater possibility for unintentional biases and cognitive errors than does evaluating an objective project or a uniformly replicable service like basic tax return preparation. As one researcher states, "Clients have to base their judgments on familiar, generic symbols of expertise . . . Do the experts speak as persons with much education? . . . [A]re the experts well dressed?"[55] Although explicit biases deeming women inferior to men are more infrequent now than they were 20 years ago, implicit or unintentional biases regarding how expertise is evaluated and perceived or how someone displays confidence have been shown to negatively impact women to significant degrees.

2. Professional service firms require very low capital intensity and are often structured as private entities (partnerships, limited liability corporations, limited liability partners/principals, etc.), which often means that there are no external Boards of Directors or other entities to provide oversight for or insight into internal practices such as an up-or-out promotion system, subjective advancement criteria, opaque compensation practices, leadership status based on revenue generation, and other processes that have been closely linked with the perpetuation of gender inequity. The professional service firms, thereby insulated from external pressures, are slower to change than publicly held companies that are governed by Boards of Directors and other regulatory agencies.

3. The consumers of professional services offered through professional service firms are large organizations and entities, not individual consumers. That makes it difficult for professional service firms to be pressured by shifting social dynamics or even calls for change by mass consumers. Although professional service firms are indirectly pressured by their clients—corporations with diverse workforces and consumer bases demand that their professional service providers develop diverse teams to serve the diverse needs of the corporations—the pressure faced by professional service firms has not been strong enough to change their overall perspectives on how success should be defined. The demand for gender-balanced teams by the clients of the professional service firms is not quite strong enough for professional service firms to veer away from the "one size fits all" model because the size available does actually fit the majority of leaders who currently lead these professional service firms.

Given these contextual factors and low representation of women in partnership and leadership, professional service firms have been publicly criticized for their lack of gender equity by women in the firms as well as the clients that utilize their services. Google searches for gender diversity in professional service firms return thousands upon thousands of reports, articles, angry ranting blogs, and proposals for solutions. Firms have responded to this outrage with women's initiatives, gender equity programs, speakers' series on gender diversity, training programs on gender bias, and even gender assessments and strategic plans to create sustainable gender equality.

In all of the noise around creating gender equity in professional service firms what you will not find is much information on firms changing anything at the core of their power centers—their business development models and related compensation systems. As a matter of fact, this is one area where firms are candidly and consistently resistant to change regardless of gender inequities.

One female partner/principal in our study assessed firms as *"committed to doing anything and everything as long as you are not asking them to touch the nucleus of business generation and comp [compensation] scales related to that . . . They will work on work-life balance, bring in trainers, wring their hands, host women's retreats, sponsor women's organizations, but you bring up changes to business generation or their comp, and you will see how much they really care about gender equity in their partnership ranks."*

Consequently, understanding and dealing with the differences in how men and women develop business in firms is critical for making progress on gender parity in these firms. The differences discussed in this chapter are the more generalized differences that set the stage for the more specific and startling differences that will be discussed in Part 2. Business development in professional service firms is different than in other arenas; however, addressing gender differences in business development is the key to achieving gender equality in these firms.

KNOWING VERSUS UNDERSTANDING

Charles Kettering, the prolific inventor and engineer who headed research for General Motors from 1920 to 1947, often said that "[k]nowing is not understanding. There is a great difference between knowing and understanding: you can know a lot about something and not really understand it."

We began the effort of identifying possible gender differences in men's and women's assessments of their own business development skills by asking individuals if they generally knew what to do to develop business. While less than 60 percent of women said that they knew what to do to develop business, almost 75 percent of men said that they knew what to do. Similarly, while 20 percent of women said that they did not know what to do to develop business, only 10 percent of men said that they did not know what to do to develop business.

When we examined this data in greater detail, we found that men and women were struggling, to different degrees, with the tension between knowing and understanding that Kettering articulates. Before Caroline found out that her brothers' gun was not the right size for her, she knew how to shoot a gun, and she actually knew how to shoot it well given how quickly she became a ranked shooter after the right gun was put in her hands. Did Caroline's knowledge of how to shoot mean that she fully understood what it took to shoot well? Not necessarily. Because her brothers and father were the only people who had coached her, she (as well as her brothers and father) thought *she* needed to do something differently; she didn't know that no matter what she did, she would never shoot as well as her brothers with that particular gun.

Women in professional service firms know the mechanics of how to develop business, but what they don't know is that no matter how well they operate these mechanics, they will not be able to develop business as well as men using the same tools. Knowing requires knowledge of what works well, but understanding requires knowledge of what works best for you.

This is also true for men. Even though an overwhelming majority of men said that they knew what to do to develop business, they also said that they didn't really understand how business development worked in spite of knowing the general steps to take to make it happen. This man's perspective encapsulated how several men expressed their perspectives on knowing what to do but not necessarily understanding how it worked:

There is a list of things that I know to do. Reach out to people. Show up at events. Talk to people. Tell people what I do. Speak at conferences. The list of things to do is pretty easy to create. There are lists galore online that are a simple search away. What I don't know is what combination of the stuff on my list I should be doing. I'm doing these things, but I don't know for sure which of the things I'm doing are actually working. The head of the firm grew up with the guy who is now our biggest client. I know that growing up with a guy who runs a huge department at a big corporation is a great business development strategy. But, I can't go back and redo my childhood, right? So, we are back to the list of what I can do. I have done everything on the list several times, but no business has come from it. Business has come from other sources but not sources I can really replicate.

Although men and women equally struggled with the difference between knowing and understanding business development, men did not discredit what they knew because of what they did not understand. The majority of men were comfortable asserting knowledge of the process while accepting a lack of understanding of what actually led to success.

Women, on the other hand, assumed that they did not have knowledge of the process if they did not fully understand what led to success. While men felt comfortable saying that they knew something even if they did not understand it fully, women expressed a greater sense of needing to understand something fully before feeling comfortable saying that they knew something. So, while only 10 percent of men in comparison to 20 percent of women said that they did not know what to do to develop business, a significant segment of that 20 percent did in fact demonstrate a knowledge of what to do, but they interpreted their lack of understanding of what actually led to success as a lack of knowledge.

These differentials in language are important because they provide clues about how reality is being interpreted and how the social context is informing the communication of that interpretation. They are also important because they influence what kinds of business development resources men and women are asking for from their firms. While men are asking for more resources to practice what they know because they want to understand it better, women are still asking to learn things that they actually know but don't realize that they know.

The language that women and men used to describe their degree of knowing and/or understanding of business development is consistent with what researchers beginning with Robin Lakoff have found for decades.[56] Women tend to answer questions with "hedges" and "qualifiers" to leave room in their answers for the potential of being wrong.[57] Men tend to answer questions more definitively even if they realize that there is potential for them to be wrong. The statistical differences between men's and women's reports of how much they knew and understood business development were as informed by these gendered linguistic patterns as they were by actual differences in knowledge and understanding.

Moreover, the lack of understanding for women more than men was not a lack of cognitive comprehension about the mechanics of how the process worked, but a lack of understanding of how the process specifically worked for them. For example, if a woman really thrives in more of a collaborative setting but the only business development model in her firm is an ubercompetitive one, she cognitively may understand what needs to be done, but she doesn't understand how it will work for her given her discomfort with the competitive style.

According to one female leader in a midsize professional service firm, *"Women know what to do. When you think about it, business development is not that difficult to figure out. What I see is that women are more reluctant to do the things they know to do but men are not reluctant. Should firm leaders be doing something that is easing that reluctance, I don't know . . . But, really smart women who have done amazing things become reluctant when it comes to business genera-tion. I think we have to do something if we don't want to lose these women who are real superstars in our field."*

A male leader in a large professional service firm had a different perspec-tive: *"We have done trainings and panel discussions and coaching sessions, but in my conversations with the female partners in our firm, I still feel like they don't know what to do. There is an 'I tried that but it didn't work' conversation that I've had with several women. And, when I listen to what they say they are doing, I'm not surprised that it isn't working. These are smart women, and what they do in this area seems clumsy, not at all elegant like I know these women to be."*

This difference, real and/or perceived, between men and women in know-ing and understanding how to develop business is also linked very closely to the differences that men and women reported in their access to the mentor-ing and training they needed in order to learn the craft and art of successful business development in their firms. Almost 70 percent of men said that they had mentors who had taught them how to develop clients in comparison to 39 percent of women. Almost 50 percent of women responded that they had never had the mentors they needed in order to learn how to develop business in the firms.

Similarly while 53 percent of men said that they had mentors and/or spon-sors who introduced them to the people they needed to know in order to start developing business, only 37 percent of women said the same. Again, over 50 percent of women responded that they had never had the mentors and/or sponsors who introduced them to people they needed to know in order to start developing business.

Finally, more than 60 percent of men said that they had the access to the training and development they needed in order to maximize their client development potential in comparison to only 33 percent of women who said that they had that type of access.

The gender differentials in access to mentors, sponsors, and training/development opportunities in business development definitely explain, at least partially, the differences in men's and women's reports of knowing and understanding what to do to develop business. I define mentors as "people who provide information, insights, and opportunities to help you advance your career," and I define sponsors as "people who use their influence to advocate for you behind the scenes." Training/development opportunities were generally defined as "opportunities in the workplace where you can learn, practice, showcase and stretch skill sets to demonstrate the full potential of business development abilities."

MENTORS
People who provide information, insights, and opportunities to help you advance your career

SPONSORS
People who use their influence to help you advance your career

While the preceding discussion answers some of the questions about the differences in business development behaviors and outcomes in professional service firms, there are additional layers of differences in personal preferences and expectations that help us understand the nuanced dynamics and differences on an even deeper level.

Men and women described the most successful mentoring on this topic to be the active hands-on type of mentoring that occurred when they were asked to participate in putting together a response to a Request for Proposals or when they were allowed to accompany a pitch team to actually see a pitch done in front of a client. The "in the field" types of mentoring activities were viewed as more beneficial by men and women than conversations in which business development was described/detailed, but men were three times as likely as women to say that they were actually receiving this type of mentoring.

Men were more likely to be invited to both informal and formal opportunities where business development activities were taking place, and women were more likely to hear about business development activities in lunches, through panel discussions, and in trainings by outside consultants. Thus, of the men and women who did feel that they were getting the information and advice they needed, the men were more likely to get it in ways that they (and women) found to be more helpful and effective.

The responses to the questions about sponsors and about training/development opportunities were remarkably similar to the responses about mentors. Men had significantly more access to sponsors than women did, and both men and women commented on the direct correlation between having mentors and sponsors and getting the training/development opportunities to grow business development skill sets.

A female partner/principal commented on this correlation: *"Firms are not places where you have a job waiting for you to come do it. You have to get work from client leads who staff you on their client projects if you don't have work of your own. If you don't have these types of people mentoring you or sponsoring you, it is difficult to get opportunities to develop and grow. These opportunities are literally in the hands of a few people, and you can't get them unless one of these people opens his hand and gives you the chance. He will give it to people he knows and likes."*

BEING TAUGHT VERSUS LEARNING

"Personally, I'm always ready to learn, although I do not always like being taught."

—Winston Churchill

Harold Geneen, the former President of ITT Corporation, said that "[l]eadership cannot really be taught. It can only be learned." Geneen's statement along with Churchill's personal declaration illustrate the distinction between learning something and being taught something. This distinction came up many times in the stories we heard through our surveys and interviews, and the primary distinction between learning and being taught was the active engagement of the "student." Learning was articulated as what happened when you were actively engaged in doing something as a result of being given the opportunity to do it. Being taught was articulated as the somewhat impersonal transference of information or insights from one person to another.

The overarching theme that emerged was that men were learning to develop business while women were being taught about business development, with the former being active and the latter being much more passive. Men were formally and informally being given opportunities to actively learn, while women were being passively taught in a disengaged way.

The majority of firms today still depend on organic methods of growing business development skills, primarily that of transference from the finders to the minders or the entrepreneurial efforts of the minders on their own. A few firms are experimenting with business development professionals who are principally responsible for generating clients without actually performing the services for which the firm is being hired. This administrative business development process is working in a few industries, but the overall landscape of service providers within firms needing to generate clients has not changed that much.

Professional service firms rely on their partners/principals to develop the clients, and when firms get frustrated with individual or collective performance levels in business development, they attempt to increase business development performance through two additional channels of effort:

1. An *internal* channel that utilizes internal professionals, resource groups, and more formal and informal mentoring/sponsoring by senior professionals with proven track records in business development, and
2. An *external* channel that utilizes external business development education opportunities, tools, consultants, and coaches.

INTERNAL CHANNELS: LEARNING AND CONNECTING

Internal Professionals
Internal Professional/Affinity Resource Groups
Internal Formal and Informal Mentoring
Internal Sponsoring by Senior Professionals and Leaders

EXTERNAL CHANNELS: TRAINING AND COACHING

External Business Development Education
External Business Development Tools and Networks
External Business Development Coaches
External Business Development Trainers/Consultants

These two channels (and the efforts contained within them) were seen as successful to varying degrees by men and women, with informal mentoring/ sponsoring in the internal channel being ranked as the most effective by both men and women. Nevertheless, as previously mentioned, while this particular effort within the internal channel was ranked highest by both men and women, men reported accessing and receiving this mentoring/sponsoring at much higher rates than women. A deeper analysis of both of these channels provides a more comprehensive picture of how firms are trying to deal with increasing business development generally and women's business development specifically.

INTERNAL CHANNELS: LEARNING AND CONNECTING

The internal business development enhancement efforts in firms center around three primary components: (1) internal professionals, (2) resource groups, and (3) more formal and informal mentoring/sponsoring by senior professionals with proven track records in business development.

The internal professionals range from business development trainers whose responsibility it is to train and develop people to develop business to people whose sole responsibility it is to develop business for their firms regardless of the fact that they don't actually provide the services they are selling. These professionals focus on the firm's overall brand in regard to the marketplace, and while they sometimes may be marketing or public relations oriented, they serve in roles that are more directly connected to helping people bring business in the door.

In addition to focusing on the overall brand of the firm, these professionals concentrate on identifying the knowledge and skills that people need in order to develop business, and they ensure the distribution of the knowledge and the training of the skills. One professional development specialist in a firm explained her role as *"the stretcher . . . professionals who are trained to do a particular thing like accounting or law don't always know how to sell . . . even if they know, they may not want to sell . . . my job is to help them stretch beyond their comfort zones and learn the habits they need to effectively develop business."*

While many women (and men) reported that they found the internal business development seminars useful, they were frustrated that *"the development people can tell us what to do but they can't actually help us do it because they can't sell for us, and most of us know what to do, but if we aren't comfortable doing it, we are on our own."*

Moreover, many of the women who had used internal business development resources commented that even business development materials that were specifically written and developed for women were not different in substance from the general materials. One woman in a technology consulting firm commented that *"the only difference that I saw in the materials designed for women was that there was an entire section in the materials for women that talked about work-life balance and gave suggestions on how to do business development and be a working mom . . . they had suggestions like making sure that you have adequate child care coverage in the evenings because a lot of events are in the evenings. They also had stern messages that even if you don't like doing some of the things suggested, you have to do them to get business. It really irritated me."*

In some industries, firms have completely taken business development out of the hands of the professionals performing direct client service and made the full process of business development a more administrative process. While this has alleviated the pressure on women in some arenas, most women in these firms also said that the administrative process did not act as a substitute for business development efforts. The process merely streamlined the efforts and standardized what the client experienced, but it did not change the inequities experienced by women in regard to being seen as business developers.

"Our business development person is great. She is seen as a part of the firm's leadership team even, but she still has to report who she is attributing certain clients to . . . There is still credit being given and gotten . . . and credit for business is the currency for success in the firm."

The second component, the resource groups (also referred to as affinity groups and networking groups), are the internal mechanisms through which women, people of color, and other minority groups such as members of the LGBTQ community create connections with other people in their "identity communities" in order to attack business development and other systemic issues in a collective and cohesive way. In many firms today, the women's resource groups operate as women's initiatives, women's leadership groups, or other such entities that focus on women getting together to talk about and work on getting women to be more successful in those firms.

Women's resource groups principally work to create "safe spaces" where women can discuss the challenges of being a woman in the firm from work-life balance issues to unconscious gender bias to the specific trials of business development. In regard to business development, these efforts do everything from connecting women with other women in the firm in order to cross-sell services or intra-firm references to identifying effective external resources to assist women with their business development.

Although such groups have been successful in pushing through other types of changes that are beneficial to women like maternity policies, work-life balance initiatives, and even an increase in the investment of firm resources in women, most women in our study did not feel that these resource groups were actually working in enhancing women's abilities to bring in and grow business of their own.

As one woman put it, *"The women's group is great at getting us [women] together. We are able to get some things done, but they are the kinds of things that benefit younger women . . . like flexibility initiatives or more transparency in evaluations . . . but, the group really can't help with business development. We get together and talk about how difficult it is, but we aren't doing anything to change it because we really can't."* Another woman talked about the difficulties in using these groups as avenues for collective business development when each of the women in the group did not have much business: *"We read this book that talked about referring business to each other so that we can benefit from each other's contacts, but that didn't work. We didn't really have business to refer, and the bottom line is that we are trying to fix the business development problem by ourselves . . . and we don't have business as a group."*

We saw almost no correlation between the participation in women's groups and increased business development even when these groups were present and active. Ironically, we did discover that the presence and activities of these groups increase the amount of revenue that enters the firm, especially from client teams led by women, but the women in the firm don't benefit from this increased revenue. In many cases, the activities of the women's groups are actually helping the men who fight for and control client relationships.

The final component of the internal support system for business development is the informal mentoring/sponsoring by senior people, especially senior people with business. Definitions of mentoring and sponsoring abound, but the one we were able to derive from the people who participated in our study was primarily that mentoring is the transference of how to do something while sponsoring is the advocacy for someone utilizing personal and professional capital. While people did differentiate between mentoring and sponsoring, men and women were overwhelmingly positive that informal mentoring and sponsoring worked whereas formalized mentoring and sponsorship programs did not work as well.

Men reported higher rates of being both informally mentored and sponsored, but women reported higher rates of actively seeking it. Men seemed to be creating these relationships with senior people more organically while women were actively seeking these relationships often to no avail.

The formal mentoring programs were viewed as generally failing by both the male and female professionals. The firm leaders also felt that the programs were failing but were hesitant to dismantle them until they had effective replacements. So, programs that are not seen as working are continued because effective alternatives are unknown, but potentially effective alternatives cannot be fully pursued because the current programs are using up necessary resources.

EXTERNAL CHANNELS: TRAINING AND COACHING

"In school, you're taught a lesson and then given a test. In life, you're given a test that teaches you a lesson."

—Tom Bodett

The irony in professional service firms is that developing business is the test that teaches you the lesson of how to develop business. Without the lesson, there can be no test, but there cannot be a lesson unless there is a test. Confusing? We thought so as well as we analyzed the stories and perspectives of the professionals in our study. The majority of men reported learning how to develop business by being given the chance to develop business while the majority of women were often told that they would be included in business development opportunities once they demonstrated business development abilities. Many firm leaders acknowledged that these types of challenges were being experienced by women in their firms, and they pointed to their firms' investments in external business development resources, especially for women, as their way of trying to minimize some of these challenges.

One leader listed the various external business development learning opportunities in which his firm invested: *"conferences, workshops using top consultants, retreats for the women's group so that they can get to know each other better and refer business to each other, coaches who work in confidential relationships with individual partners, and other efforts . . . we are trying a lot of things, and I can't tell you for sure what is working or what isn't working, doing something is better than doing nothing."* Interestingly, the majority of external resources for business development were not utilized by people who were actually successful in developing business. Additionally, the people who utilized these resources did not feel that the resources were significantly helpful in assisting them with developing the business they were seeking to develop.

The data painted a picture of two types of learning business development—the external route and the internal route, with the latter leading to far greater success than the former. That said, the one resource that people who were not able to access the internal networks found helpful was access to individual coaches. While men and women equally valued the benefits of working with a coach, women were far more likely than men to actually engage a coach.

Of those professionals who worked with external business development coaches, women worked with coaches because they wanted to be held accountable for doing what they needed to do while men worked with coaches to plan and stay organized. Women were very comfortable planning and organizing their business development plans on their own, but they were uncomfortable executing those plans, primarily because they did not enjoy the activities needed to execute. Men, on the other hand, were comfortable executing activities once these activities were identified and integrated into an organized plan, but they were more uncomfortable actually creating a plan.

The business development coaches who graciously agreed to speak with us shared their insights into the challenges that professionals face in developing business and the differences they saw between men and women in developing and executing a business development plan. According to the business development coaches, the following are the business development challenges faced by professionals in firms. Following the outline of challenges are the gender differentials that the coaches have observed between their male and female clients.[58]

Business Development Challenges
(as Reported by Business Development Coaches)

- Professionals see their professional skills as requiring a high degree of intellectual effort and professional integrity, and business development feels like a skill that is incongruous with what they do as professionals, so they don't like it and often resent it.
- Business development feels unpredictable and out of the realms of personal control, and feeling out of control or doing something without predictable achievements does not feel attractive to professionals in firms.
- Business development is very time consuming, and professionals are already frustrated with the pressures of working long hours to serve clients. Business development falls off the priority list when people get crunched for time.
- Business development requires extroverted tendencies, especially in networking, and it is difficult for introverted professionals.

Gender in Business Development
(as Reported by Business Development Coaches)

Business development coaches generally teach business development techniques as applicable to all equally regardless of gender, but they commented on how their female clients were not able to achieve the same results as their male clients using the same business development techniques.

- Women talk about scheduling conflicts more than men do, but underneath the conversations about schedules were expressions of discomfort and difficulties around engaging in traditional business development activities (sporting events, golf games, events involving copious amounts of alcohol, etc.) as women.
- Men are more direct and open about their ambitions around business development and what they will gain as a result of getting more business. Women are more hesitant to express explicit ambition, and the indirectness of their approach makes it harder for them to develop and execute ambitious business development plans.

The perspectives of the business development coaches allowed us to hear the concerns and anxieties expressed by those who had actively sought out expert assistance to enhance their business development skills and increase their business development outcomes. When men and women who actively seek out this assistance implement the expert advice they receive with relatively equal vigor and end up with significantly different outcomes, the impact of gender on business development behaviors and outcomes cannot be ignored.

According to the coaches, the women were as motivated and committed as their male counterparts, but when they implemented the same strategies as their male counterparts, they got different outcomes. One coach told us directly that *"women need to be doing something different, but we don't yet know what that different thing is . . . we do know that what we are doing right now is not working for women as much as it is working for men."*

One female partner/principal who had used a coach (she loved the experience of working with a coach) told us that *"I've been a high achiever my whole life. I worked hard and reaped big rewards. Ivy League education. Great jobs. This business development challenge is the first time in my life when hard work does not lead to rewards . . . of any kind, not big or small. So, I'm frustrated. I've listened to people. I've created checklists. I check things off my list. It doesn't work. I know what I'm doing. It just isn't working."*

Several women also talked to us about feeling further demoralized and depressed after working with a coach because their work with coaches had been their last-ditch effort to get better at business development. When nothing changed after the coaching, they felt worse than they had before the coaching. One coach shared with us that he often saw this trend in female professionals, and he opined that men were better at translating relationships into business whereas women lingered in relationships without translating them into clients. We actually found that this was, in fact, happening, and you can read more about the experiment and findings in this area in Chapters 7 and 8.

KNOWING VERSUS DOING

For the men and women who felt that they did indeed know and understand what to do to develop business, we wondered if there was a difference in how men and women actually executed on this knowledge in order to develop the business they needed. What we found, simply put, is that men executed and women did not, but the reasons for this difference were far from simple.

We took a closer look at the gender differences in men's and women's perspectives on business development as a professional strength and analyzed whether the differences in perspectives explained why men executed on their knowledge of what to do more than women did.

Although we did not specify a particular context for these perspectives, many of the survey respondents and interviewees offered assessments of their business development with the qualifier that they were specifically responding in the context of how business development was currently defined in their firms. For many people, especially women, it was important to differentiate between business development as a general competence and business development as defined, recognized, and valued in their respective firms. The following perspective was one that we heard consistently from women who work or had worked in women-owned professional service firms.

"I worked in a woman-owned firm before I came here. The process there was very different. So, if you had asked me these questions then, I would have answered differently. It is very different as a woman to get business in a firm where the majority of partners are men. I know how to get business, but I can't seem to get it right here."

Within the context of business development in men-owned (interesting how it looks strange when framed this way) firms, 60 percent of men agreed or strongly agreed that business development was a strength for them in comparison to only 40 percent of women. Furthermore, only 24 percent of men actively said that business development was not a strength for them in comparison to 43 percent of women. While the 20 percent differential between men and women in feeling that business development was a strength for them warrants a closer look, the almost 20 percent differential between men and women who actively said that business development was not a strength for them warrants equal attention.

When asked specifically about whether business development activities were difficult for them, 48 percent of women said that business development activities were difficult for them in comparison to only 31 percent of men. The 17 percent differential is noteworthy, and the reasons presented by the men and women for their difficulties with business development were also noteworthy.

The men who found business development activities difficult primarily focused on time and a lack of structure in the process as constraints. Women also mentioned time constraints and unstructured processes as challenges, but they also noted that the business development activities within their firms such as golf outings, "boondoggles" or "junkets," and sporting events were events where men were actually uncomfortable if their female peers participated. The following two stories provide some experiential insights into the difficulties faced by women in traditional (and common) professional service firm business development events.

"At our golf events—we have about two to three a year—we invite our current clients and maybe some potential clients. A few years ago, these golf events were expanded to be golf/spa events where female partners/directors could invite female clients. Given that there aren't a lot of us female partners/directors or a lot of female clients, the firm opened up the event for the men at our firm and our clients to invite their spouses for the spa activities. Let's talk about all that went wrong with this. First of all, the firm did not open up the golf activities to any spouses, and that was awkward for some of the women from the firm who actually golfed—their husbands were not invited to golf—and the women from our firm who went to the spa activities could not invite their husbands to golf either. So, it basically turned into a situation where men could invite their wives, but it was very very awkward for a woman to invite her husband. We had one female client who asked if she could bring her husband because he loved golf, and she told me later that he had a miserable time because of how uncomfortable every-one acted when he told them that he was a writer and worked from home so that he could be there for their children. And, the conversa-tions at the spa were ridiculous. The majority of the women in the spa are the wives of the men playing golf so "who is your husband" is one of the first questions they ask of any woman they see. The awkwardness of trying to talk business with a client in this environment was too much. I stopped going to the events."

"The firm had a client development event at a concert, and each of us got four tickets for the concert. I invited three women—one was the head of marketing at a huge company, one was the superintendent of a nearby school district, and one was chief of staff at a large hospital. All three of these people had budgets to hire firms to do exactly what we did. They were all mothers, and all of our kids were around the same age. The firm had a cocktail reception before the concert, and the four of us were talking about our children when one of the leaders of the firm pulls me aside to tell me that he is disappointed that I took this event as an opportunity to have a girls' night out. I was pissed. He didn't even ask who they were. And, I couldn't get into it with him right then and there because I had to get back to my guests. The worst part was that the guy who said this to me brought his 20-something son and his son's girlfriend to the concert. That's why it's hard for me. I can do what I'm supposed to do just like anyone else, but it's hard to put up with those types of assumptions and comments."

There were several men as well who noted that business development events in their firms were not appealing to them because they were not golf or sports enthusiasts. As one man commented, *"I know that women say that it's an old boys club the way we develop business, but not all of us boys are included in that club either. There is a lot about the system that needs to change, not just for women but kind of for everyone."* Another man reflected on how hard he had to try to fit in: *"I don't like golf. I don't really like sports. One time when I suggested to a couple of my partners that we should think about adding performances at the symphony and the opera as possible events to which we can take clients, one of my partners asked me if I was gay."*

While the men who do not share an interest in the more traditional business development activities like playing golf, attending sporting events, and having drinks with colleagues may have a harder time developing business than the men who do share an interest in these activities, women have particularly thorny social expectations and constraints to navigate that make business development especially difficult. If they know what to do and intend to do it, they aren't always allowed (explicitly or implicitly) to actually do it.

On July 21, 2010, the *New York Post*'s Page Six ran a story titled "Pols Told to Be Wary of Female Lobbyists."[59] The following excerpt from the story highlights the social complexities of developing business as a woman.

Some Republican congressmen have been warned to keep their distance from the female lobbyists who prowl Capitol Hill.

Sources say House Minority Leader John Boehner has told GOP congressmen who partied with lobbyists "to knock it off" . . . While there's no evidence of anything more than friendly flirtatious behavior, the lawmakers have been told to keep partying to a minimum in this midterm election year.

GOP Rep. Lee Terry of Nebraska—who's in a tough race against Democratic opponent Tom White—was witnessed by Page Six in close conversation with a comely lobbyist at the Capitol Hill Club in DC recently.

"Why did you get me so drunk?" Terry asked the giggling woman, among other personal remarks. When Terry realized he was sitting near a reporter, he quickly changed the topic of conversation to his three children and the struggle to pay their college tuition.[60]

Journalistic accuracy and integrity aside, the word choices of "prowl," "friendly flirtatious," "partying," "comely," and "giggling" imbue a story about a networking event between lobbyists from lobbying firms and politicians with a social meaning based on gender. None of these words would be used to describe a man from a lobbying firm networking with another man, and coverage like this makes the case that women cannot fit into the business development models in which men comfortably play.

Underneath the slightly salacious content of the story, there is an unspoken question of why the Republican politicians are being told to stay away from the female lobbyists instead of being schooled in exercising good judgment and appropriate behavior around men and women in professional settings. Boehner's actions almost make it seem like bad behavior is inevitable thereby making it necessary to avoid the trigger for the bad behavior—women.

In October 2010, The Hill ran an article on this issue from the female lobbyists' perspectives that was titled "Female Lobbyists Cry Foul as Republican Lawmakers Keep Their Distance on the Hill."[61] An excerpt from this article follows.

> The concern about the appearance of impropriety is not new on Capitol Hill. Perception, after all, is everything in politics.
>
> But female lobbyists are raising new concerns that access to male Republican lawmakers has been further hampered by a warning made earlier this year by House Minority Leader John Boehner . . .
>
> Some women on K Street, who say they are already at a disadvantage to their male counterparts, are upset about the reports of Boehner's edict and say it represents yet another obstacle.

The subtle and not so subtle social currents surrounding men and women socializing with and being around one another impacts what women can do in business development. A senior male firm leader in our study talked about how uncomfortable it made him to take a woman from his firm to a business development event with a client, especially if the event was in the evening: *"I know it's not right, but it's just uncomfortable to walk into a restaurant to meet two men from the client team and have a young attractive woman with me. I've done it before and gotten comments that I can't repeat here. I don't need comments like that said about me. That doesn't happen when I take a young man to these meetings. These issues affect women surely, but you should also be looking at how men are affected."* Other men expressed other assumptions about why women were not always invited to client development events ranging from stereotypical (*"do women really want to attend sporting events"*) to paternalistic (*"I assumed that she wouldn't want to be out late because she has kids . . . I was looking out for her"*) to explicitly exclusive (*"I know these guys and where they want to go . . . . .places where women are there to be entertaining to men, if you know what I mean . . . not a place where a woman would want to go, trust me."*) Female partners/principals were very aware of many of these assumptions, and their reactions ranged from *"what can I do about it"* to *"ask me and let me make up my own mind . . . don't decide for me."* One woman talked about how her firm entertained current and potential clients at basketball games and how their assumptions about her interest in basketball were *"infuriatingly wrong because I'm a huge hoops fan, and I actually played, in high school and col-*

lege, and none of the guys here played in college . . . we had tickets to some March Madness games, and my school, the one I played hoops for, was playing, and I had a fit when I wasn't invited and when I asked for tickets, they told me the tickets were all gone."

Another female partner gave the example of being told to "show up." *"We had this business development training where we were told that the first rule of rainmaking was to show up. Showing up is the hard work—that's what the speaker said. But, that's only true for men. For women, showing up is the least of it. I have to show up and not be too friendly to be a flirt but friendly enough so that I'm not seen as cold and not overtalk the guys but not be a wallflower and be cool enough to have a few drinks but not drink so much that it's in poor taste and talk about my family enough that I don't come across as a spinster but not talk about them too much so that I don't seem like I'm having a conflict with work and family . . . these are not hypotheticals . . . it's not as easy as just showing up . . . if it was and I could be myself when I showed up without worrying about how I'm coming across to the guys, I would probably show up more."*

Social context and meaning can create a huge gap between knowing what to do and actually being able to do it not because you don't have the capacity to do it, but because you may or may not be allowed to do it from a social perspective. Even if men and women equally knew exactly what to do, the social contexts of gender norms and gender expectations would make it more difficult for women to do what they know to do because their actions would not be perceived or received in the same way as the actions of their male counterparts.

INITIATING VERSUS INHERITING

As Epstein, Sauté, Oglensky, and Gever report, "Women, like men, make contacts with and secure clients through several routes: one is business obtained from internal referrals made by senior partners within the firm; another is from clients and former clients of the firms who refer new work to a lawyer; yet another is from new contacts from the outside. The latter most closely resembles the conventional model of 'rainmaking.'"[62]

Many of the professionals in the survey and interviews discussed the difference between inheriting clients and having to initiate clients, the former being comprised of being integrated in succession plans for client relationship management and internal referrals and the latter being *"clients developed from scratch."* Men and women alike perceived that women underperformed men with both inherited and initiated clients, but the reasons for the underperformance differed for each category.

The primary reason cited by women for their underperformance in inheriting clients was that no matter how much they wanted to get the business, they were not pulled into and included in the informal networks within the firm through which critical relationships necessary for inheritance were created and nurtured. While men generally agreed that women had less access to key sources that allowed them to inherit clients at a rate equivalent to that of their male peers, some of the men noted that they felt that the women in their firms *"did not act like they wanted to deal with client development."* The difference between these two perceptions lay in the behaviors that men and women were using to describe women's ambitions and abilities to inherit clients; while women were pointing to how they went above and beyond in the work for the clients, men were looking at women's presence and participation in client development activities like attendance at athletic events and participation in golf games.

Unlike the gender differences in the inheritance of clients that were attributed by men and women to a lack of networks for women and by men to a lack of desire on the part of women, the gender differences in the initiation of clients were attributed to a lack of ability for rainmaking. Our data analysis resulted in findings that were, again, very similar to those of the "Glass Ceilings and Open Doors" study:

> Very few women have the reputation for independent rainmaking, and women in general are not regarded to be as good rainmakers as men by both men and themselves [women] . . . Although many senior men tend to dismiss the notion that women are disadvantaged by their gender, only a very small number of them could imagine any woman partner they knew—in the firm or outside—filling the shoes of the senior rainmakers of their firms.[63]

The perception that women were not good at rainmaking was compounded by men's and women's views of successful female rainmakers as *"exceptions"* or *"lucky."* Most interestingly, even the women in our study who were successful rainmakers saw themselves as the exceptions and pointed to unique circumstances around a particular relationship or a specific specialty that resulted in their business development. When I asked them how their success in developing clients had been different from that of their male counterparts, they were not able to give any specifics.

When women were successful in initiating their own clients, the prevailing presumption that women were not good at rainmaking made the successful ones into anomalies instead of using their examples as evidence to take apart the presumption itself.

Women reported getting less business than men in both the inheritance and the initiation categories for all of the reasons just mentioned, and many of these women noted that they were frustrated because their underperformance in this area was not for the lack of trying. One female partner/principal started crying in the interview when she was talking about how much she had tried and how frustrated she was with the process: *"I would not be as frustrated if I was not doing well and I was not trying. I am doing everything I know to do, and it isn't successful, and I'm being looked at like I don't want to be successful. They [the leaders] don't want to hear that it is very different for women. We get judged by standards that we cannot meet."*

◢ MARIE

Marie is a partner/principal in the most profitable division of a midsize professional service firm. She has been with the same firm for her entire career, and she was advanced into partnership because the partner/principal for whom she did most of her work generated a very high amount of revenue for the firm. When this prolific business generator insisted that Marie be elected into partnership, no one argued.

"I became partner because of him, but once he retired, of course I became very vulnerable. I have never felt like I am truly a partner at this firm because there has always been a qualifier for me. I am a female partner because we only have one other female partner, and we are never just partners, we are always the female partners. I've been told that I am a 'service' partner because I don't have business. I know that I am one of the least compensated partners because I am a 'service' partner."

Marie does much of the work for the two biggest clients in her division. The clients call her directly, and they communicate their trust and confidence in her to the partner/principal who "gets credit" for the client. *"When he thanks me for doing a great job on 'his' clients, it always feels like he's patting my head as if I was a child. He barely does any of the work for the client. He takes the two key people at the company to games and dinners and even on a trip, I think. I've never been invited to those things.*

"I'm a female service partner," she jokes. *"That makes me officially the thing you never want to be in a firm."*

A few days after our interview, Marie sent me an e-mail with the following quote from Elizabeth Cady Stanton: "I would have women regard themselves not as adjectives, but as nouns." The message from Marie that accompanied the quote simply said, *"We need to stop being adjectives."*

PART 2

THE FITS
& THE
MISFITS
(AND A FEW REFITS)

CHAPTER 5

SUPERSTAR SIZES VS. TEAM SUCCESSES

In the 2004 Olympic Games in Athens, Greece, the USA Basketball Men's National Team (USA Men's Olympic Team) lost three out of eight games and settled for a bronze medal. Although any Olympic medal is a great achievement, the three losses were more than the USA Men's Olympic Team had ever suffered in all previous Olympic Games . . . combined. This was also the first time that Americans did not get a gold medal in this competition since professional basketball players were allowed to join the 1992 team.

The team, comprised of professional basketball superstars like Carmelo Anthony, Carlos Boozer, Tim Duncan, Allen Iverson, Stephen Marbury, Amare Stoudemire, and Dwayne Wade, first lost to Italy in an exhibition game and then to Puerto Rico. A *USA Today* article described the game against Puerto Rico this way: "This is the Olympics, and the U.S. men's basketball team was rocked, shocked, humiliated and exposed on sports biggest stage Sunday as Puerto Rico, a Commonwealth of 4 million residents, pulled off the upset of all Olympic upsets with a 92-73 drubbing of the Americans."[64]

The USA coach, Larry Brown, focused on how the Puerto Rican players "'played as a team'" and said his star-studded team needed "'to come together and see if we really are a team.'"[65] The USA team had stars who could each achieve amazing things, and a few individuals even set records at the 2004 games, but those individual performances were not enough for the team to win. Every team has a few superstars, but superstars don't make a team, and as global competition in basketball heated up, the USA needed a team, a strong one.

Citing the team's challenges in 2004 and the increasing "strength of the competition in international basketball,"[66] the USA Basketball Executive Committee created a Managing Director position for the team and hired Jerry Colangelo, the Chairman and CEO of the Phoenix Suns, to fill that role. One of Colangelo's first statements after getting the position was to stress that the USA needed "'a team not of individual stars, but athleticism, shooters, role players and distributors.'"[67]

Keeping his eye on the ever-increasing international competition, Colangelo selected coaches and players who weren't just strong individuals but would collectively make a strong team. He upset many NBA players and fans by not selecting many of the superstars of the day, but he focused on the whole, not the parts.

The USA Men's Olympic Team won the gold medal in 2008 with an 8–0 record, and they won the gold medal again in 2012 with an 8–0 record. The superstar size looked like the right size when the players were viewed individually, but in order for the team to win as a unit, adding different sizes—players who weren't necessarily superstars but could collectively play all the roles necessary to win as a team—was essential.

◢SUSAN

Susan is a partner/shareholder in a professional service firm that works primarily in the engineering arena. She is an engineer by education and training (a Ph.D. in a highly specialized area of engineering who trained in an elite invention laboratory), and she was highly sought after by professional service firms when she decided to leave the laboratory and go into consulting. She selected the firm that she is currently in because the majority of partners/principals with whom she had met had talked about how supportive the firm was of individual partners'/principals' business development efforts.

Susan had a strong connection to a particular technology company, and she set up a meeting with the CEO to get the conversation going regarding the company's hiring of her firm as its primary consulting firm. The day before Susan's meeting with the CEO, one of the other partners/principals at the firm had a conference call with one of the members of the corporation's Board of Directors, an individual with whom this partner had done business several years earlier.

When Susan proceeded to officially begin the relationship between her firm and the corporation, she realized that the "relationship" with the client had already been opened by the other partner who had spoken with a Director from the Board of Directors. When Susan protested that the Board had nothing to do with the engagement of the technical consulting firm, the firm's leader said that there was nothing he could do about who first *"opened the project."*

Susan quickly realized that the *"credit"* for business development was a *"vicious battle,"* and she did not know if she wanted to fight back or find ways *"to get along."* She settled for the latter, not because she didn't want to fight but because she didn't want to do anything that might be seen as *"not being a team player."* She felt good about the decision initially until several male leaders stopped by individually to tell her that her actions (or lack thereof) had secured her status as a "service partner," not a "rainmaker."

Susan, after several years of being in the lowest quadrant of the firm's business developers, better understands now why she consistently finds herself at the bottom of the client development heap even though she manages the key projects for several of the firm's top clients. *"I want to work as a team, and I will have to work differently if I want to rank differently or throw my hat in for a leadership position. Do I want to work differently and not get the accolades or do I want to work in a way that makes me happy? I don't want the rankings or the accolades, but then, I realize that those rankings and accolades are the only paths to leadership. Not because I want the leadership for [the] sake of the leadership or even the compensation, but because I want to make a difference. The higher up you go, the more you can make a difference."*

SUPERSTARS WITHOUT TEAMS

Many professional service firms operate like the 2004 USA Men's Olympic Team where the big revenue generators are the superstars, and the firms don't realize that those superstars, no matter how successful they are individually, will not lead to the sustained success of the firm if other models of getting, serving, and keeping clients are not acknowledged and rewarded. Bronze medals are great, and if there are professional service firms that want to play for bronze, the superstar game plan may work. If professional service firms, however, want to go for gold, the superstar game plan needs to be replaced with a team game plan.

Brent Adamson, Matthew Dixon, and Nicholas Toman, in a recent article, wrote about a Corporate Executive Board study that found that there has been *"an extraordinary shift in the relationship between individual achievement and business unit profitability. . . . From 2002 to 2012, the impact of individuals' task performance on unit profitability companywide decreased, on average from 78% to 51%. But the impact of employees' 'network performance'—that is, how much people give to and take from their coworkers—increased from 22% to 49%."*[68] Individuals, even the stars, bring down the collective performance unless they are actively collaborating with others in the organization. Moreover, if they are being asked to collaborate with others but are still being rewarded via their individual contributions, individuals will not collaborate as much as they will when their compensation is tied to collective success.

Human beings, though, generally don't like change until change is no longer a choice. The USA Men's Olympic Team would not have been open to change if not for the fact that they lost miserably in 2004. One of the firm leaders I interviewed, the head of a department in a large firm, recalled when the two biggest rainmakers in his department left to go start a firm of their own. The approximately 18 people left in his department were devastated and demoralized when the firm put them on warning that unless they brought in some revenue, the firm would have to let them all go. The head of the department decided to do something radical and told everyone that the department would work to bring in revenue as a team. Everyone in the team would get paid a base salary based on experience and tenure at the firm, and all bonuses would be dependent on the overall performance of the department. People were energized by the "all for one" approach and enthusiastically began working on client development, including reaching out to the clients who had tentatively agreed to leave with the departing rainmakers. They were able to convince a few clients to stay and brought in enough business as a team to stave off any terminations. This leader, admittedly, would never have made this change if the change had been a choice, but he left the system in place even after the crisis was over because the new system worked better and his team was more engaged than they had ever been.

The leader described it as a "moneyball experience," referring to the book *Moneyball: The Art of Winning an Unfair Game* by Michael Lewis in which the Oakland A's—one of the poorest teams in Major League Baseball—put together a team of average players that played as a team and achieved one of the longest winning streaks in baseball history.[69] No stars, just a winning team.

As John Wooden, the legendary UCLA basketball coach, once said, "The main ingredient of stardom is the rest of the team." Professional service firms forget this main ingredient in identifying the full depth of their strengths. Moreover, they make the superstars the leaders, and by doing so, they perpetuate a process in which the superstars become the leaders who only recognize the next generation of superstars as the next potential leaders. So, not only do professional service firms overvalue their superstars, they underestimate their superstars' abilities to lead all people in the firm.

One professional service firm leader laughingly admitted that professional service firms are *"the only industry that takes their best salespeople and make them CEOs."* Another leader acknowledged that professional service firms *"don't promote people into leadership because they have proven themselves as leaders . . . they promote people who have proven themselves as business developers. If they have business, they get to lead . . . yes, regardless of leadership skills, per se."*

As Sian Beilock, Ph.D., a psychology professor at the University of Chicago, has found in her research on brain performance under pressure, "the best players don't make the best coaches."[70] Beilock finds that as "you get better at what you do, your ability to communicate your understanding or to help others learn that skill often gets worse and worse." Therefore, those who are successful at business development in professional service firms, *"intellectual athletes"* as one professional service firm leader told me, may be the worst choices to lead the firm, especially if the leaders have any responsibility to teach, facilitate, or encourage business development in those that come after them.

Similarly, Andris Zoltners, P. K. Sinha, and Sally Lorimer, in their research on salesmanship behavior in contrast to leadership behavior, found that "[w]hat it takes to succeed in sales is different from what it takes to succeed in management."[71] Whether you follow the sports research demonstrating that the best players don't make good coaches or the business research demonstrating that the best salespeople don't make the best leaders, the practice of using business development success to determine access to leadership creates a conundrum for women. Women are not succeeding at business development in the current model and therefore cannot access the leadership positions to change the model to better fit their needs.

THE ONE SIZE THAT IS SUPPOSED TO FIT ALL

In spite of the abundance of research that has demonstrated that it's teams and not superstars that win big, the one size for business development in firms is based on the superstar. Teams, by design, need different players to play different roles and therefore have multiple sizes for shoes that need to be filled.

If you search for materials on the characteristics of great business developers, you will find many articles, blogs, and other resources that explain how rainmakers come in many shapes and sizes, that great business developers are built not born, that it is the daily practice of certain behaviors that leads to successful business development. The majority of the 72 leaders of professional service firms that we interviewed, however, had a very different perspective.

We asked these leaders to select the 10 business development characteristics from a list of 35 that they felt were most critical to success in their firms.[72] The following diagram illustrates their selections.

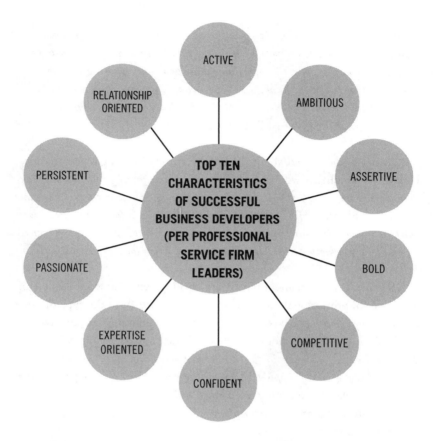

The additional commentary that the leaders provided to emphasize what successful business development looks like creates a fuller picture of the one size in firms and who is most likely to fit that size.

One firm leader surmised that a successful client developer—he included himself in this group—in today's market needed *"ego, delusion, and greed."*

I know I'm using terms that upset people, but the words are what they are. And, I'm not suggesting that people who are this way are not nice people. But, if you don't have these characteristics, you won't have the stamina you need to do this day in and day out. You need to have a serious ego because you have to believe that you are not only good but that you are better than everyone else. It goes beyond confidence because confident people know that they are good, but confident people aren't focused on being better than others.

Having an ego is also about being extremely competitive. You don't just want to win. You want to compete against others and win. And, you have to be delusional because every time something doesn't pan out, you have to convince yourself that it was them, not you. You have to be greedy. There is no end to client development. You don't set a goal and stop at that goal. You have to be greedy because there is no goal. There is only more.

Another leader talked about the good fortune of having a personal network in which clients were easy to develop. *"Your family, your friends, your alumni network . . . all of these are places where you get your clients. For some people, these places are rich—literally—with resources and for others, these places won't yield much. In addition to what you do, of course, it is about who you know . . . and how you know them. Meeting a CEO at a networking event is different than being that CEO's kid or nephew or best friend."*

A few leaders talked about how client development that led to leadership and power in professional service firms was different from the type of rainmaking that individual lawyers, accountants, consultants, financial advisors/managers, and architects would do. As one leader noted, *"Selling to individuals who are buying your service for themselves is very different than selling to an individual or a group of people who are buying your service for a large company. Some of the things that you hear from coaches, trainings, and such work on a small scale, but that's not what firms are looking for. Are there people who amass a large amount of business by stitching together a whole bunch of small clients? Yes, but it's rare."*

When asked directly about what they noticed regarding gender differences in business development in their firms, the leaders answered the question in various ways, although the consistent theme in their answers was that women just had more difficulty and less success getting clients than men did. The following examples illustrate the range and variance in the leaders' responses to the question of what, if any, gender differences they noticed in the business development behaviors and outcomes in their firms.

"I don't think women want it [to be seen as a rainmaker, to have access to leadership, to be one of the most highly compensated in the firm] as badly as some men do. A lot of men don't want it that badly either, but you really notice that almost no women do."

"Of course women want what having business will get you, but they don't want to do what it takes to get the business. That's not to say that the system is fair, but women are not restricted from doing what it takes. They just choose not to."

"We have an initiative for women to help them develop business. I think they do trainings and things like that. We want the initiative to work because we have some great women in the firm. They just don't bring in business, and without the business, in this type of a firm, it is just not going to be successful."

"Women are fighting for the wrong thing. They want to be equally included in client pitches so they get mad when they are left out. They want to be equally in line to inherit clients when the relationship person retires. They don't realize that what they are asking for only makes them seem even more like they can't do it on their own. They need to put together a pitch, not ask to be included on one. They need to bring in their own business, and when they do, everyone will scramble to include them in their pitches."

"Yes, the women bring in less business on average. Yes, they get paid less because of that. I'm not saying that can't change, but that is what it looks like today. If it is going to change though, it has to start with the women."

Interestingly, the female leaders' perspectives were very similar to those of the male leaders. Of the female leaders in the study, the majority were, in fact, some of the highest revenue generators in their firms. They were very conscious of their visibility as the "only one" or the "one of few" rainmakers in their firms, and they struggled with reconciling their perspectives on what women needed to do and why so many women were either not doing what they needed to do or not succeeding in their attempts.

Many of the female leaders had mixed perspectives on their high visibility in their firms. As one female leader summarized,

You are visible but not understood. The men are trying to figure you out, especially the men who don't have a lot of business. The women see you as their voice at the table but many of them don't actually think you represent their voice, so they are kind of glad that you are at the table, but they want to constantly tell you what your voice should be. You are asked to be a leader for all things women while still actually doing your job. If you say yes, you get hit with a ton of additional work and time commitments. If you say no,

then you are the b word because you don't care about women's success overall.
The guys don't have that added responsibility.

The perspectives on business development as articulated by different leaders of professional service firms are starkly consistent with each other on what successful business development looks like (individual credit/big clients/clients = power), how it is done (independently/visibly/competitively), and who is more likely to succeed at it (assertive men). The following chapters demonstrate how this one size is not compatible with how women (and many men) actually develop business. This one size leads to a firm's succeeding through the output of a few superstar business developers instead of succeeding as a firm, a cohesive unit that works together to grow together.

The individual superstar model may have worked when the supply-and-demand equation for professional services favored professional service firms, and it may even continue to work if you want to merely survive. However, in this global hypercompetitive market where the supply–demand equation no longer favors professional service firms, dependence on a few superstars without teams is not a good strategy for any firm's long-term success, especially if you want to transcend survival and thrive in a sustainable way.

◢ LISA

Lisa is a senior partner in a firm where she is the only female partner of color. The firm has a women's leadership initiative and a diversity initiative, and she is active in both, though she feels like she really doesn't fit in very well with either group.

"When I'm with the women, they look at me with some confusion because I'm a woman but they can't really relate to me. They have no idea what my life is like when I leave here, what my home is like, what I do on the weekends, and they don't ask me these questions like they ask each other. The other partners of color are all men, so when we get together, they say all sorts of sexist stuff and don't realize it. Every single one of them has children, and none of them [has] work–life balance issues like I do. This is the context in which I have to live and breathe my client development efforts."

Lisa was recruited from another firm because a client of her current firm had recommended her highly when this firm was thinking about recruiting new people at a more senior level. That client, a white male, has put Lisa's name up for consideration many times for positions ranging from civic boards to high-profile political appointments.

"I jokingly told [the client] that he was the strongest advocate for diversity that I had ever met the way that he throws my name around. He responded by saying that he wished that I was not a minority because he hated that he constantly had to explain to people that he wasn't recommending me because I was a woman or a minority but because I was smart and the hardest worker he had ever met. That took me a second to digest . . . he wished that I was not a minority. I didn't know how to respond because I understood . . . I think I did . . . what he was saying, but it was still difficult to process."

Lisa has a few clients, but all her clients, according to her, are *"not really clients I pitched."* She has been a part of a few client pitches that other partners have organized, and she laughingly calls herself the *"two for one diversity token." "I would invite me if I were them . . . our clients are asking for diversity, and I am as diverse as diverse gets. But, I don't get treated as an equal on the pitch team. The diversity role is never quite as profound or powerful as the best in class role."*

The head of the firm approached her a few months ago and told her that he wanted to start grooming her for a leadership position. He told her that they had to start with getting her business generation numbers up. She asked him how he thought she should do that, and he told her that she was not aggressive enough, and that she needed to focus on "getting in there and getting the kill" because he knew she had it in her.

"'Get in there and get the kill.' Could he have said anything that I connected with less? I like to compete, but for me, it's about competing against an ideal . . . being better than I was before or competing as a member of a team because I want to see my team win, but competing against my other partners . . . that doesn't turn me on.

"I don't want to kill. I don't want to fight to kill. This doesn't make sense. We are in a field that is about innovation and creativity, and fighting to kill isn't anything that I know how to do . . . or want to do. But, it's hard to say that, right, because he is saying it like it's a compliment. He also uses the phrase 'hunger in the belly' often, and all that makes me think of is indigestion. Hunger in the belly sounds like what you get after you fight to kill."

CHAPTER 6

THE FITS & THE MISFITS OF THE ONE SIZE

Although much has been written on the general differences in how men and women communicate,[73] not much research has been done on what, if any, specific differences exist in communication styles and behaviors within the context of developing business. In order to better understand what the "one size" in professional service firms looks like, we reached out to leaders and professionals to identify some key characteristics that are used to describe business development styles in firms.

In the previous chapter, we briefly looked at the list of the top ten characteristics that leaders felt represented the most successful business developers in their firms. In this chapter, we will go behind the scenes of that list and see how the full set of characteristics were identified and how leaders culled the longer list to arrive at their top ten list.

We began the creation of the list by asking the 72 professional service firm leaders to list the communication characteristics that they believed great business developers needed. We also asked 35 partners/principals (19 men and 16 women) in various firms to identify the characteristics that best described their own client development styles. This method—identifying the ideal characteristics sought by the leaders and the actual characteristics professionals felt that they had—allowed us to create a list of 24 that was both aspirational and realistic and allowed us to explore to what extent male and female professionals reported having characteristics that aligned with the ideal.

We compiled the characteristics provided by both groups into one list for the survey that we conducted. The list—a varied, multifaceted, and sometimes contradictory mixture of characteristics—is presented in alphabetical order:

Active	Ambitious	Assertive	Bold
Cautious	Collaborative	Competitive	Confident
Creative	Direct	Expertise Oriented	Extroverted
Formal	Indirect	Informal	Introverted
Motivated	Passionate	Passive	Persistent
Relationship Oriented	Reluctant	Service Oriented	Team Player

We then asked the firm leaders to identify the ten characteristics from this list that they felt were most necessary for success for business development in their firms. As discussed in the previous chapter, the leaders identified the following as the ten most important characteristics.

We began our analysis by examining the gender differences, if any, in how men and women reported and evaluated their own business development characteristics in relation to the characteristics listed in the preceding figure. Our findings revealed that not only were there differences in whether or not men and women saw these characteristics in themselves, but there were also significant differences in how men and women were actually defining the characteristics.

When the ten ideal characteristics are compared to the characteristics that men and women report as representing their individual styles of business development, an interesting picture emerges.

The shaded characteristics—confident, persistent, and relationship oriented—were the only characteristics that men and women equally reported as representing their business development styles. The remaining seven characteristics—active, ambitious, assertive, bold, competitive, expertise oriented, and passionate—were reported significantly more by men than women as being representative of their individual business development styles. There were no characteristics in this top ten list selected by leaders that were reported by women more than men. We did not see any deviations from this for women of color.

The leaders' list of the ten essential characteristics for successful business development is the "one size" for business development in firms today. One way to frame these findings is that men are more likely than women to fit 70 percent of the key characteristics identified by firm leaders as necessary for successful business development, and men are as likely as women to fit the remaining 30 percent of these key characteristics. There are no key characteristics that women are more likely to fit than men.

The following figure presents the data in the "one size" model. The majority of this "one size" as articulated by firm leaders is comprised of characteristics that more men report having in comparison to women. The few characteristics that women report having are ones that they report having in equal numbers to men. There is no part of this "one size" that is comprised of characteristics that women report having more than men do.

MEN
ONLY

ACTIVE
AMBITIOUS
ASSERTIVE
BOLD
COMPETITIVE
EXPERTISE
ORIENTED
PASSIONATE
CONFIDENT
PERSISTENT
RELATIONSHIP
ORIENTED

MEN AND
WOMEN

The "one size" more readily fits men than women. We can, of course, explore whether the size emerged first, thereby ensuring a majority of men in these firms, or whether the majority of men in these firms created the size that now exists not as the male size but as the only size. Based on the numbers of women in firm partnerships and the high level of attrition that is occurring from professional service firms overall, the exploration of what came first— the size or the men—is less important than the discussion of how we create more sizes to expand the participation and success of women in firms.

CAN THE ONE SIZE EVER FIT ALL?

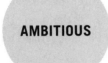

Of men, 54 percent described themselves as active in comparison to only 48 percent of women. Although that difference of 6 percent is relatively small, the activities attributed to being active were very different for men and women.

While men attributed being active to outward-facing activities such as networking, setting up meetings with potential clients, and attending and speaking at conferences, women attributed being active to inward-facing activities such as actively learning more about the industries in which they worked, seeking feedback from senior people, managing their schedules, and engaging in professional development activities to increase their knowledge and skills.

Of the men, 32 percent felt that they were ambitious in comparison to only 25 percent of women. Men primarily described their ambitious styles in the context of wanting to get more business to get ahead in their firms, but women primarily described their ambitious styles in the context of wanting to succeed against the odds and wanting to develop business in order to be taken seriously in their firms.

It is interesting to note that 68 percent of men and 75 percent of women did not feel that their style was ambitious even though firm leaders identified this characteristic as one of the top characteristics necessary for business development success in professional service firms.

With 39 percent of men describing their style as assertive in comparison to only 24 percent of women, the 15 percent differential between men and women was initially surprising given that there was only a 7 percent differential with the ambitious characteristic. A deeper look into how men and women defined "assertive," however, sheds light on why the differential was so high.

Men and women both described "assertive" as an outward-facing characteristic in that being assertive was about the style involved in dealing with other people. For men, this style was an offensive style in that they described being *"assertive from the start"* and assertively asking for what they wanted. Women had a much more negative association with this word, and the women who chose this as a descriptor for themselves described being assertive more as a defensive mechanism to protect themselves from stereotypes in the workplace, to correct perceived misconceptions about them, and to make themselves heard in meetings.

It is important to note, as with the word "ambitious," that 61 percent of men and 76 percent of women did not perceive this word as describing their individual business development style. Yes, men see themselves as more assertive than women see themselves, but the majority of men don't see themselves as assertive.

BOLD

The overwhelming majority of people in the study did not describe their communication style as bold, but of those who did, there was a significant differential between the men and women. Of the men, 19 percent described their style as bold in comparison to only 8 percent of women.

Again, the definitional differences added texture in that men generally defined "bold" as taking risks and women defined "bold" as not being afraid. In some ways, the definitions were very similar in that they were both pointing to being courageous, but the men were more likely to assume the presence of courage to take the risks they wanted to take whereas the women were acknowledging the presence of fear and seeing boldness as the act of moving past the fear. It was a subtle but meaningful difference in how men and women shared their stories in connection to this characteristic.

In order to fully understand how the characteristic of competitive was chosen by people, it is necessary to also bring in the characteristic of collaborative to provide context through comparison. Many of the professional service firm leaders emphasized that good business development required a competitive communication style, but only 21 percent of men and 10 percent of women described themselves as competitive. Conversely, although collaborative was not a characteristic listed by the majority of the professional service firm leaders, 65 percent of men and 80 percent of women described their styles as collaborative.

The differentials between what the professional service firm leaders think is necessary and how people actually see themselves are staggering, and the gender differentials within those descriptors are very significant. The 11 percent differential between men and women in selecting competitive as a characteristic of their communication style and the inverse 15 percent differential between women and men in selecting collaborative as a characteristic of their style are central to the difference between men and women in business development behaviors and outcomes. We will discuss this particular issue in greater detail in the next chapter.

A relatively equal number of men and women selected confident as one of their communication styles in business development, with 67 percent and 64 percent, respectively. Unlike with many of the other characteristics, there were more similarities than not in how men and women defined "confidence," primarily as belief in oneself.

Firm leaders definitely felt that expertise-oriented business development netted great results, but they varied in their articulations of how this expertise-oriented style manifests. For example, while some professional service firm leaders focused on stressing expertise and experience in business development meetings and conversations, other leaders focused on expertise-oriented activities such as speaking at conferences and being featured in articles and other public relations/marketing materials.

Of the men, 54 percent felt that their style was expertise oriented compared to only 38 percent of women. The men who selected this characteristic as part of their communication style were equally as varied as the professional service firm leaders in pointing to various ways they manifested this characteristic. The women who selected this characteristic, however, not only differed from the men dramatically in terms of their definition of the term, but they were surprisingly unvaried within the group. Women defined this term as how they were perceived by others, not as how they expressed it in their conversations or otherwise. Several of the women discussed how stressing expertise in a conversation can be perceived as *"bragging"* and being *"too self-important."* A few women discussed how it was harder for women to be expertise oriented because they first had to overcome the perception that they were not experts while men could jump into a conversation about their expertise without worrying about jumping over that initial hurdle.

Overall, the women who selected this characteristic agreed that they were expertise oriented in that they understood how important it was for them to be viewed as experts, but they struggled with the challenges of being seen that way and what they could do to change that.

PASSIONATE

The gender differential for passionate as a characteristic was exactly similar to the differential for expertise oriented—men with 54 percent and women with 38 percent. The primary definitional difference was that men described the characteristic as the passion they felt for business development itself, the firm, or the area of work. Women, on the other hand, described the characteristic more as the passion they felt for earning their client's trust and the opportunity to serve their clients.

PERSISTENT

Men and women equally selected this characteristic as applying to their personal style at 18 percent and 17 percent, respectively, and there were not any significant differences in how men and women defined this characteristic. It is interesting to note, however, that more than 80 percent of the professionals in this study did not feel that they were persistent in their business development communication styles.

RELATIONSHIP ORIENTED

Seventy-five percent of women and 72 percent of men felt that their communication style was relationship oriented. The relatively bare differential between women and men did not carry over into the differentials in definitions. Men defined their relationship orientations in business development as the need to develop relationships in order to develop business as well as the need to continue to grow the relationships with current clients in order to keep those clients happy and loyal. The women's definitions of being relationship oriented focused much more on the need to get to know the clients personally in order to retain them as clients. The women's definitions also focused heavily on how to balance the ability to develop relationships in order to develop business with the need to not "use" the relationships solely to get business. Many of the women discussed the ease with which they were able to develop relationships and the challenges they faced in extracting value from the relationship in the form of business. The men's responses did not hint at all at these tensions.

A CLOSER LOOK AT THE MISFITS

Let's now explore some of the gender differences in the characteristics reported by professionals that were not selected as key criteria by professional service firm leaders. Eight characteristics—creative, direct, extroverted, introverted, motivated, reluctant, service oriented, and team player—displayed no significant gender differences at all. There were also no notable differentials in definitions except for the team player characteristic. Men were more likely than women to see themselves as leaders of teams while thinking about being a team player, and women rarely mentioned leading the team, only being on the team and being a team player.

The characteristics discussed next are the six remaining characteristics from the full list of 24 characteristics included in the survey. To quickly summarize, there were ten characteristics on the leaders' list, seven of which were dominant in men and three of which were equally found in men and women. There were eight characteristics not on the leaders' list that were equally found in men and women, and those are stated in the preceding paragraph.

The remaining six characteristics were not on the leaders' list but had notable gender differences in regard to impact on business development styles.

COLLABORATIVE

We have already discussed how women were significantly more likely to select collaborative as a communication style than men. It is also important to note that many of the men who selected this characteristic defined collaborative as asking another person to help with something while women defined collaborative as working on a shared goal with a group.

CAUTIOUS AND PASSIVE

Men were more likely to say they were cautious in comparison to women, with 17 percent and 11 percent, respectively. Men related to being cautious in the context of "not stepping on toes" in regard to other people's business development efforts in the firm in comparison to women who related to being cautious in approaching personal and professional relationships for business development reasons.

Men were also more likely than women to report passive as being one of their communication styles at 12 percent to 3 percent. This differential for passive is somewhat contradictory given that men reported active as a communication style more than women, but women had a more visceral reaction to the word "passive" in that they strongly felt that being passive led to failure. Even the women who selected this style as part of their own style commented on how they wished they were not passive but found themselves being that way because they felt intimidated by the process. The men who selected this style talked about being passive in a less personal sense in that they described finding passive ways to generate business like practicing in a niche area where there was not much competition. Because men and women defined both active and passive so differently, the fact that men would report being both more active and more passive is less a contradiction and more a divergence in definitions.

INDIRECT

Women were considerably more likely than men at 14 percent to 1 percent to report that their client development styles were indirect. Since there was no difference between men and women in the selection of direct as a client development style, the differential in the selection of indirect is an interesting one, especially since there were so few men who selected the trait at all. Men seemed to have a similar visceral reaction to the word "indirect" that women had to the word "passive." Women focused on the word "indirect" as a way to describe word-of-mouth and referral-based introductions while men focused on the word in a more "lack of courage" type of manner.

FORMAL VERSUS INFORMAL

Men were more than twice as likely as women to select formal as a communication style at 22 percent to 10 percent, but women were more likely than men to select informal as a communication style at 45 percent to 38 percent. Even though men and women generally reported being more informal in their business development styles, men categorized taking potential/current clients to sporting events, golf clubs, and such as part of an informal style, whereas women categorized these types of events as part of a more formal style. Men and women equally considered sharing meals (outside large events that involve meals) as part of an informal style.

Of the 24 business development communication styles surveyed, 11 characteristics had no discernible self-selection rates between men and women: confident, persistent, relationship oriented, creative, direct, extroverted, introverted, motivated, reluctant, service oriented, and team player. Men reported ten characteristics significantly more frequently than women: active, ambitious, assertive, bold, competitive, expertise oriented, passionate, cautious, passive, and formal. Women reported only three characteristics more frequently than men: collaborative, indirect, and informal.

Our survey respondents and interviewees offered some descriptors of their own personal styles in addition to the characteristics that made the full list of 24. For some irreverent fun, see if you can guess whether men, women, or both were more likely to select the following characteristics as consistent with their business development styles.[74]

CHARACTERISTIC	MEN	WOMEN	BOTH
Aggressive			
Determined			
Effective			
Friendly			
Helpful			
Loyal			
Reluctant			
Strong			
Tenacious			

THE LEADERS' REACTIONS

We showed the data on the characteristics to a small sample of the firm leaders who participated in compiling the list of characteristics, and they were not pleased with what the data showed, but they were also not surprised. One leader commented on how *"abnormal the normal seems when you look at it in this way."* Another leader focused on the tension between competitive and collaborative as business development styles:

> *We focus on being competitive. That's how we frame everything. It seems like we have to differentiate between being competitive with other firms and people in our firm competing against each other, but that's hard, because even in the firm, it is a competition. And, not everyone is going to win. So, how do you communicate that without stressing the competitive because we also want people to collaborate with each other? We cannot win as a firm without collaborating internally, but not everyone internally is going to make it.*

If the characteristics that leaders of firms say are critically necessary are far more likely to occur in men than women, should leaders take this data to mean that women cannot be good client developers or should they understand this data as describing a size that men are reporting as a good fit and women are reporting as a bad fit? In other words, are the ten characteristics the only way to develop business, or are the ten characteristics the only way to develop business in the current business development model that exists in most firms today?

If leaders lean toward the former by validating the one size in existence, then it is an urgent imperative for the firms to let women know that their natural self-reported styles of communication will not be successful in business development, the gateway into sustained success and leadership at these firms. That would not go over very well with women, but it would be honest.

If the leaders lean toward the latter, they need to ask themselves whether they will continue to require women to wear a size that does not fit them or whether they will make additional sizes of success available. In the following chapter, we will take a deeper dive into the gender differences between a competitive business development style and a collaborative business development style. This difference was where we saw some of the most profound evidence of the impact when one size is expected to fit all.

CHAPTER 7

A NEW SIZE: AN EXPERIMENT

One size never fits all. In many ways, we intuitively know that to be true. Yet, when our intuitive knowledge clashes with the deeply engrained status quo in professional service firms, it is difficult for us to understand what the misfit between reality and the "one size" really looks like.

We designed a micro experiment to better understand and illustrate what the "one size" looks like when it fits and when it doesn't fit. We wanted the experiment to reflect what we knew to be the reality in professional service firms: that women and men equally understood the urgency for business development and equally aspired to and worked toward generating revenue at a competitive level. Given that reality, we wanted to identify why women were originating less business than similarly situated men if they were putting in the same amount of time doing the same amount of things.

This experiment allowed us to probe and examine the differences in perceptions and behaviors between men and women in a structured business development process. While most business development activities in professional service firms are not this structured, the results are nonetheless revealing and insightful about where men and women are diverging when it comes to business development perceptions and behaviors.

METHODOLOGY

We recruited volunteers from our various firm clients in professional service industries to identify 12 women and 12 men who (1) were senior enough to be evaluated for their business development efforts as part of their overall compensation requirements and (2) had generated less than $200,000.00 in the previous billing year. As we found qualified volunteers, we asked them to follow the protocol shown in the following figure. While all of the volunteers participated in the same study, they did not necessarily do so at the same time given our rolling enrollment into the study. Each volunteer spent approximately four months in the study.

Each volunteer was asked to identify a high-value networking event that would have high numbers of potential clients in attendance. The next step was for the volunteer to attend the event, meet individuals, and collect business cards from people with whom she or he planned to follow up. After returning to work, participants were to follow up with the new contacts via e-mail, social media (such as LinkedIn, Twitter, etc.), and/or telephone. Subsequent to this follow-up, the volunteer was to ask her or his contacts for in-person meetings to discuss a potential business relationship. At this in-person meeting or immediately thereafter, the volunteer was instructed to ask for business from the contact directly.

BUSINESS DEVELOPMENT PROTOCOL

Attend a selectively targeted networking event. ▶ Seek out and meet individuals who have the potential to be clients and collect their business cards. ▶ Follow up with contacts via e-mail, social media, and/or the telephone. ▶ Ask for an in-person meeting to discuss potential business relationship.

We interviewed the volunteers before they attended the networking event to examine how they prepared, and we followed up after the networking event to identify how many cards they had collected. (We initially hoped to better understand the networking process in which they engaged at the event, but the variations between individuals were so substantial that we focused only on the number of cards collected as an objective outcome.)

We connected with each volunteer 30 days after his or her respective event to see how the e-mail/social media/telephone follow-up had gone and to determine whether an in-person meeting had been set up. We reconnected with each individual again 60 days after his or her respective event to note behaviors and outcomes in executing the protocol. We completed two additional follow-ups at 90 days and 120 days to discern whether the in-person meetings had occurred, the request for business had been made, and objective outcomes from the implementation of the protocol (Business Development Behaviors) had been realized.

All interviews with the volunteers were confidential and conducted via telephone. There were several points of additional correspondence (primarily via e-mail) between the interviews based on questions or concerns about the protocol and its implementation from the volunteers.

GENERAL FINDINGS

- There was no significant difference between how men and women prepared for the networking events. Men and women equally researched the host organization, the organization's leaders, past attendees, and past speakers online.
- Individuals collected an average of 12.5 cards, which resulted in an average of longer-term relationships with 5.2 people. There was no significant difference between men and women in the number of cards collected or the number of relationships developed. (Both men and women of color were more likely to connect with other people of color, but there were no other significant differences between their behavior and that of their white counterparts.
- Men and women were equally likely to contact all of their contacts via e-mail. Women were more likely to have a greater number of e-mail communications (5.2 e-mails per contact for women versus 2.8 e-mails per contact for men).
- Of the 12 men, 5 reported difficulties in actually developing interpersonal relationships with their contacts, while only 2 out of the 12 women reported similar difficulties.
- Men were three times more likely (73 percent to 24 percent) to have an in-person meeting scheduled within 60 days with at least one contact.

At the end of our time with the individuals, 10 out of the 12 men had scheduled at least one in-person meeting in comparison to 6 out of the 12 women.

- Of the ten men who had in-person meetings with their contacts, eight asked for business. Only two of the six women who had these meetings asked for business.

- At the end of 120 days after their respective networking events, three men were in active negotiations for potential business. No women were.

ANALYSIS AND DISCUSSION

Our interviews with the volunteers revealed that despite similar ambitions to develop business and similar preparation for the business development protocol, gender differences in business development behaviors gradually emerged, leading to differences in business development outcomes.

When we asked individuals for their perspectives, perceptions, emotions, motivations, and other thoughts about their behaviors in implementing the protocol, we found that although the behaviors at the beginning of the protocol seemed similar on the surface, **the women and men were actually undertaking the relationship development process for very different reasons.**

The women were focused on developing relationships for the intrinsic value in developing relationships—the building of the relationship itself was the "transaction" in which they were engaged. The men, on the other hand, were focused on developing relationships that would yield business transactions—the building of the relationships was the means to an end, not the end itself.

This key difference of a relationship as the end itself (value in relationship) in comparison to the relationship being the means to an end (value in the yield of the relationship) was the source of subsequent behavioral differences once relationships were forged. The majority of women in this study reported feeling "guilty" (regardless of the gender of the contact) when the time came for them to request an in-person meeting and/or ask for business from the contact. The following statements from a few women illustrate the emotions reported by the majority of the women:

"I almost did. I almost asked for business, but I felt guilty like I had been using him all along just to get business. It caused me too much stress, so I didn't ask."

"We had e-mailed back and forth several times. I felt like we were now friendly . . . not strangers. I felt like if I now asked for a meeting, it would look like I had been getting to know her only to get business, not for who she is, and I really like who she is."

"I didn't want to be seen as a user. I asked to meet in person but I framed it as 'it would be great to get together over lunch.' Once we were at lunch and we had talked about our families, where we grew up . . . I just felt awkward turning the conversation into a formal business conversation about getting business from him."

The majority of men, on the other hand, did not report any emotional concerns about asking for in-person meetings or asking for business (regardless of the gender of the contact). When the men hesitated to ask for business, they hesitated because of business concerns:

"I had a feeling that we may be conflicted out so I didn't want to put him in the situation where we talked about business and I had to come back and say that we can't do business together anyway because of our other clients and possible conflicts from that."

"I wasn't sure about the fit between what they needed and what we did, but I asked for the meeting anyway. Who knows who she knows, right?"

The women were more likely to see the "asking for business" as a unilateral request for a benefit from the contact whereas the men were more likely to see the "asking for business" as a bilateral relationship with mutual benefit for themselves and the contact. This difference in the perception of reciprocity in the development of business seemed to be a root cause of the differentials in behavior.

The women were also more likely to see the business development process as "selling" themselves to the potential client, which they were not comfortable doing. The men were more likely to see the business development process as "telling" the potential client about what they did and what kind of services they could provide for the potential client. This framing of "selling" versus "telling" was another root cause of the differentials in behavior.

KEY TAKEAWAYS

Women are more likely to enter into the business of developing professional relationships for the intrinsic value of building good relationships; therefore, they are more likely to see the business development process (the asking for business) as potentially violating the relationship because the "asking" would be a unilateral extraction of benefit from the relationship. While women excel at the building of the relationships, they don't get business from the relationships because their behavior in not wanting to extract personal benefit from the relationship drives the outcome of having rich relationships but not necessarily extracting business value from the relationships.

Men are more likely to enter into the business of developing professional relationships as a transactional process that will be mutually beneficial to themselves and their potential clients. Men may initially appear as though they are building more "superficial" relationships in comparison to the relationships built by women, but men build interpersonal relationships to specifically transition the relationships into business transactions, while women build interpersonal relationships to deepen the connection in the relationship.

The concept of *relationship value versus relationship yield* is a useful framework for understanding possible ways to develop professional development programming in the business development arena. Further, the framework of *"selling" versus "telling"* in communication perceptions of women and men, respectively, also offers useful insights in developing institutional programming and support for business development.

Even in the context of this small study, it became clear that differentials in outcomes were not rooted in unequal implementation of similar behaviors. Men and women were framing the process, choosing behaviors, and implementing communication strategies that were so different from each other that differentiated outcomes can be easily predicted as a by-product of these different frameworks and behaviors. In other words, men and women were not doing the same things differently—they were doing such different things that expecting anything other than different results would be unreasonable. In analyzing the data, we did see that if men and women of color attended events where there were no other people of color with whom they could net-work, that would affect their initial collection of contacts, which may impact the overall outcomes that result from behaviors that might be exactly the same as those of their white counterparts.

The differences in developing relationships for what they yield instead of for their intrinsic value are consistent with the differences we found in regard to being in business development versus selling and being competitive versus being collaborative, concepts that are explored in the next two chapters.

This experiment is by no means an exhaustive exploration of this topic, but it does provide us enough new insights to understand the findings that are detailed in the chapters that follow.

CHAPTER 8

COLLABORATIVE FEET IN COMPETITIVE SHOES

com•pete | *intransitive verb* |\kəm-ˈpēt\: to try to get or win something (such as a prize or reward) that someone else is also trying to win; to try to be better or more successful than someone or something else[75]

col•lab•o•rate | *intransitive verb* |\kə-ˈla-bə-ˌrāt\: to work with another person or group in order to achieve or do something[76]

On the surface, the 11 percent differential between the 21 percent of men and the 10 percent of women who described their business development styles as competitive does not seem very significant. It actually seems like the bigger story here is that 79 percent of men did not describe their style as competitive, especially because 65 percent of men and 80 percent of women described their style as collaborative. It seems like the story to tell is that the overwhelming majority of men and women describe their business development styles as collaborative, not competitive. Unfortunately for gender parity, this story does not give us a full or even accurate picture of what is going on in professional service firms.

The real story emerged when we dug deeper into this data through the narratives offered by respondents in the survey as well as the experiences shared by the interviewees. Upon closer examination, we discovered that although only 21 percent of men described their business development styles as competitive, over 70 percent of men desired to compete and said that they would thrive in competitive environments. Only 12 percent of men said that they would evaluate a workplace negatively simply because it was competitive. Sixty-five percent of men said that they were more collaborative by nature, but only 15 percent of them said they felt that they would thrive more in a collaborative environment than in a competitive environment. Thus, men reported being more collaborative in comparison to being competitive when asked about their business development styles, but the majority of men did not feel that the quality of their work environments and their abilities to succeed in those work environments were hindered by competitive cultures, and many said that, in reality, they desired competitive environments.

The narrative comments from the men reflected the complexities that emerged in the quantitative survey responses. As one male partner said, *"It's tough for me to see myself as competitive because I'm generally not a competitive person. I'm not that guy that has to win everything or beat others, but I do love the competition at work. I like keeping score because I like being the best. I don't want*

people to lose so I can win but I definitely want to win." We heard many similar sentiments about competition and winning from men. Another male partner, for instance, described himself as *"collaboratively competitive . . . I will work with others because I am a collaborative person, but when it's a competition, I play to win."*

While 10 percent of women described their styles as competitive and 31 percent of women felt that they would thrive in competitive environments, 63 percent of women said that they would evaluate a workplace more negatively because it was competitive. (The 63 percent included women who said that they would be willing to compete as well as women who said that they would not be willing to compete.) Eighty percent of women said that they were more collaborative by nature, and about 75 percent of women said that they would thrive in a work environment that was more collaborative than competitive. Unlike the men's responses that diverged in this area, women's descriptions of their business development styles converged with their perspectives on the types of environments in which they would thrive.

80% of women described their business development style as collaborative.

75% of women said they would thrive in a collaborative environment.

Women's narrative comments also differed from the men's in significant ways. For example, one female partner discussed how she would enjoy business development more if it was not a competitive ranking process in her firm: *"I don't mind the business development itself, and I might even be more enthusiastic about it, but the ranking of who brought in the most money or the biggest client irritates me. It's not like any of these guys brought anything in all on their own, but that is how they act. And, it feels like a pissing contest the way they talk about it and go on and on about it, and I don't want any part of it."* Another female partner expressed how the competitive environment in her firm made her feel less like it was truly a firm: *"I sometimes feel like we are individuals who work in the same office instead of being one firm because of how much competition there is between the partners. When someone brings in a big account, you see that the other guys are irritated even as they are congratulating the person. If we were truly one firm, we would be competing with other firms, not each other."*

MEN		WOMEN	
21%	of men described their business style as competitive.	**10%**	of women described their business style as competitive.
70%	of men wanted to compete.	**31%**	of women wanted to compete.
12%	of men would evaluate a workplace more negatively if it were competitive.	**63%**	of women would evaluate a workplace more negatively if it were competitive.
65%	of men said they were more collaborative than competitive in nature.	**80%**	of women said they were more collaborative than competitive in nature.
15%	of men said they would thrive in an environment that was not competitive.	**75%**	of women said they would thrive in an environment that was not competitive.

The shaded boxes of data in the chart illustrate the immense differences between what men and women expect from and prefer in their workplaces and how these expectations and preferences are not always aligned with how they define their own business development styles.

For example, while there is only an 11 percent differential in the number of men versus the number of women who see themselves as competitive, there is a 29 percent differential in the number of men who are willing to compete in comparison to the number of women who are willing to compete. Similarly, there is a 51 percent differential between men and women in their likelihood to evaluate a workplace as negative if it was competitive.

Again, although there was only a 15 percent differential in the number of men versus the number of women who see themselves as collaborative, there is a 60 percent differential in the number of men who felt that they could thrive in an environment that was not competitive in comparison to women who said the same. Men and women may be much more in agreement about whether their business development styles are collaborative, but their perspectives on needing competition in the workplace to thrive differ significantly.

THE NATURE VERSUS NURTURE DEBATE REDUX

As many people questioned throughout the course of this study, are we really suggesting that men are biologically different from women, or are we simply saying that men and women do things slightly differently because of how they are socialized? We are saying both or either, sort of, and we are saying that it is complicated to answer that question, but it is not necessary difficult to do so.

The gender differences that emerged in our study on competitive and collaborative styles of business development are very similar to gender differences that have emerged in other research studies that have examined men's and women's perspectives on competition and collaboration. While our research does not attempt to solve the nature (born different) versus nurture (raised different) debate on gender differences, recent studies on neurological differences between men and women and the impact of these differences in workplace outcomes suggest that some of the differences in behaviors between men and women may, in fact, be driven by the structural differences in male and female brains.

A vast amount of research is currently available on this topic, and you can explore many additional resources.[77] For the purpose of better understanding gender differences in business development behaviors within the context of professional service firms, we will focus primarily on the differences between men and women in the amygdala (the fear center), the prefrontal cortex (the executive decision–making center), and the anterior cingulate cortex (the worry center) in the brain. The following section highlights the various studies conducted in the financial, legal, and accounting industries that demonstrate correlations between collaborative styles and better outcomes even though the competitive environments have not yet made room for these collaborative styles to get the full credit that they deserve.

As the studies have demonstrated, women are generally (not stereotypically) more collaborative, more focused on achievement instead of winning, and more cautious than men. While this model has not been accepted as a legitimate size that can be worn for success in professional service firms, this size is achieving the types of successes that firms may want to embrace in order to stay competitive in today's marketplace.

THE RESEARCH ON THE NEUROLOGY OF COMPETITION AND COLLABORATION

John Coates, a former trader who worked at Goldman Sachs, Merrill Lynch, and Deutsche Bank, wrote a book with the interesting title *The Hour between Dog and Wolf.* Coates left the financial services industry to research and teach the intersection between neuroscience and finance at the University of Cambridge. In his book, he discusses in detail the correlation between increased levels of testosterone, risk, and bad decision making, and he logically argues that hiring more women on the trading floors of financial exchanges would reduce the impact of testosterone-induced risky behavior and stabilize decision making in the marketplace.[78]

Coates writes that "women were relatively immune to the frenzy surrounding Internet and high-tech stocks. In fact most of the women I knew, both on Wall Street and off, were quite cynical about the excitement, and as a result were often dismissed as 'not getting it,' or worse, resented as perennial killjoys."[79] He describes many of the frenzies that have occurred in financial markets over the past couple of decades and argues that men and women responded very differently because of neurological reasons, not just socialized reasons.

Coates's research and arguments are further supported by recent research on hedge funds. Hedge funds have one of the highest rates of female attrition and one of the lowest rates of female leadership among any other category of firms that we studied. According to Re:Gender (formerly the National Council for Research on Women), "75 percent of women in private equity said their gender was a major impediment to success in the field. These stereotypes, combined with the highly competitive culture and the long hours and travel often demanded by these jobs[,] render the field uninviting, causing talented women often to look elsewhere for opportunities."[80] Subsequently, less than 3 percent of hedge funds are led by women, and only about 20 percent are managed by women (in male- and female-led firms).[81]

It is a common problem faced by many firms—they have competitive environments, and women don't like those ubercompetitive environments, and they leave. If you listen to the firms talk about how to better retain and advance women, the conversations center on how to make the women more comfortable in these environments, not how to change the environments because the current way may not be the best way. Hedge funds are using this logic and focusing on how to make women more comfortable in hedge funds so that they will stay longer, but what if the hedge funds have it wrong and the women have it right?

According to the *New York Times* coverage of a study released in early 2014, "From the beginning of 2007 through June 2013—a period that includes the dark days of the crisis—a Rothstein Kass index of women-run hedge funds returned 6 percent, the report says. By comparison, the HFRX Global Hedge Fund Index, released by Hedge Fund Research, fell 1.1 percent during that time, according to the report."[82] According to the Rothstein Kass study, there were no female partners/principals in 42 percent of the firms surveyed, and there were no women on the investment committees in 40 percent of the firms. The dearth of women in the general arena of hedge funds may explain why the index of women-run funds had a 9.8 percent return in comparison to a 6.13 percent rise in the broader index.

Other studies have demonstrated similar results—that female money managers and investors yield better results than males ones. According to Re:Gender, "Researchers . . . found that, on average, women tend to be more consistent investors, holding investments longer and processing a greater level of informational detail, including contradictory data, in making decisions. On the other hand, men tend to manage actively, trading often and basing decisions on overall schema. This research debunks the myth that women are less effective money managers than men. Systematic management of risk needs to benefit from the talents of both genders to create a sustainable, stable system."[83] This study found that the caution that women exercised along with their ability to collaborate with people who may disagree with them led to better decision making and better results.

Research in the legal profession demonstrates very similar results. When litigators were asked to predict outcomes in real litigation cases, the correlation between the litigators' predictions and the actual outcomes demonstrated that women were better predictors than men of what would actually happen in cases.[84] The female litigators were more likely to filter their predictions through reasoned caution and take more points of view into consideration before solidifying their predictions.

In the accounting arena, research by the American Accounting Association has found that organizations with female CFOs had a higher quality of accruals (more reliable accruals and less abnormal accruals) on their balance sheets than did organizations with male CFOs. According to Abhijit Barua, one of the lead researchers of the study, "A large amount of abnormal accruals in a company statement may suggest financial manipulation or fraud or it may simply suggest aggressive accounting . . . What our study makes quite clear is that firms with women CFOs are associated with significantly lower amounts of abnormal accruals than those with male CFOs. In other words, companies with female CFOs tend to have higher accruals quality, which, all else being equal, means higher earnings quality and more reliable accounting."[85] The study also found that when female CFOs replaced male CFOs in organizations, the quality of accruals of the organizations' financial statements improved significantly regardless of what model of accrual quality was employed. As Professor Barua reported, "A number of studies have shown women to be less aggressive or more cautious than men in a variety of financial decisions . . . female CFOs have been found to be more cautious in evaluating company acquisitions and in issuing debt. Such evidence led us to hypothesize that firms with female CFOs would have higher accrual quality than companies with male CFOs, and this clearly turns out to be the case."[86]

The research on the differences between men's and women's brains has been consistent over the last couple of decades. We know that men's and women's brains develop differently, and we know that men and women utilize different parts of their brain in solving the same problem. While there is no difference in the intelligence levels between men and women, we know that each group's intelligence manifests differently. In addition to the differences just discussed, we now know that

- **two different brains are better than one.** Women's thought processes use both sides of their brains, and more parts of their brain are active during problem solving. Men's thought processes use more of one side of the brain, and while there is less overall activity in problem solving in comparison to women's, men's thought patterns are more linear, focused, and concentrated. Women collect and analyze details faster, and they can generate many more possible solutions that run the gamut from linear to intuitive, but men tend to ignore data that doesn't fit with their thinking because they are driving toward a solution. If your firm is putting together a business development pitch to attract a particular client, it is the integration of the two types of thinking—generation of many ideas and a focused drive to make a decision—that will benefit you the most. If only one of these approaches is accepted as a viable option, the probability of getting and keeping that client are similarly limited. The bottom line is that neither of these options is great by itself, and the two need to go together and be assessed as a collective effort in order for firms to fully reap the benefits of the talent they have in their partner (and associate) ranks.

- **not all cues are caught the same way.** Women generally tend to have higher levels of emotional intelligence when it comes to recognizing and understanding nonverbal cues such as subtle changes in facial expressions, variations in voice and tone, and body language patterns. Especially when a team is pitching to a potential (or current) client team that includes women, the women on that client team expect their nonverbal cues to be recognized and understood, and they feel ignored when those cues go unnoticed or unmet.

- **I and we are not always we and I.** Women tend to shy away from competitive communication and expressions such as ordering people around, making decisions without asking for input/advice, sitting at the head of the table, using their power to silence others, and so forth, because women report these types of behaviors to be indicative of someone who is seeking to establish authority or superiority over another person. For example, women are more likely to say "we" when they mean "I," and men are more likely to say "I" even when they mean "we."

The studies just discussed are only a representative sample of how the alternative sizes worn by women are actually producing the kinds of results that firms would want to embrace, encourage, and advance. By digging a little deeper into the three main neurological patterns that are relevantly different for professional service firms, we will get a better idea of how to create the different sizes necessary to allow women to succeed without contorting themselves into molds made for men.

FIGHT OR FLIGHT VERSUS TEND AND BEFRIEND (THE AMYGDALA)

Starting in elementary school, we learn about the fight-or-flight response—an instinctive reaction we have when we experience (or perceive) being threatened in some way. When the threat is felt, we charge toward it to fight and defeat it or we run as fast as we can away from it. Our actions during fight or flight are guided by a hormone-induced directive from our amygdala (the fear processing center of our brain that is much bigger in men than in women and is especially sensitive to high levels of testosterone), not by conscious, deliberated decisions that we make after weighing the pros and cons of each option. (This fight-or-flight response was recently changed to fight or flight or freeze because studies showed that there is a group of people who don't fight or flee . . . they freeze.)

As we all learned about this universal fight-or-flight instinct based on the work of Walter Bradford Cannon in the early 1900s,[87] we were generally unaware that the majority of work on this reaction triggered by the amygdala was done on male subjects. Thus, while the reaction is a very real reaction, it is far from a universal reaction. It is primarily a male reaction.

When the amygdala's reaction to danger was studied in women, the female subjects did not fight or flee or even freeze. They tended and befriended.[88] Although the parasympathetic nervous system in men and women responded to stress in the same physiological way—increased heart rate and blood pressure, dilated pupils, shortness of breath, and the like—the behavioral responses to these physiological changes were dramatically different. Men adopted a competitive (win-lose) stance while women adopted a collaborative (better together) stance.

The evolutionary analysis for this difference is this: when women were attacked hundreds or even thousands of years ago, fighting was not a reasonable answer because most women were not taught to fight, and flight, from man or animal, was not reasonable because the chance of most women outrunning the danger was equally slim. So, women did what they had been biologically or socially programmed to do—tend to the children in order to keep them safe and befriend other women because the collective response to the danger was more likely to succeed than an individual response.

Whether or not this evolutionary proposition is a persuasive one for you, we know that the neurobehavioral response to stress today is different in men and women. If we take this insight and apply it to business development scenarios in professional service firms, the "get business, become powerful, become leader" model is one that works very well to trigger a competitive response from men, but the inherent challenge (the workplace version of threat) in that model drives women into collaborative behavior.

Coates discusses this in his book to explain why women don't react to economic swings the way men do: "Women's stress response is triggered by slightly different events. Women are not as stressed by failures in competitive situations as are men; they are more stressed by social problems, with family and relationships."[89] Many of the women in our study wanted to bring in more business, but the more competitive the firms made the process, the less the women wanted to engage in it. The more collaborative the business development processes, the more likely the women were to engage in business development and even lead the efforts.

Almost all the firms the leaders in our study represented reported that the tactics their firms used to get women to compete involved bigger competitive rewards (more money, more power) and bigger threats (no equity, no access to leadership, potential loss of income). Not surprisingly these tactics not only failed, but they made the women focus even more on tending and befriending behaviors instead of competing.

The same tactics that made men more competitive made women more collaborative, but that did not mean that the women were not competitive. The women were just not competitive in a model where they had to compete as individuals. When firms created teams that competed against other teams for key business, the women's competitive instincts actually kicked in strongly because they were now competing as a collective, and they were committed to giving their all to the collective.

When the women's amygdalas were triggered through competition, they tended and befriended instead of competing, but when those whom they had tended and befriended were threatened, the women's competitive instincts were fully and fiercely activated. Women are extremely competitive . . . in a team, as a team, and for the team. Most firms, unfortunately, do not allow for this collaboratively competitive model of success.

One size doesn't fit all. And trying to make that one size fit all not only doesn't work, but it denies the firms the opportunities to gain the benefits that can be brought in through other sizes.

WINNING VERSUS ACHIEVING (THE PREFRONTAL CORTEX)

The neurological check on the amygdala, the prefrontal cortex, is the rational decision-making center of the brain. The prefrontal cortex is larger in women, and it utilizes emotional information and reasoned analysis to make decisions. In contrast to the amygdala, which triggers decision making from the perspective of winning a conflict (win-lose), the prefrontal cortex triggers decision making from the perspective of reaching a solution (win-win). While the amygdala drives more of men's decisions, the prefrontal cortex drives more of women's decisions. Therefore, when men are confronted with a problem, they are more likely to try to find a win for themselves in contrast to women who are more likely to try to find a solution, even if it means a significant compromise on their part.

These neurological differences are by no means static nor do they apply to all men and women equally, but they play a significant role in how we connect in and with our workplaces. Our neurology informs our behaviors in order to drive us to do things that make us feel good, and the neurological differences between men and women drive us to exercise different behaviors in order to achieve the outcomes that make us feel good.

Winning feels good to men, and achieving a solution feels good to women. We are more likely to repeat behaviors that lead us to feeling good, so regardless of what the workplace may be demanding, men are more likely to keep wanting to win, and women are more likely to keep wanting to achieve a solution through compromise or consensus.

Differences in the prefrontal cortex are thought to be the reason why the presence of women in a group increases the collective intelligence of the group more than the presence of men. When researchers studied how teams work together to design solutions and achieve goals, the presence of women was one of the key factors that increased the collective intelligence of the team. "In two studies with 699 people, working in groups of two to five, we find converging evidence of a general collective intelligence factor that explains a group's performance on a wide variety of tasks. This 'c factor' is not strongly correlated with the average or maximum individual intelligence of group members but is correlated with the average social sensitivity of group members, the equality in distribution of conversational turn-taking, and the proportion of females in the group."[90] The three factors that the researchers correlated with high group performance mattered more than the individual

IQs of the group members. The researchers also made the point that it was the presence of women that raised the levels of social sensitivity and equality in distribution of conversational turn-taking.[91]

Social sensitivity (empathy, connection with someone else's feelings and emotions, reading people's faces, etc.) as well as listening to others before interrupting them (conversational turn-taking) are all behaviors that arise from the brain's prefrontal cortex. Women excel and thrive in group environments like this because the victory lies in the collective achievement of the group, not the winning by beating someone else to the answer.

Therefore, even in a highly competitive environment, if an organization wants to perform better as a collective, the neurobehavioral tendencies of women will lead to greater performance than the collective achievements of individual high performers . . . even if you have a lot of them.

CAUTION VERSUS RISK OR CAUTIOUS RISK (THE ANTERIOR CINGULATE CORTEX)

If the amygdala governs the response to threat and the prefrontal cortex moderates the response to threat by decreasing the guidance of the instinctive amygdala, the anterior cingulate cortex generates the options that can be considered in formulating the response to threat. The anterior cingulate cortex is a part of the brain's overall decision-making apparatus, and it is the part that gets most involved in the weighing of options prior to making a decision. The anterior cingulate cortex is larger in women's brains than in men's brains, and it is affectionately referred to as the "worrywart." It is more active in women than in men and contributes greatly to the higher levels of anxiety in women.

The anterior cingulate cortex is heavily involved in the detection of errors, the anticipation/organization of tasks, and connections between motivation and attention.[92] This part of the brain has a high level of influence in moderating risky decisions such as the ones discussed earlier with female investors, female litigators, and female CFOs. The risk tolerance versus risk aversion analysis that occurs here lasts longer and is more thorough in women. Furthermore, because this analysis in women is not competing with the amygdala demanding immediate action, more cautious responses tend to come from women than from men, especially in a highly competitive (or at least perceived to be competitive) context.

This neurological difference is understood to be the reason why women generally are more cautious (worrying about risk) and collaborative (collective action reduces risk) in their decision-making processes than are men. Men, on the other hand, tend to take greater risks and do so often in the pursuit of a competitive win. A competitive approach organically fuels the drive to take more risks whereas the need to build consensus organically drives more collaborative behavior.

Of course, these differences do not occur in the absolute in men or women, and most of us have our own individual formula of how much risk and how much caution we want to employ in different decision-making contexts. Generally, men will gravitate toward a formula with more risk and less caution in it, and women will lean toward a formula with less risk and more caution.

In contexts where success is defined singularly as being competitive and taking risks, women's tendencies to lean toward collaboration and caution would deem them lacking the potential to be successful, but the studies that we have explored are telling us something quite different. While many firms are still debating whether they want their associates to exercise more caution or more risk, it may work best if the conversation steered to cautious risk—a middle ground where women (and many men) thrive.

THE PLASTICITY OF NATURE AND THE INFLUENCE OF NURTURE

The brain is remarkably responsive to its interactions with the environment. The temptation to understand behavior in terms of either nature or nurture has become considerably less compelling in recent decades, in part because of the recognition that experience induces measurable, morphological changes in cells of the brain, both neurons and glia, and in their connections with each other.[93]

The neurological differences between men and women discussed in the previous section help us understand why men and women may differ in their behavioral patterns . . . generally. The neurological differences, however, should not be construed to serve as stereotypical labels or absolute predictors of anyone's behaviors. Each of us knows enough exceptions to each of the differences discussed to know that these neurological insights are not absolute in any way. That said, these insights do provide enough data that supports some of what we see in professional firms today, and these insights are extremely consistent with what we heard from men and women in our study. The differences are not absolute, but they do matter.

They matter because they are partially biological in nature and partially formed by the environments in which we are raised, educated, and socialized. There are neurological differences in men's and women's brains, but our brains do change their neural networks based on our experiences, even in adulthood. Although the majority of our brains' changes occur in our infancy and adolescence, our brains continue to learn new things, experience new realities, create new memories, and understand new perspectives by changing old neural networks and building new neural networks.

While men and women are born with the tendency to behave in different ways, they actually learn to behave in those different ways throughout their lives. This interplay between nature and nurture is especially important to understand in the context of deconstructing behavioral differences in elastic characteristics like competition and collaboration.

For instance, consider the recent research by Uri Gneezy, Ken Leonard, and John List that bends the arc of the competitive versus collaborative debate toward the nurture argument.[94]

Gneezy, Leonard, and List studied gender differences in the Maasai, the seminomadic people who live in Kenya and Tanzania, and the Khasi, tribal people who live in the state of Meghalaya in northern India. Maasai society is very patrilineal and patriarchal and is structured "such that wives are said to be less important to a man than his cattle."[95] Maasai men don't count daughters when they are asked how many children they have, and they have many wives, the majority of them decades younger than the men they marry. The women are not educated in parity with the men, and their lives are governed by men, from their fathers and brothers to their husbands. All inheritance is passed down from father to son(s).

The Khasi, in contrast, are a matrilineal culture where all inheritance is passed down from mother to daughter(s). Social, cultural, and economic decisions are primarily made by the women, and the households are run by women. Unlike in traditionally patrilineal societies, a Khasi man leaves his mother's house upon marriage to live with his wife near his wife's family, and he moves back with his family upon his wife's death or a divorce. Khasi women live in homes where mothers and grandmothers are the decision makers and wielders of power.

The researchers found that in the Maasai culture, the men were far more competitive than the women, but in the Khasi culture, the women were far more competitive than the men. In a cross-cultural comparison, the researchers found that the Khasi women were actually more competitive than the Maasai men! Men and women, when raised and expected to be in positions of authority, power, and control, become more competitive.

While my objective in this book is not to settle the larger nature versus nurture debate, the research on neurological differences combined with the research on the Maasai and the Khasi peoples gives us solid data through which we can begin to understand how our perspectives on competitiveness and collaboration are malleable. They are shaped by who we are born to be as well as how we are socialized, and they are honed through our experiences. They are indeed malleable, but they are also very real, very influential in our thought processes, and they drive our behaviors.

The contemporary social realities in the United States and most other countries that are patriarchal in nature operate in ways where women react to competitive triggers very differently than men. Since 2000, researchers have consistently found that not only are women less likely to want to work in competitive environments,[96] they perform worse than men (and their own potential) when they compete in these environments.[97] There are many neurological, sociological, and experiential reasons posited about why women don't prefer competitive work environments, but the analytical reasons, although important to know, matter less than the reality that they don't, a reality that is playing out daily in professional service firms in various industries.

In studies conducted by Peter Kuhn and Marie Claire Villeval, women were more likely to choose team-based work and compensation systems than were men. When men and women were given the freedom to choose their own teams, women's self-selected teams performed much better than men's self-selected teams.[98] After studying men and women in competitive and collaborative groups, Kuhn and Villeval concluded that "replacing tournaments by team-based incentives in highly paid jobs [m]ight increase women's representation in these jobs."[99]

Evren Ors, Frédéric Palomino, and Eloic Peyrache continued along this line of thought in their research by studying whether "gender-based differences in performance during competitive tournaments may be contributing to the underrepresentation of women."[100] By controlling for potential self-selection (opting out), childbearing, and discrimination, the researchers found that women outperformed men in noncompetitive environments and underperformed in relation to the men when competition was introduced.[101] Their research found "no evidence of differences in ability or in risk-taking behavior between male and female candidates. Hence, consistent with earlier experimental studies, we believe that the difference in performance is explained by the competitive aspect of the contest."[102]

Another study by Radosveta Ivanova-Stenzel and Dorothea Kubler found that "men perform worst when the benefits are shared with another man in a cooperative [collaborative] environment."[103] Men performed poorly when they were collaborating with other men, and their performance increased significantly when intragroup and intergroup competition was inserted into the team's working process. Interestingly, when men and women worked together in groups, the men's performance increased, but the women's performance decreased. The women also generally performed better when they worked in teams of women in collaborative settings. A finding of particular import in this study was that women performed at their best when they were in all-female teams competing against all-male teams—intragroup collaboration among the women and intergroup competition against the men.[104]

In a summary of several other research studies, Muriel Niederle and Lise Vesterlund found that two primary reasons impact women's performance in highly competitive workplaces even when men and women have the same ability to perform: (1) men are attracted to competition, and competition makes men overestimate their abilities, which leads to a greater eagerness to compete (and win); and (2) while women are confident in their abilities, they are not attracted to competition and will explicitly or implicitly choose to not engage in the competition if at all possible.[105]

The research on gender differences in competitiveness and collaboration relies on and expands generalizations, and we should be careful to not use these generalizations to stereotype women or men. There are many women who seek competition and thrive in hypercompetitive environments, and there are many men who avoid both. The goal of our research in this area is not to suggest that women and men are inherently drawn to or suited for particular environments but to recognize that women and men are socialized differently when it comes to competition and collaboration. This socialization has led to different preferences, styles, and behaviors in the workplace, and if these differences are not accounted for in how workplaces that are dominated by men work, these workplaces will not work as well for women as they do for men.

THE BOUNDARIES OF BEHAVIOR CHOICES

Viewing our respondents' perspectives in the context of a larger body of research on gender differences in competitive and collaborative styles of working gives us a more nuanced perspective on how business development works in professional service firms and why it may not be working as well for women as it does for men. A particularly unyielding dimension of this competitive/collaborative scale is the difference in responses received by men and women when they are perceived as being competitive.

Similar to the nature versus nurture debate on gender (are gender differences innate or socialized?), the structure versus agency debate provides us additional tools to understand not just how men and women behave in workplaces but how these behaviors are encouraged or discouraged by others through their responses to the behaviors.

Social scientists have been studying this structure versus agency debate for over a century now in trying to understand human behavior patterns and motivations. Generally defined, structure is the set of established social rules, patterns, behavioral expectations, and such that influence and/or constrain the choices and opportunities available to individuals.[106] Agency, in contrast, is the desire and capability that individuals have to free themselves from structure's constraints and take independent action to exercise free choice.[107] The structure versus agency debate (I prefer to call it a negotiation instead of a debate) is fundamentally about the extent to which we behave in socialized ways consistent with social structures and the extent to which we behave in autonomous ways that indicate an exercise of free choice irrespective of social constraints. Structure and agency are constantly negotiated and evolving in that individual agency exercised by many that is contrary to social structures can sometimes change the structures. Likewise, social structures can moderate individual behavioral choices through social rewards and punishments.

Social movements such as those for women's suffrage and civil rights illustrate the complexities of this structure versus agency negotiation. Social structures can impose certain behavioral mandates (i.e., women cannot vote, black and white children have to attend separate schools, etc.) until enough people exercise their agency to speak up against these mandates. Collective exercise of individual agency against social structures eventually erodes the existing structures, and new structures (i.e., women have voting rights, schools have to be integrated, etc.) replace the old structures.

These structure versus agency negotiations around gender in workplaces are not explicit or evident as negotiations are in massive social change movements. The negotiations on expected ambitions and behaviors for men and women are more implicit and subtle, but they have been researched enough for us to start understanding how structural rewards and punishments play a role in moderating behaviors along gender lines.

In this growing body of research, scientists refer to women (or men) who defy structural norms and expectations as "agentic," and the research on agentic women highlights the true complexities in how women (and men) make choices along the competitive/collaborative spectrum. The structure-agency negotiation in this area looks something like this:

There are some jobs that have historically been held by men. Socially accepted male traits (individualistic, assertive, competitive, etc.) become attached to the job as characteristics necessary for success in the job.

When men want to get hired in these jobs, the masculine traits that are perceived as necessary for the job are naturally manifested during the hiring process. After they are hired, when they continue to manifest these traits, they are seen as "natural leaders" because the traits that are deemed necessary for success in these positions are also traits that are socially accepted and even required of men. The more the men manifest these traits, the more they are seen as leaders, and they advance accordingly into leadership positions.

When women want to get hired into these jobs, they are initially rejected because they have more feminine traits (communal, empathetic, collaborative, etc.) that are not seen as conducive to being successful in the job. Women, then, manifest the more male traits while interviewing for these jobs, and, slowly, they start getting hired. Once they are in these positions, the manifestation of these more male traits rubs people the wrong way because the women are behaving in contradiction to structured norms of male/female behavior. These women are then labeled as difficult to work with or disagreeable, which makes them socially unfit for leadership. The more women manifest the masculine traits that they needed to manifest to get hired, the less they are seen as leaders, and they are marginalized accordingly.

Although the preceding is a slightly hyperbolic explanation of what happens to women in male-dominated environments, it is the cycle that Sheryl Sandberg was referring to in *Lean In* when she wrotes, "Success and likeability are positively correlated for men and negatively for women. When a man is successful, he is liked by both men and women. When a woman is successful, people of both genders like her less."[108] The Heidi/Howard case study,[109] cited by Sandberg to emphasize the point, illustrated how the same résumé (Heidi Roizen's actual résumé) provoked negative reactions when Heidi's name was on it and positive reactions when Heidi's name was changed to Howard. When given a résumé highlighting the stellar accomplishments of a Silicon Valley CEO and a successful venture capitalist, people reacted positively when the name on the résumé was Howard Roizen and negatively when the name was Heidi Roizen. Howard was likeable and had the ability to get things done, but Heidi was selfish and disagreeable.[110]

Women like Heidi Roizen are seen as agentic women who are successful in traditionally male-dominated fields. Agentic women are respected for their successes but disliked for the behaviors they manifest to become and stay successful. As Laurie Rudman describes this "backlash effect" in her research, "simply by acting in an agentic manner, women may be seen as violating the female-niceness prescription because agency and communion are viewed as opposing (though not completely irreconcilable) traits. Thus, female agency can simultaneously increase perceived competence but decrease likeability."[111]

Women in professional service firms are required to be agentic if they want to be successful in developing business in the business development model that is in most firms. Women have to choose between being successful and being liked while men don't have to make that choice. Given that the majority of human beings have a need to be connected to other people who like them,[112] the choice that women are being asked to make is, at best, an untenable one.

Several female partners/principals made this point emphatically in our study. One specifically referenced the phrase "difficult to work with" in her comments: *"So many female principals in my firm are considered difficult to work with . . . we do the exact same things as the men, and the men are considered strong but the women are seen as difficult to work with . . . there is this one male principal in my firm who battles for credit for every project that he works on, and they call him 'Pitbull.' He knows that's his nickname, and he loves it. He will even sign his e-mails that every once in a while. I fought for credit on a project that I worked on with him, and I was told that I was not being a team player and that I was setting a bad example for the younger people by focusing on credit instead of the client."*

Another partner told me that *"the cliché that if a man stands up for himself, he is confident, and if a woman stands up for herself, she is a bitch, is alive and well in firms . . . I've made peace that people will see me as a bitch if I do what I need to do to get business in the door and hold on to my clients. Not all women make that choice because it is not a fun choice."*

In order to enhance women's business development capabilities, models of business development need to be expanded to align with behaviors that fall within the structural norms for women's behaviors in our social environment. If women can develop business without having to be agentic, not only would they be very successful at it (see our experiment in Chapter 9), but they would not have to choose between developing business and being liked.

Dr. Benjamin Spock, America's most famous pediatrician and the man who encouraged mothers and fathers to trust their intuitions and raise their children as individuals, also cautioned that when "women are encouraged to be competitive, too many of them become disagreeable"[113] because "biologically and temperamentally, I believe women were made to be concerned first and foremost with child care, husband care and home care."[114] This issue of women being disagreeable when they are competitive becomes especially intense when women are in competition against men, as they are in many professional service firms. Recall the 1976 Olympics example from Caroline's story when the shooting competition was segregated after a woman tied a man for first place. It is not socially acceptable for women to act competitive, but it is really not socially acceptable for women to act competitive against men.

Let's bring this logic (or lack thereof) into the 21st century. In 2011, the International Association of Athletics Federations (IAAF), the governing body for track and field competitions, implemented a rule regarding record setting in road races (i.e., marathons, half marathons, 10K races, etc.) that banned women from being able to set records in marathons when they run alongside men.[115] Women can only set road race records now when they run in women-only races. The IAAF not only implemented this ban but did so retroactively, effectively wiping out two world records that Paula Radcliffe set in the 2003 London Marathon (2:15:25) and the 2002 Chicago Marathon (2:17:18) for no reason other than she ran those races alongside men. The current record was one that Radcliffe set in the 2005 London Marathon (2:17:42), a race in which women began 45 minutes before the men so that the elite female runners could not pace with the men.

One of the reasons proffered by the IAAF for this ludicrous rule was that women ran faster when they paced with men because men ran faster at the elite level. The women performed better because they paced themselves with runners who ran faster than they did, and those runners happened to be men, so the women's race times should not count. The logic not only defies reason, but it explicitly distinguishes between the male and female competitions as if to say that it's fine for women to compete against each other, but it is not okay when they compete in any way that suggests they can compete alongside men.

Another reason proffered by the IAAF was that women who were paced by men ran behind the men, and given the fact that men are generally bigger than women, the men's bodies block the headwinds, thereby giving the women an unfair advantage. This reason defies even more logic than the previous one because the assumption would have to be that a woman can then also not be paced by a woman who is bigger (measured by height? weight? girth?) than she because it would be an unfair advantage. The IAAF did not answer that question or the question of whether the ruling was legitimate if the male pacer was smaller than the female runner.

These are but a few examples that help us better understand the structural and cultural constraints that women face when they consider the choice of competing or not. Of course, there is a percentage of women who will nonetheless choose to compete, and these agentic women carefully negotiate the balance of competing successfully or being successfully liked. Men can compete *and* be liked. Women can compete *or* be liked.

Regardless of how men and women described their individual business development styles in professional service firms, more men were willing to compete than women (70 percent to 41 percent), and more women said that they would thrive in an environment that was not competitive (75 percent to 15 percent). The business development size in professional service firms is one that is deeply rooted in tournament-style competition where the rewards for winning the competition are increased compensation and power, rewards that resonate better with men than they do with women. All of the research points to the reality that this size fits the majority of men, and it does not fit the majority of women. Of course, there are women for whom this size is a great fit, and there are men for whom this size is a severe misfit, but gender differences between the majorities in each gender demonstrate that the current size fits men more easily than it does women.

When we showed a few of the professional service firm leaders this data, they were again frustrated but not surprised. While some leaders felt that firms do have the responsibility to make structural changes to accommodate these differences between men and women, other leaders felt that women need to make different choices given their lack of attraction to competition. The majority of the leaders agreed, however, that this type of structural change would be difficult to catalyze and implement in their firms.

One leader talked about how his firm was very committed to advancing women, but addressing these depths of gender differences felt too radical for him: *"We are not trying to fix a crack in a wall. The cracks are coming from a foundation that is not working. I'm not saying that I don't recognize that, and I'm not saying that I don't want to fix the foundation, but I don't know how to do that without tearing the whole structure down. It's like our government. We know it's broken, and we keep trying to fix the cracks. But our government needs to be overhauled, and that only happens in the wake of a revolution. My firm is not about to agree to a revolution."*

Another leader agreed that the problem was a difficult one to fix, but he did not agree that it was a problem that needed to be fixed by the firm: *"The data paints a bleak picture. Yeah, the numbers are bad, but if the women are choosing not to compete, is it our responsibility to make this all nice for them or is it their responsibility to figure out where they would be happy?"* This leader's perspective was echoed by others who discussed how the "value proposition" or "business case" for gender diversity incentivized change but only to a certain point. Although changes in recruiting, hiring, mentoring, and even talent development processes could be changed through the incentives presented by the business case, those incentives are not reported to be strong enough to motivate change in the business development efforts and their consequent compensation practices.

The leaders were not necessarily in disagreement that they were operating in a "one size fits all" model, but they did vary in whether they felt this was truly a problem that they needed to address. For those firms that have decided that the lack of representation of women in partnership and leadership is indeed a problem that they want to fix, the "one size fits all" model will impede their progress in solving this problem.

If different sizes are not offered, women will continue to underperform their male counterparts in business development efforts in firms. If the amount of business generated were not the primary precursor to compensation and leadership, maybe this size misfit would not be a big deal. That is, however, not the case in firms, so the misfit becomes a critical piece of any gender equity strategy.

CHAPTER 9

SIZING UP BUSINESS DEVELOPMENT AND SALES

Earlier, we parsed business development into its various definitional and working parts and explored gender differences in how men and women received, comprehended, and executed on business development information and advised actions. We worked with the general definition of business development offered by Scott Pollack from *Forbes* as "the creation of long-term value for an organization from customers [clients], markets and relationships."[116] We focused on the difference between knowing and doing business development, specifically on how men and women can know the same thing but do very different things depending on social context and personal choices.

We also explored the gender differences in how business development is perceived, characterized, and internalized by men and women in firms and why the different choices that men and women make between competitive and collaborative business development strategies can impact how individuals approach, engage in, and enjoy business development activities. In addition to the gender differences in competitive versus collaborative business development styles, the gender differences in how men and women defined and understood business development in comparison to sales also played a critical role in creating differences in preferences, behaviors, and outcomes between men and women.

In this chapter, we will delve into the particularly strong divergence between men and women in their perceptions of and responses to selling as a part of business development. The gender differences we saw in the preceding chapter in regard to competitive behaviors were raised by one firm leader in thinking about business development and sales: *"Business development is sales. Sales means there are buyers and there are sellers and not every buyer will buy from each and every seller. Buyers will make choices. They have to make choices. You work to be the one they choose which means that others won't get chosen. That's competition. The data [on competition] definitely describes what's going on in my firm . . . I'm not surprised by it, but we cannot take away the competition in this work."*

Professional service firms are not necessarily any more or less competitive than other types of organizations, but they are different in what they are competing to sell. Women seem to be much more comfortable being competitive when they are selling something outside themselves instead of selling themselves. One female partner who had actually been in sales before she transitioned into consulting talked about this difference in connecting sales and competition: *"In sales before, I had to sell financial service products. I was comfortable comparing the products I was selling with other products on the market. I did great at talking about the positives and the limits of the products, and I was good. I cannot seem to translate that into selling myself . . . The skills are there . . . I just cannot use them to sell myself . . . One partner at the firm told me to sell the firm, not myself, but if I sell the firm, I have to sell that there are other people who do what I do, and I will still have to sell why I should be selected above others in my firm."*

While men's responses did not vary whether the term "develop business" or "sell" was used, women's responses diverged greatly in ways that illustrated that women had a clear and strong dislike for "selling." In one question that directly inquired whether or not people like to sell as part of their client development efforts, 52 percent of women said that they did not like to sell in comparison to only about 20 percent of men who said that they did not like to sell. Men and women in our study struggled with understanding how selling differed from business development and what exactly the relationship was between these concepts.

The intricate and complicated relationship between business development and selling has garnered much attention in the business world generally, and not understanding the differences and the relationship between the two can have particularly negative consequences for women in professional service firms.

Neal Kielar, a consultant who works on strategy, marketing, and business development for professional service firms, advises his clients to distinguish between sales and business development before they create a definition of either. The key differences between sales and business development according to Kielar[117] are summarized in the following table:

SALES	BUSINESS DEVELOPMENT
Tactical	Strategic
Transactional	Consultative in approach
Immediate outcomes expected	Immediate and longer-term outcomes expected
Revenue growth is primary success measure	More flexible measurement of value
Sustainability of sales is more uncertain	Higher value outcomes sustained over time
High emphasis on short-term objectives	Success measures anchored in strategy
Financial motivation is paramount	Service orientation along with financial focus

When we showed this table to firm leaders, the consensus among the leaders was that their firms really tried to focus on business development but that the focus on sales had definitely been increasing considerably in the last 10 to 15 years due to competition from other firms, client demand for flexibility in fee structures, the unpredictability in movement of partners/principals from one firm to another, the focus on partner compensation as a key indicator of firm performance, and the impact of the economic downturn of 2008–2009.

One leader articulated the reality in his firm: *"the ideal is 75 percent business development and 25 percent sales, but it doesn't break down that neat in reality . . . bottom line is that there are people who excel at business development and client relationships and others who excel at sales . . . as much as we value the developers, we mostly reward the sellers because sales, the dollars, are easier to measure than development, the relationships."*

The leaders also talked about how professionals in firms generally steered clear of language involving "selling" because it felt like framing their services in sales language minimized the tailored problem solving and creativity required of their work. One leader summarized this avoidance of sales language: *"People in my firm see themselves as partners to our clients, not vendors . . . we don't sell something that can be prepackaged and mass distributed . . . every client is different, and we treat them that way . . . so, thinking of it as selling cheapens what we do."* Another partner discussed how the actual terms used in the client development process in his firm mirror sales language even though the process was not defined as sales per se: *"We open deals and close them. We cross sell and measure dollars. We are selling, but we don't call it selling because selling is not part of our tradition, our history."*

Scott Pollack, the writer for *Forbes* whose definition of business development is highlighted in Chapter 3, frames business development as being comprised of three interrelated but independent pieces—strategy, sales, and relationship management:[118]

- **Strategy**: Being able to assess an opportunity for its potential to create long-term value, determine the paths available to you to pursue it, and understand the trade-offs and risks of one path vs. another, are core [business development] functions.
- **Sales**: The process of navigating through an organization, identifying decision-makers and uncovering their unmet needs, and concisely demonstrating the value of what you can offer are core sales skills needed whether you're selling a product, service, or partnership.
- **Relationship Management**: Business development requires not only having an expansive network to help you facilitate a deal, but also a deep understanding of how to build and maintain new relationships to leverage them when needed. Relationships with partners/principals, customers, colleagues, and even the media, can all be crucial factors in not only getting in the door to a [business development] opportunity, but keeping it open.

In both their survey and interview responses, women responded positively to the strategy and the relationship management aspects of client development, and they responded to the concept of selling with a strong dislike that was articulated in various ways. This was very consistent with how they viewed the development of relationships in our experiment. Women overwhelmingly focused on developing relationships for the intrinsic value of developing a relationship, and this focus felt contrary to the act of selling for many women.

Men, on the other hand, responded to all three aspects in a relatively similar manner, and they did not respond with a dislike for any particular aspect. Again, this was consistent with our finding that men developed relationships not just for the value of the relationships but for what the relationships could yield; focusing on relationship yield was consistent with the act of selling. The comments from men reflected an array of perspectives of which aspects they considered to be strengths and which aspects they felt were more challenging for them. All three aspects were mentioned as strengths and challenges in the aggregate responses from men. One man noted that *"I can sell but am not good at maintaining relationships . . . I prefer to get the work and do the work instead of tending to relationships,"* while another said, *"Love the strategy and planning pieces, doing the research . . . could do without the selling, but do like to see the pitches come together after taking the time to pull all the research."*

The comments from women focused on the strengths they felt they had in strategy and relationship management and the challenges they faced with selling. Not a single woman identified selling as a strength. Women were most likely to select relationship management as a strength and selling as a challenge, with strategy being listed more as a strength than a challenge. Although there were men who talked about not liking the selling process, women, like this female partner, were emphatic about disliking the selling process: *"I don't like to sell. I did not become a [professional] to sell. I'm good and my work speaks for itself. It feels cheap to have to sell people on my craft and profession. I honestly hate it."*

Women also differentiated between selling a product and selling a service, especially when they were the service providers they were selling. For example, one female partner framed it like this: *"When people think of selling generally, it's about selling stuff. I have done sales before, but selling myself is very different. I feel like I'm cheapening the process of what I do by having to sell."* Another partner said, *"Selling myself sounds wrong and feels wrong."*

A few female partners/principals raised a socially charged perspective on "selling" that is captured well with this perspective: *"Even saying 'selling myself' starts the conversation wrong for me . . . selling yourself has a different connotation for women. Some of that connotation is conscious and some of it is unconscious, but it's there. I remember a few years ago, I asked one of my colleagues how I could sell myself better, and he responded with 'shorter skirt, taller heels.' I was really upset for weeks. I almost left the firm after that."* Whenever female partners/principals brought up the discomfort of using the language around "selling yourself," they did so with an expressed fear of sounding like they were too sensitive or thin-skinned, but they wanted to bring it up because it was heavily influencing how they thought about this and why it was difficult for them to talk about it with their male colleagues.

On one hand, it may be tempting to dilute these women's perspectives by talking about their tolerance levels, but we heard enough stories from women about how men reacted to the language around women selling themselves that these women's perspectives deserve to be evaluated and understood at their fully concentrated levels.

Men's responses in this area were far less intense in regard to their focus on selling, and men's comments about selling were subsumed into their overall comments about the difficulties of business development. Where the reactions to selling were internal and emotional for women, they were external and detached for men.

For instance, one male partner focused on selling being difficult because of the competition involved: *"It's difficult to sell myself or the firm because the competition is so intense. The competition now is not just about the firm down the street but the firms in India, in China and in Europe. The competition is the digital firm that has no address but is always in your face. It's hard to sell in this environment."* Another partner talked about the time constraints involved: *"Selling myself today seems to be about always having to be everywhere and that's a pain. There are so many events and meetings and conferences, and there is this pressure that if you don't go to everything, you are not doing your best to develop business. If you like that kind of stuff, you are good, but I don't, so it feels like a chore."*

The business development versus selling dynamic was something that many women focused on intensely in their surveys as well as their interviews.

Business development was perceived by women as relationship building and relationship nurturing, and investing in a relationship. Selling, on the other hand, was perceived by women as taking from a relationship. Women consistently reported being more comfortable with the former and not the latter.

Although a lot of research has been done on the differences in how to sell to women in comparison to men, there has not been a lot of inquiry into whether women sell differently than men or if they even perceive the selling process differently than men do. Before conducting an extensive study entitled "How Women Decide" on the purchasing patterns of female decision makers in large corporations, Cathy Benko and Bill Pelster, principals at Deloitte LLC, did an internal survey within Deloitte and found that "70 percent of our senior managers told us they perceived that selling to women was different from selling to men."[119]

Many of the firm leaders and partners/principals we talked with discussed the importance of selling to female purchasers of professional services very differently than selling to men. For example, one male firm leader talked about a woman who was one of the primary decision makers at one of his firm's largest clients: *"We almost didn't get the business the first time we did a presentation for them because we had women on our team, but she commented how none of them had talked during the presentation. She also gets to the point a lot faster than the men in her group. A lot of our female clients are that way. They don't indulge in as much small talk as our male clients do, and they don't want to go to dinner and drinks . . . the men do. We definitely spend more business development dollars on our male clients."*

Many firms had given a lot of thought to how their female clients made purchasing decisions differently than their male clients, but there had been no focus on whether their female partners/principals may sell very differently than their male partners/principals. When one firm leader thought about the proposition that women may sell very differently than men, he said, *"Of course, that makes sense . . . if they buy differently, it is logical to think they may sell differently . . . we just have not thought about it like that."*

A study done by Trulia, an online residential real estate tracking database, found that male real estate agents list more homes on average than female real estate agents although there are more women than men registered as agents in residential real estate.[120] Although men list more homes, women are far more likely to list homes more expensive than the ones that men list.[121] Why do female real estate agents net the more expensive homes when they net less homes overall? We interviewed a few male and female real estate agents to get more insights into this data, and their views highlighted how the male and female agents thought about the process of selling very differently.

Female real estate agents were less likely to take on homes that they didn't connect with and felt that they couldn't sell, but men saw the listing of homes as a numbers game in that the more homes they listed, the more they were likely to sell. Women concentrated less on the volume and more on their ability to truly sell a particular home because they saw each house much more individually than the men did. There are more women in real estate, but the women are reporting to be more discerning in what they will list, so they, collectively, list fewer homes, and they are reporting connecting with the more expensive homes because of the individuality, character, and connectability of the more expensive homes.

The female partners/principals in our study generally noted discomfort with selling, but the process of selling was easier if the women really believed in the outcomes they were trying to achieve. One senior female partner expressed how she came to think about sales in a slightly different way: *"I have never thought of myself as a sales woman. I am a professional, and I realize that I have to develop clients, but I honestly don't know what to do and I don't like to sell. One day, one of the senior leaders in my firm asked me why I wasn't using my salesmanship skills in getting more business. I was honestly surprised. When he pointed out to me how much money I had raised for our scholarship program, it really threw me for a loop. I would have never seen fund-raising for a scholarship program as selling, and he didn't see any difference between what I was doing for the scholarship program and what he wanted me to be doing for client development. It still doesn't compute, but I'm open to how I may need to see selling differently than how I see it right now."*

This disconnect in women between "this isn't selling because I really believe in it" and "I don't like to sell" was an interesting one because it focused less on the behavior of selling and more on the thing being sold, which is consistent with our previous discussion on women's discomfort with "selling themselves." When women were selling something outside or other than themselves, they did not see it as selling per se. When women were commenting on selling themselves, their time, or their skill sets, the framework of "I don't like selling" really kicked in.

As one woman noted, *"I can sell anything outside of me. I can sell a product or even my colleague's expertise, but I cannot go out there and ask people to buy me. It feels awkward and bad and generally not very appealing to me."* Men, to the contrary, did not differentiate between selling a colleague's expertise and their own expertise. One male leader asserted that *"selling is selling . . . I don't understand how you say you can sell in one situation but you can't in another situation. If you know how to sell, you should be able to sell anything anywhere."*

In *To Sell Is Human: The Surprising Truth about Moving Others*, Daniel Pink makes an impassioned case for thinking about selling as persuasion instead of traditional sales.[122] By focusing on topics like persuasion, service, and even empathy, he argues that the traditional perspective on selling is outmoded and ineffective. This model of selling exists in professional service firms, and women are both attracted to it and good at it, but this model exists after the clients are officially signed up as clients. The translation of contacts into clients is a process that still involves some aspects of traditional sales, and these aspects are the ones that create the greatest gender differentials in business development outcomes.

"I HATE THIS HORN"

I hate when people tell me to "toot my own horn." What does that even mean? I don't have a horn. None of the people who tell me this even play the horn. My firm brought in a speaker to talk to the women about business development, and she spent the majority of the time talking about how women need to toot their own horns more. I wanted to scream. Seriously, what does the phrase really even mean? I hate this horn that everyone wants me to toot.

—FEMALE PARTNER IN A LARGE PROFESSIONAL SERVICE FIRM

This partner's emphatic take on the phrase "toot your own horn" was similar to what many women said (maybe not as emphatically) they did not like about the traditional sales aspect of business development. This commentary from women was a close second to how much women focused on not liking the process of selling. This inspired me to do some research on the phrase and what it actually means.

"Toot your own horn" or "blow your own horn" is derived from the slightly more archaic phrase "sound your own trumpet." History has been recording the presence and function of trumpets since 1500 B.C. because trumpets were not just musical instruments—they were the attention getters for something important. Trumpets were sounded before the arrival of highly important people or the announcement of important messages. Trumpets heralded importance, so trumpeters were sent ahead of the important people or news so that people could be called to attention in order to receive the people or news with appropriate reverence.

Therefore, blowing your own trumpet (or horn) evolved to mean that you were announcing your own importance or promoting yourself, which has often been considered a negative thing, from Matthew recommending in the Bible that "when you give to the needy, sound no trumpet before you," to Jim Collins reporting his findings in *Good to Great* that self-promoting leaders are less sustainably successful in the long run than leaders who don't blow their own horns.[123]

Given the phrase's roots in more negative connotations, it is fascinating to see how "blowing your own horn" today has not only become associated with a positive and self-empowered outlook but one that is necessary for success. The following two quotes by prominent men illustrate the message that people hear these days.

- *Blow your own horn loud. If you succeed, people will forgive your noise; if you fail, they'll forget it.*—William Feather (Journalist)
- *If you don't blow your own horn, someone else will use it as a spittoon.*—Kenneth H. Blanchard (Author/Leadership Consultant)

Compare the preceding quotes to the next quote by Kathryn Erbe, a prominent actress: *"I think that I have never had the confidence to really aggressively get behind myself, and so what I do tends to be . . . I don't want to say sheepish, but there is a sheepish quality to my ability to toot my own horn . . . I just do what I like to do, and what I think I do well is not very loud, necessarily."*

As I was researching the history and social dialogue around this phrase, the female partner's strong statement that "I hate this horn!" continued to push me into examining whether women truly had a very different reaction to this concept of "blowing your own horn" than men did.

Self-promotion, according to Laurie A. Rudman, includes "pointing with pride to one's accomplishments, speaking directly about one's strengths and talents, and making internal rather than external attributions for achievements."[124] Research conducted over the past couple of decades definitely illuminates the reality that women see self-promotion very differently than men do, and they are treated very differently when they engage in this behavior. As Sophia Dembling wrote for the American Psychological Association, "Both women and men fear that people won't like them if they are self-promoting, but women are more likely to let it stop them."[125] Perhaps men and women feel queasy about tooting their own horns, but men seem to find it easier than women do to move past this queasiness.

Dembling also cited a study done on women and salary negotiation and quoted the study's researcher, Hannah Riley Bowles: "Women pay a higher social cost and particularly career cost for attempting to negotiate for higher compensation."[126] The study "showed that when women came to the bargaining table with an offer from another possible employer—a common and usually effective negotiating tool—potential employers were turned off."[127] Bowles explained this phenomenon in simple terms: "Everybody knows if you have an outside offer, it's totally appropriate to negotiate." And yet, when women do this, people respond with an, "'Ugh, I don't think I want to work with her' feeling."[128]

When Laurel Bellows became the President of the American Bar Association (only the fifth woman to do so in over a century of the organization's existence), she talked often about the need for women to deal with this difficulty to promote themselves so that they can maximize their career potential and success:

Sixteen percent of the equity partners in the top 250 law firms are women. Ten years ago the number was 14 percent; that's only 2 percentage points improvement in 10 years. Equity partners are those given the opportunity to own a share in a large firm. In the top 250 law firms in the country, there are only about five managing partners [who are women] . . . women and men in the legal profession are not treated or paid the same or given similar opportunities for advancement.

The senior-level women that I represent in negotiations about employment, promotion, separation or job title are very reticent to push. So often, a man walks in and says, "I'm a senior vice president and you've just made me executive vice president and put me on the executive committee of this huge corporation. That's wonderful. What's my new salary? What's my new bonus? How many people are going to report to me?" They just go in there and ask. Women generally don't do that, and they should. But when they do they are much more frequently seen as being self-serving and greedy. There remains this stereotype barrier to the women who do ask; there's this danger of being thought aggressive that we have to overcome. But on the other hand, if you don't ask, you don't get, ever.[129]

While people lauded her advice and perspectives in theory, Bellows was roundly criticized by many female lawyers when she talked about her own self-promotion behaviors in her life. In an interview, Bellows called work-life balance "a fraud" and joked about how her husband laughs at her because she takes her business cards with her even when she goes to the restroom.[130] The article itself was far less interesting than the commentary provided by readers offering their often angry and hostile reactions to the interview. Take, for instance, the message blogged by Victoria Pynchon, a consultant and trainer on negotiation skills for women:

This is a plea for Bellows to rethink her position as a leader not only of America's lawyers, but as a woman leader in a profession in which institutional barriers to women's retention and advancement are acute . . . Bellows, like many a rainmaker male and female, loves to market, to self-promote, to make a lot of green from every relationship she enters into . . . She doesn't believe she is sacrificing anything. She likes her life and she either doesn't see the unnecessary barriers women face or she's chosen to ignore them. That's great for Bellows personally. It's just not great for the women leader of lawyers where the professional wage gap between male attorneys and the few women who survive long enough to become equity partners is 60%.[131]

While male partners/principals talked about self-promotion in terms of *"being uncomfortable at first but getting over it"* and *"it's not bragging if it's true,"* female partners/principals talked about *"never seems like the right time,"* *"bragging has always felt uncomfortable to me,"* and *"my work should speak for itself."* There was a much greater reluctance by female partners/principals than male partners/principals to promote themselves, and for the majority of these women, this reluctance was based on witnessing negative consequences for other women and their own perceptions of potential negative consequences, not actual experiences with negative consequences.

A number of the women recollected how other women in their firms were perceived when they spoke up about themselves. One female partner recalled a luncheon meeting that she had attended with several of the partners/principals from her firm. She and another female partner were the only women in attendance, and when the topic turned to speeches that people had recently given at conferences, *"she [the other female partner] talked about how she had given this great talk based on a case study that she had completed with a client and how well the audience responded to her talk, and the guys just stared at her. It was uncomfortable and a completely different reaction than when the men had gone on and on about speeches they had given. She had talked at the most prestigious conference in our field. She should have been proud, but she was clearly embarrassed by the guys' reactions. They didn't say anything to her . . . just stared at her and moved on to another topic like she hadn't said anything."*

Another woman discussed how women in her firm were consistently told that they were not team players when they touted their own successes, but she never heard that criticism aimed at the men when they did the same.

Some of the women reported such a strong avoidance of self-promotion that they experienced physical symptoms like nausea, sweaty palms, and dry mouths when they even attempted to talk about their own accomplishments in front of their colleagues. *"I wouldn't even be good at talking about myself in that way, about what I did or what I was really good at because of how nervous I get to do it. I would probably stutter if I tried. It's better for me to not go that route. There has to be another way."* The female partner who told me this laughed nervously after she made the comment and then told me that she had felt uncomfortable even talking about how uncomfortable she was with this topic.

Women who promoted themselves were similarly perceived as competitive women in regard to being agentic—violative of social norms of how modestly and humbly women are supposed to act.[132] Corinne A. Moss-Racusin and Laurie A. Rudman found that "[w]omen experience social and economic penalties (i.e., backlash) for self-promotion, a behavior that violates female gender stereotypes yet is necessary for professional success."[133] Moss-Racusin and Rudman did not find any backlash effect for men who self-promoted or for women who promoted their peers instead of themselves.

The research on women being seen as more competent but less likeable if they self-promote is especially important to understand in the context of research that shows that men are seen as less competent and less likeable if they don't self-promote.[134] If women are penalized for not being self-effacing and men are penalized for being self-effacing, the defensive reactions by both groups is to work hard for their actions to be congruent with socially expected norms. When you introduce the kind of competition that is pervasive in firms into this mix, the defensive reactions of both groups intensify, and the gap in self-promotion behaviors between men and women grows.

One male partner in our study talked about how he didn't understand why the female leaders in his firm did not feel comfortable being more self-promoting in their communications inside and outside the firm. *"These women are tough negotiators, great with tough clients. These are tough cookies, but they won't talk about their successes. They even play down what they did and roles they played to get something done."* Consistent with the research discussed in this chapter, women are penalized for self-promoting, but they are seen as both competent and likeable when they promote the interests of others. This quirk in the stereotype empowers women to be strong advocates and negotiators for their clients and effective promoters of their colleagues and creates confusion when they don't use those proven skills for their self-interest.

Even the most successful and powerful women in these firms talk about self-promotion carefully. In March 2013, *The Accountant*, an online publication for accounting professionals, published an article entitled "Top Female Accounting Leaders Share Their Views on Gender." The article featured RSM Chief Executive Jean Stephen, ACCA Chief Executive Helen Brand, Morison International Chief Executive Liza Robbins and Ernst & Young (E&Y) Fraud Investigations and Dispute Services Partner Maryam Kennedy.[135] Overall, the female leaders talked very positively about being women in the accounting profession while acknowledging that the profession had a long way to go to retain and advance women. On the subject of succeeding as a woman and the need for self-promotion, Kennedy attempted to reconcile the tensions we have discussed thus far in this chapter: *"When you blow your own horn, recognise the orchestra.' You'll only get so far by yourself. Build a team around you as you go to be collectively powerful and successful."*[136]

Women are right to hate that horn even if they mute some of the noise from the horn by recognizing the orchestra! Women suffer penalties for not self-promoting because the model of success requires self-promotion, and they suffer penalties for self-promoting because the behavior is violative of how women are supposed to act. When women in firms are advised to "toot their own horns," they resist not because they don't want to or don't know how to self-promote but because they know that they will pay a heavy price for following that advice.

E-DIFFERENCES

Given that the majority of communications in professional service firms are conducted electronically (e-mails, web updates, professional blogs, etc.), we examined what happens to the gender differences we have discussed thus far when the communications, sales pitches, and other business development activities occur in the electronic realm.

We gathered business development e-mails from 23 male and female partners/principals in our study, and we also looked at a sample of about ten professional service blogs, of which six were hosted by men and four were hosted by women. We found many of the differences we have discussed over the past few chapters in the electronic communications as well.

For example, women were almost twice as likely as men to say "we" instead of "I" in their e-mail communications with potential clients. Women were also more likely than men to talk about ways in which a team from their firm would be able to service the client's needs in comparison to men who focused more on what they could provide the clients as individuals. Men were significantly more likely to compare themselves and/or their firms directly to perceived competitors whereas women were more likely to use general terms such as *"I know you have many choices"* or *"there are a lot of great options in this field."* In many instances, women would use general terms and not state directly why they would be better options than the other choices available.

Men were far more likely than women to end their electronic communications with specific questions and/or desired actions to advance the business development process such as requesting a meeting, asking for a direct response to a business question, and so on. Women were more likely to end their electronic communications in a more open-ended manner that did not require a response. For men, the specific actions arose from a desire *"to make it easier for the client to respond,"* and for women, the open-endedness was rooted in the desire *"to not be seen as presumptuous or demanding."*

Women's electronic communications and blogs also tended to be much longer than men's and have longer introductory statements and paragraphs. One female partner commented on this by telling me that *"I'm always concerned that they don't remember me or that they are wading through so many e-mails and I don't want them to have to place my name or where they met me."*

Our informal exploration of gender differences in the electronic aspect of business development communications is consistent with what other, similar studies have found. One study, for example, found that " there is a clear difference in the language used by males and females online . . . women used far more expressions offering support and a deepening of their relationship with the readers. Men used only six 'supportive' expressions, while women used eighteen. In addition, women used much more open expressions of appreciation and thanks, while men used 'tighter' and less direct expressions. Furthermore, men were found to be more interested in presenting their personal point of view in order to present an 'authoritative' contribution to the discussion, while women were more interested in the contribution itself."[137]

The competitive versus collaborative differences as well as the different perspectives on selling and self-promotion were as visible in the electronic communications as they were in the live interpersonal interactions recounted by the majority of our survey respondents and interviewees.

While the consistency of this data informs us about the significance of these differences in business development behaviors and outcomes, it also offers us guidance on understanding that strategies to neutralize gender differences in business development cannot leave out the universe of electronic communications.

In Part 3, you will read about an experiment in creating a new size for business development in professional service firms, and you will find a variety of strategies for individual women as well as for firms and firm leaders. We have spent the majority of this journey understanding the problem. In Part 3, we can move on to what really matters—solving the problem.

DESIGNING NEW SIZES (AND ALTERING THE ONE SIZE)

CHAPTER 10

BUSINESS DEVELOPMENT - NOW AVAILABLE IN MORE SIZES

In 2013, Warren Buffett penned an opinion piece for *Fortune* in which he discussed how the future of the U.S. economy depended on our collective ability to integrate women as full and equal participants in workplaces and leadership across all industries.[138] He asked us to consider how far our nation had come utilizing only 50 percent of its talent and how much more success was possible if we started utilizing all of our talent. Buffett's words on the need for more opportunities for women were quoted, tweeted, and repeated for weeks in headlines that shouted things like "Buffett Is Bullish . . . on Women," but there was a critical message in his piece that was quietly and just as repeatedly ignored. This ignored message was about the reality of the challenges we face in creating the change for which he was advocating:

> Resistance among the powerful is natural when change clashes with their self-interest. Business, politics, and, yes, religions provide many examples of such defensive behavior. After all, who wants to double the number of competitors for top positions? But an even greater enemy of change may well be the ingrained attitudes of those who simply can't imagine a world different from the one they've lived in.[139]

Who, indeed, would want to double the number of competitors for top positions, especially in environments that are already ubercompetitive? While professional service firms are committed, in theory, to increasing the opportunities for women, there is resistance to changes in areas like business development because business development is what defines the powerful as powerful. It's generally difficult to get people to change what they are used to doing, but it's really difficult to get them to change something that is working well for them. In addition, change in how business development gets done, gets recognized, and gets rewarded goes against the ingrained beliefs, attitudes, and behaviors of those who are currently in leadership in these firms.

This resistance is real, and it is strong. This resistance is what has led many firms to gently tweak their business development models instead of catalyzing the deeper and more comprehensive change that is actually needed. This resistance is what continues to perpetuate the idea that if only women could be taught to be better business developers, this "women's issue" could be resolved, because as long as it's the "women's issue," women are seen as responsible for fixing it. Initiatives and programs to fix "women's issues" are the tweaks; upending the business development model is comprehensive change.

Buffett's advice on creating change in environments that are resistant to change is this: "Should you find yourself in a chronically leaking boat, energy devoted to changing vessels is likely to be more productive than energy devoted to patching leaks." Professional service firms today are chronically leaking boats when it comes to women and business development. The firms' resistance to change has engendered solutions that are "devoted to patching leaks," but what we need—what will work—is to change boats. Fixing the "women's issue" is a patch; changing the business development model to equalize opportunities for everyone is a change to a new boat. There is not much resistance to patching leaks. There is considerable resistance to changing boats. We can't take what we are currently doing and do it slightly differently. We need to do different things altogether.

The strategies in Part 3 are focused on changing boats, not patching the leaks in the one that has not brought us very far. Changing boats, in comparison to patching the same leak over and over again, is definitely more difficult in the short term but will yield greater results in the long term.

Individually, each strategy in this integrated process involves a small but tangible change. Collectively, they offer an alternative way forward for women (and men) who want to develop business but don't want any part of doing it the way it is currently being done.

CREATING NEW SIZES: AN OVERVIEW

The secret of change is to focus all of your energy, not on fighting the old, but on building the new.

—SOCRATES

When I started researching gender differences in business development, I was surprised to discover how aware most people were that there was such a significant gap between business development outcomes for men and women. As I learned more about people's perspectives and the contexts for business development that exist in many firms today, I was equally surprised by how little interest there was in making the big changes necessary to do something about this gap.

As we experimented with strategies within firms to address the problems we identified through this study, we began to see that doing something different and new was often more successful than ideas to fix what was broken. Once we demonstrated that one size never fits all, the effective solution seemed to be to create new sizes that will fit more people, not to alter the one size that currently dominates the business development models in professional service firms. Fixing patches just did not work as well as starting anew.

Creating new sizes required a comprehensive shift in how to conceptualize and implement new business development paradigms that still result in successful outcomes. Extensive experimentation with different behaviors and structural changes identified five core areas through which new sizes of business development can be constructed.

The following five areas are ones in which active and deliberate changes in business development behaviors correlated with positive changes in business development outcomes.

1. Reframe Your Perspective: *Change what you see.*
2. Refocus Your Goals: *Change what you choose.*
3. Revise Your Vocabulary: *Change what you say.*

4. Reshape Your Methods: *Change what you do.*
5. Review Your Successes: *Change what isn't working.*

The suggestions for possible changes in each of these areas range from those specifically designed for individual women (and men) to those devised for leaders seeking to change what their firms are doing on an institutional level. These five areas can be understood and explored separately, but their full power lies in their collective impact. Imagine what you can achieve if you see, choose, say, do, and change differently than you did before.

CREATING NEW SIZES: A PILOT PROGRAM

We took these five core areas for behavioral change and developed a pilot study for "one size never fits all so let's create a new size that fits us" thinking based on what we heard from female partners/principals in our study. We worked with a female firm leader to run the study in a large department within her firm. I hope that the findings will give you ideas, inspiration, and lots of food for thought on creating your own "new size" efforts.

THE PROGRAM

Eleven women in the department volunteered to pilot this "new size" business development program. We divided them into three groups of three, four, and four and asked each group to grapple with what they currently saw, chose, said, did, and changed in order to identify how they could do so differently. Interestingly but not surprisingly, all three groups reported very similar patterns of responses:

1. They *saw* business development as difficult, and they saw men as more successful at it than women. They also saw that men seemed to enjoy business development activities more than women did and that women did not seem to have the same amount of time as men because of family obligations.
2. They *chose* to not be involved in many of the informal business development activities, and they felt that they were not given the opportunity to choose to be involved in the more formal business development opportunities like pitches to clients. They also felt that they did not

have the choice about how much business they could develop because they were not being involved in the efforts by the men who dominated the processes.

3. They *said* that business development was more difficult, less enjoyable, and more of a burden for women. They also said that business development was more difficult, less enjoyable, and more of a burden for themselves personally.

4. They *did* what they thought they were supposed to do (attend firm events, attend client development events, network, etc.), and they did a lot of things that they did not enjoy.

5. They *did not change* what they were doing even though they were not getting the results that they wanted. When they sought out resources such as articles, training programs, and words of wisdom from successful male business developers, they implemented and imitated what was supposed to be successful even if those things were not working for them.

The challenge we set forth for the women was to change all of the above in a way that allowed them to see if different perspectives, different goals, different vocabulary, different methods, and different measures of success could actually net for them better outcomes. They struggled at first, but each group came up with alternative ideas for the five core areas just discussed that they were excited to implement. When we got the groups together to discuss these alternative ideas, they focused on these options:

1. *Seeing themselves and business development differently by focusing on past successes instead of current challenges.* As one woman explained, *"We are amazing women, and we have been hoodwinked into thinking we are failures. We are not failures. We are successes that they don't see coming."* Many of the women focused on how they had been seen as trailblazers and overachievers their whole lives, yet after they became partners in their firms, they began feeling like failures. The change in perspective from "Why am I having such a hard time at this?" to "I am a superstar. Bring on the next challenge!" was a significant shift for many women, and they committed to approaching business development by seeing themselves as capable and seeing business development as doable—not

in the way that it was currently being done but in the way they were going to do it.

2. ***Choosing to redefine "wins" by shifting to team goals and client service.***
When many of the women started talking about refocusing their goals, they talked about how empty and unfulfilling their current goals of business development felt to them. The subtle shift from "I" to "we" produced a not so subtle shift in enthusiasm. *"I don't know why this is so hard for me"* suddenly became *"We can do some damage!"* Choosing a team goal immediately raised questions of whether the outcomes would be accepted in the firm even if they were successful or whether the "radicalness" of team goals would hurt the women. (Not only did the firm in which the experiment was taking place not have any form of team-based client development model, none of the women in the pilot had heard of any other firms that did. These women were truly blazing new trails!) They decided to create team goals and chose to divide team earnings equally among all team members.

They also chose the goal of ensuring that the client had a great experience in the process instead of choosing a purely numerical monetary goal of success.

By redefining the wins, they were able to focus on collective achievement and a positive impact on the client. This shift ignited an enthusiasm for the process that was lacking when the goal was to develop business individually as measured solely by income generated.

3. ***Changing their vocabulary from a "sales" model to a "service" model.***
This vocabulary shift was a natural one based on the women's new perspectives and new goals. The "sales" model did not have the connection to collective achievement and client impact that resonated with the women. The "service" model, on the other hand, connected well with feeling both that the client was at the center of the process and that the team was collectively impacting the client with great service.

One woman vocalized this change by differentiating between the service you get at a store when the salesperson is on commission and when he or she is not on commission. The former is focused on selling something to you whereas the latter is focused on helping you make the best decision for you. The groups wrote down their perspectives on selling by focusing on service language such as *help the client solve problems that we can truly help her solve, reduce the client's stress in finding a service provider he can trust, help the client get the information she needs in order to make the choice that works for her,* and the like.

4. **Changing how they identified, communicated with, approached, and followed up with potential clients.** Group members identified potential clients who were already in their networks. They decided to reach out to these potential clients to let them know they would like to get together, and they decided to ask them their preferences for events/meetings. Members divided up client development tasks like researching the client, putting together the pitch materials, and so on based on who wanted to do each piece so that they could maximize their collective strengths. As one woman commented, *"We have tried to cross-sell each other before, but it was awkward and a little stilted. This wasn't anything like that. This was us creating something together. It was very different and much better."*

5. **Changing the review process from "did we close the deal" to "did the client get what she needed to make the best decision for her" and "did we work well as a team."** As the female partners started thinking through what their new perceptions of themselves and their goals were, they realized that analyzing by dollars alone was not consistent with how they were starting to think about business development. So, they adopted an *"if we work as a team and the client has a good experience with us, the money will follow"* model of evaluating their work.

THE RESULTS

Within two months, each of the teams had arranged for or already completed at least one in-person meeting with a potential client. All of the groups decided to conduct the meetings with at least two members of the team in attendance. One of the teams had already been asked to submit a formal proposal to be considered for a potential client's "preferred provider" network.

The teams of women were moving forward beyond the discomforts of any individual woman on the team by drawing strength (and enjoyment) from the collaborative process and the focus on collective success.

We debriefed the individual teams approximately 90 days after the teams had begun their work, and their responses were overwhelmingly positive: *"It's the first time I haven't dreaded business development." "It was fun because I was doing it as part of a team." "I can talk about how phenomenal [my colleague] is, but if I had to talk about myself that way, I would have never been able to do it." "I think we are going to land this client, and if we do, we are going to go out for drinks. It feels so good to know that we will be able to celebrate together." "When I've gone on pitches before, there is tension if one person is getting too friendly with the client if that person didn't have the initial contact. That dynamic was not there." "Why haven't we been doing it like this all along?"*

THE FEEDBACK FROM PROFESSIONALS IN FIRMS

The feedback to the data from this pilot program from women and men in various professional service firms was much more varied than the feedback from the women who had participated. There were notable differences in the feedback between men and women, with women showing significantly more enthusiasm about the possibility of developing and implementing an initiative like this in their own firms. Interestingly, the primary focus of feedback from men and women was the team-based model.

Although some men were interested in the potential benefits of such a business development process, the majority of the feedback from men focused on skepticism that people would truly be comfortable with a team-based system and concern that the team-based system would work to their detriment. The men were also skeptical about a review process that did not focus purely on revenues.

Comments like *"how exactly is it a team thing if you are the one with the contact," "no way everyone would be good with everyone getting the same credit on the team,"* and *"it sounds good in theory but the whole holding hands and singing Kumbaya doesn't work in real life"* represented the feedback from the men who felt that neither men nor women would really be comfortable with a team-based model in the long run. The majority of these men did feel that men would be more uncomfortable with the model than women would.

There was also a contingent of men who truly believed that they would be negatively impacted if a team-based model were implemented because they would be bringing more to the team than everyone else. *"I would rather go it alone. I don't need hangers on weighing me down,"* stated one male partner who felt not only that he performed better in a competitive system but that he was actually motivated to better his performance in a competitive system and would not feel the same way in a more collaborative system. Another male partner poked at the topic by saying, *"Do women want to do this in teams because they really want to do this in teams or because they can't do it alone? . . . Teams work when they have strong individuals but weak individuals together don't make a strong team."*

The feedback from women varied among the women themselves but was very different from the men's feedback. The majority of women expressed enthusiastic interest for alternative opportunities that would expand the ways in which they developed business. The women who had concerns about alternatives like this were focused on the challenges of teams going awry because of the composition of the teams and the potential burden faced by women in mixed-gender teams.

According to one female partner, *"teams sound good but it depends on the teams . . . There are women at my firm and men that I would never want on my team."* This focus on the success of a team being dependent on the character of the individuals involved was a significant issue for many women. Another major area of concern for many women was the amount of work that women would end up doing in mixed-gender teams. One female partner remarked that *"I work in teams with men now, and they look to the women to make sure everything actually gets done while they get the credit . . . I would be very scared that the same thing would happen in these client development teams."* Several other female partners/principals echoed variations of this sentiment with concerns that this new size may work with all-female teams but would be more vulnerable to the same problems as the competitive focus of the current size in firms.

KEY TAKEAWAY

The results from this experiment were consistent with women's stories that their efforts to change the business development model in their firms were often futile, but achieving success outside their firms' traditional processes did, in fact, work to get their voices heard. The caveat to this alternative was that working outside the accepted model was mostly successful when it was done in the collective as opposed to being implemented by individual women.

"We don't yet have a critical mass where we can afford to not stick together and be seen as a cohesive unit," said one woman. *"It's hard to stay cohesive as one unit because we are all different and we have different needs, but they [the firm's leaders] take us seriously when they see [us] as one strong unit."*

While some individual efforts were successful, it was the collective efforts in which women focused on setting goals as a collective, achieving success as a collective, and reaping the rewards as a collective that seemed to have the highest probability of success in regard to outcomes.

FOOD FOR THOUGHT

Although this pilot program was limited in scope and nuanced for a particular context, the application of the steps involved in creating a new size instead of merely trying to fit into the size currently in the workplace can work in any professional service firm with just a few adjustments for industry, size of firm, geographic location, and so forth. The results from these and other pilot programs/experiments helped us identify which strategies have the highest probability of changing outcomes, and we share those strategies with you within the framework of the five core areas through which you can have the greatest impact.

While there are other resources that focus more generally on business development[140] or on women's abilities to negotiate and ask for what they want,[141] the strategies in this chapter specifically address how you can

1. Neutralize the challenges that arise from developing business in a very narrow model that may not fit your strengths, skills, and preferences, and
2. Create new ways of developing business that will leverage your strengths, skills, and preferences and that still work within the current model's constraints.

Many of the strategies are supplemented with additional research from our study as well as other studies, and the strategies should be viewed as rough drafts that can be finalized by you for your unique contexts and circumstances.

CHAPTER 11

CHANGE WHAT YOU SEE
(REFRAME YOUR PERSPECTIVE TO RESIZE BUSINESS DEVELOPMENT)

STRATEGIES FOR WOMEN (AND MOST MEN)

All of the strategies in this section focus on women (and men for whom the current size does not fit) resetting their business development efforts by seeing themselves and business development differently. I was surprised and saddened to see how many phenomenal, talented, and highly successful women started to internalize the feeling that they were failures because they were judged by their firms as not being able to develop business. Seeing themselves differently included reminding themselves that they were, in fact, superstars who had beaten more odds than could be named to be in the positions that they were in currently. Seeing business development differently was focused on recognizing that business development—as it was currently done—seemed difficult and unappetizing, but business development did not need to be done as it was currently done in order to be effective. Business development could be enjoyable, productive, and consistent with women's personalities and preferences if done differently, and reframing perspectives was about figuring out how to do it differently instead of writing off one's ability to do it at all.

The following are additional specific strategies that came out of our interviews and experiments.

UNDERSTAND AND USE THE DATA. DON'T INTERNALIZE THE DATA.

Reframing your perspective means using data to understand the world around you without seeing yourself differently because of that data. While women generally thought they saw the data in their own firms objectively, they internalized more of it than they realized. The deliberate focus on understanding and using data on gender differences without internalizing it is a strategy that nets substantial dividends because of something called stereotype threat.

Research on a phenomenon called stereotype threat has demonstrated that the more people are aware of underperformance in an area by a group that they belong to, the more likely people are to underperform their own abilities.[142] For example, when women were reminded of the stereotype that men are better at math than women, the women's performance on math assessment tests declined significantly.[143] When women were told that they were taking a test that had been shown to have no gender bias, their performance skyrocketed.[144] When we look around and see people like us not well represented in a particular area, we unconsciously wonder if it's because we are not capable of performing as well as the people who are well represented or even overrepresented in that area. If we are made aware of a perception or stereotype that people like us generally tend to not do well in this area, we will severely underperform our own abilities and potential.

Stereotype threat creates an ironically thorny environment for women who want to actively work to advance women in male-dominated environments. When women realize that they are underrepresented, they start gathering information and resources about the underrepresentation in order to reverse it. However, the more they consume the information about the underrepresentation, the more likely they are to underperform their true and full abilities and potential.

The data on gender differences in business development needs to be understood and used to change the possibilities of success for women, but the data can be a powerful trigger for stereotype threat for women who are studying the data. One way to neutralize the challenge of stereotype threat is to consciously see the data as a snapshot taken to capture a moment in a long timeline of change instead of unconsciously taking it in as a reflection of an unchanging reality.

One of the senior female partners/principals in our study told me how disheartened she was with much of the data and how depressed she was after reading some of our preliminary findings. We talked about using the data to understand the progress that has been made but not internalizing the data as a personal reality. We had been discussing this idea for several minutes when she grabbed her smartphone and showed me pictures of a landscape that she was designing for a friend. She had taken a picture after every specific component of the design was completed. The landscape was stunning, and watching it change picture by picture really gave me a full appreciation for her creative talent. *"I take these pictures to remind me where I am on the project so that my creative juices can flow for the next phase. These pictures, they are data. They are not the finished landscape."* I agreed wholeheartedly and then immediately asked her if I could use her insight to highlight this strategy.

Data as a tool for change is empowering. Data as unchanging reality is both depressing and destructive. Understand the data, use it, and watch it to see what can change it, but don't internalize it. Data is merely a snapshot of what the landscape looks like today, not what it will look like when we are done working on it!

ASK QUESTIONS

What you see is influenced heavily by what you know. Many of the women (and men) in our study focused on data, but they did not necessarily have the best or most updated data from their firms. In most situations, women and men did not have the data they needed because they had not asked for it directly or consistently enough to apply pressure. In order to understand and use data to create more business development opportunities for women, asking questions is critical.

Professional service firms respond to pressure. They may not always respond well, but asking questions is one of the best ways to sustain the high prioritization of an issue within a firm. The more firms are questioned about what they are doing regarding gender parity in their ranks, whether what they are doing is working, and how they plan to move forward to ensure increased gender equity, the more actively they will address the issue. We also found that the more questions on this issue were being asked in firms, the more these firms had to deal with the answers, which made these firms more likely to be open to women (and men) who wanted to experiment with different ways of developing business.

The following is a sample set of questions that the professionals in our study felt were important for women (and men) to be asking in and of their firms:

- What is the attrition rate for female professionals in comparison to male professionals?
- At what point in their careers are women most likely to leave, and is this point different for women and men?
- What is the percentage of women in the partnership, and how has this rate changed (or not) over the past ten years?
- Is there an exit interview process in place at the firm that objectively captures people's reasons for leaving the firm? If so, are there differences between women and men as to why they leave?
- What are the primary business development requirements in the firm, and how are these requirements measured, arbitrated, evaluated, recognized, and rewarded?
- What percentage of the most highly compensated people in the firm are women, and how has that changed over the past ten years?

Answers to these questions may not immediately result in changes, but asking the questions does seem to make individual women feel more empowered and firms more likely to support alternative models of developing business.

WRITE A STORY . . . THE STORY YOU WANT TO WRITE

Sometimes reframing your perspective involves stepping out of your analytical brain and engaging the creative juices that are so essential in helping you solve problems and overcome challenges. The part of your brain that controls your responses to fear and insecurity loves to be self-critical and risk averse. Unfortunately, this part of the brain is very active in women when we are asked to describe or evaluate our past, present, or even future selves. Writing a fictional story about yourself, however, utilizes the part of your brain that governs imagination and a more daring exploration of risks and possibilities. When you write a story (not a memoir!) about yourself, you bypass the self-critic and engage the dreamer in you. Where the self-critic loves to say no and tell you all that you can't/won't/shouldn't do, the dreamer focuses on what you can/will/should do.

Write a fictional story about yourself as the top business revenue generator in your firm. Write about how you got your clients, the leadership opportunities that this success has brought you, and what you are able to accomplish with those leadership resources. Write in detail about what a typical day looks like in your life as the top business developer in your firm. Where is your office? How is it decorated? Who calls you? Who do you call? How many e-mails land in your inbox that day? Who are the e-mails from? How do you respond to these e-mails? The more details you add, the better, and you don't have to finish the story in any particular time frame, but you should read what you have written thus far at least a couple of times a week.

Women and men who have done this exercise have loved the results in terms of the new insights, understandings, and ideas for action they have gained from it. If you want to really push yourself, give the story to someone you trust and ask her or him to give you feedback on the story.

Find ways to slowly integrate the fiction into your reality through your expectations, your actions, or just your words. One female partner decided to have some fun with this exercise. *"In my story, I imagined myself as the power partner in my group because of how much business I brought in . . . the guy who heads our group right now always sits at the head of the conference room table. It's so silly but I realized that I saw that chair as the power chair and I never sit in it even when he is not in a meeting. So, I started with going into that conference room a couple of times by myself and sitting in the chair while I did some work. I had a couple of meetings with associates and then with some vendors, and I sat in the chair. I had a meeting with a couple of other partners in my group, and I got there early so I could get my chair. The only time I wouldn't try and sit in that chair is when [the head of the group] was there. I know what the view is from that chair. It's silly and funny and the game is mostly in my head, but it has made me more confident."*

I have learned that there is power in Ralph Waldo Emerson's words: "Fiction reveals truth that reality obscures." Writing a story (right brained) about something that is more logical (left brained) connects the two hemispheres of your brain as you think about business development, and a whole-brained approach is definitely going to take you farther than a half-brained approach.

BECOME YOUR OWN CLIENT . . . AND TREAT YOURSELF AS YOUR BEST CLIENT

Reframing your perspective—changing what you see—involves drawing on all the ways in which you already know how to see the world. We conducted a small experiment with four of the female partners/principals in our study—two lawyers, one accountant, and one engineer. I asked each of these women to write down her challenges with business development in the most objective, dispassionate, emotionless language that she could. For example, one of the women wrote, *"I am executing necessary steps to achieve desired goal. While these steps have generally been proven to achieve this goal, my efforts are not yielding much success."* The other women's problem statements were very similar to this one.

Then, I asked each of them to rewrite the problem statement replacing herself in the statement with "client." The preceding example, then, was rewritten as, *"Client is executing necessary steps to achieve desired goal. While these steps have generally been proven to achieve this goal, the client's efforts are not yielding much success."*

The shift from "I" to "client" made the women look at the problem very differently. All of the women reported feeling more empowered and able to do something when they became the advocate for a client. I asked them to stay in the role of the advocate and write up a strategic plan to help the client solve her problem. The plans for the "clients" were very different from what the women had originally drafted for themselves.

Reframe what you see by seeing yourself as deserving of your influence and advocacy skills. Become your own client and advocate and create for yourself as passionately as you would for a client! You already give your clients your best—it's time to include yourself in the category of people to whom you give your best.

SEE "WE"

The lens of individual business development and individual rewards is not the only way through which to see how business development can be done, recognized, and rewarded. Change what you see by seeing "we" when you envision how you will develop business. Working with other women to collectively develop and benefit from business generation is a significant reframing of how business development is currently viewed, and that reframing is exactly the different kind of thinking and seeing women need to do in order to create alternative models of business development success in their firms.

The pilot program at the beginning of this section explores this reframing in greater detail. As the saying goes, *when you change the way you look at things, the things you look at change.* See "we" and see how you think differently about business development when you do.

STRATEGIES FOR FIRMS AND FIRM LEADERS

START WITH YOUR CLIENTS

Currently, the focus on women and business development in many firms is articulated as a "women's issue," a deficiency in how women develop business that needs to be fixed in women. This focus is wrong, and it is not working. When firms reframe their perspectives on this issue as a deficiency that needs to be fixed in the firms' structures and culture—not the women—the firms not only create more opportunities for women, but they develop more business overall. In every industry, women's representation on the client side is growing faster than women's representation in firm partnerships, and the women on the client side are making decisions based on these issues. Beyond that, clients are also asking for the alternative models of business development and client service that work for women because these models give them better service. Reframing women and business development from the perspective of better client service changes firms' efforts from "helping the women" to creating a better firm.

Business development is about your clients . . . getting them, serving them well, earning future work from them, and inspiring them to recommend you to others. Yet, the majority of professional service firms do not consistently ask their clients what brought them to the firm, what keeps them there, what keeps them coming back, and why (if at all) they recommend the firm to others.

Astonishingly, several firm leaders told us that even though they engage in client feedback processes, the information is rarely used to reshape how business development is done. Research by organizations such as Hinge Marketing that specialize in professional service firms consistently has found that clients assess their professional service providers as teams, not as individuals.[145] Likewise, Das Narayandas and Robert Eccles at Harvard Business School discuss the reality that "[c]hallenged by faster commoditization, greater consolidation, and higher client expectations, smart professional service firms are rethinking their approach to business development."[146] I was surprised by how many of the professional service firm leaders we interviewed had heard very specific feedback from their clients that those clients wanted to feel that their service teams were in fact acting more like teams, but the firms had not changed fundamental business development practices to give their clients what they were actively requesting.

According to one leader, *"Our clients do ask for a team feel in how their work gets done, and we try to do that in how our people communicate with the client and the events we do with our clients. We have changed the business development interface that our clients see, but we haven't changed how credit and ownership for clients is handled internally in our firm. I can see how people may feel that business development credits affect the feeling of being on a team, but I think real team players should look past that."*

A female partner offered a different perspective: *"I'm not allowed to say 'our client' when I talk to the person who manages this relationship. He actually told me one day to stop saying 'our client' because it was his client. He doesn't get that I don't work for him. I work for the client, but if he keeps making me feel like I'm working for him, like I'm his employee, then, I don't see how I can make it here. I am here to serve our clients, not egomaniacs."*

Start with your clients. Ask them what they want and what makes them happy. Then, examine your business development system to see if it is aligned with your clients' needs, expectations and desires. One firm with whom we worked took this recommendation a step farther and created a task force to revamp their business development system from "soup to nuts," as the firm's chairperson liked to say. The idea of a task force was not that revolutionary, but this firm put representatives from a few key clients on the task force to help shape their client development, client service delivery, and client satisfaction protocols. That was a game changer for the firm and for the women in the firm because the clients' voices regarding relationship building and maintenance prioritized the strengths that the firm's women were bringing to each engagement.

There were, as expected, many concerns, consternations, and complaints about the changes. A few partners/principals threatened to leave the firm if the changes were implemented, and a small percentage of them did indeed leave the firm. The changes were not at all simple or easy to implement, but the clients who were involved in the process stayed committed and loyal to the firm.

Reframe your perspective by starting with your clients. Their needs are more likely to be aligned with a team-based business development system than with the system that is in most firms today.

STOP BEING AN OSTRICH

There is nothing more direct than the image of an ostrich with its head stuck in the sand to serve as a metaphor for changing what you see as a firm and/or firm leader, and the "ostrich instruction" used in courts provides a great reminder that ignorance is not always bliss—especially when you are trying to understand and resolve a complex challenge like changing your business development model to be more inclusive of how women develop business.

The "ostrich instruction"[147] is an instruction given by the judge to a jury to guide them in making a decision about a defendant. The direct instruction is a variation of this: *"You may infer knowledge from a combination of suspicion and indifference to the truth. If you find that a person had a strong suspicion that things were not what they seemed or that some had withheld some important facts, yet shut his eyes for fear that he would learn, you may conclude that he acted knowingly."*[148] This instruction is used in corruption trials of business leaders, most recently in such high-profile cases as those of Kenneth Lay (Enron), Jeffrey Skilling (Enron), and Conrad Black (Hollinger International).

Bad leaders and the law aside, the metaphor of the "ostrich instruction" is a great tool to help leaders think through what knowing something really means, especially when actions need to be taken to accomplish an expressed objective. Not knowing is still knowing if you should have known and could have known. If you know what your firm is doing and you know that it's not working, then, it's time to know that you cannot keep doing what you have been doing. You may not know exactly what to do next, but you should know that doing more of what's not working isn't the answer.

Reflect on the following statements to see if many, most, or all of the statements are true for your firm:

- Women are underrepresented in your firm's partnership and/or leadership.
- Business development is a key ticket for entry into the partnership/leadership.
- Women, generally, are not developing business at the same levels as their male counterparts.
- Women are underrepresented among the firm's highest compensated partners/principals and overrepresented among the firm's lowest compensated partners/principals.
- The firm has communicated clearly to the women in the partnership that they need to develop more business in order to advance.
- The firm is committed to increasing the representation of women at all levels.
- The firm has not been successful in increasing the representation of women at the highest levels.

If four or more of the preceding statements are true for your firm, you should know that a radical change is necessary. Apply the "ostrich instruction" candidly to the firm and the firm's leaders. Are you doing things you know aren't working simply because it's easier to do them than to create real change? It's not good leadership if you simply preside over the maintenance of the status quo. Change involves conflict, and resolving that conflict requires good leadership. Good leadership begins with being honest about what you do know and what you should know so that you have the information you need to facilitate the necessary change.

Challenge yourself to identify ways in which the firm has chosen to hide its head in the sand, and ask yourself what realities need to be spotlighted in order to better understand and eventually change the realities of gender inequity in the firm, especially at the highest levels.

GET TO KNOW THE "ONE SIZE" FOR SUCCESS IN YOUR FIRM

If you could create new avenues by which clients walk through your firm's doors, would you? Creating new sizes of business development models results in building these new avenues, and creating new sizes requires knowing what the current size is.

Do you know what the "one size" is for your firm? Do you know if it is a size that fits men more easily than it fits women? Have you ever closely examined exactly what it takes to be a successful business developer in your firm?

Several of the firm leaders in our study took a brief summary of the data we have reported in the preceding chapters and sat down with people in their firms to gather perspectives on what, if any, size was most prevalent in their firms.

The majority of these leaders were surprised by how many people in their firms did indeed feel like there was only one size for success. The leaders were even more surprised when people described this size for them in detail because they had never fully realized how deeply engrained some of these views were in the cultures of their firms. The women's perspectives were especially difficult for the leaders to hear because the women articulated clearly and loudly how the size did not fit them well at all.

One firm leader used our list of characteristics to do an internal assessment of what people perceived to be the top characteristics for successful business development in his firm. He asked people to list the characteristics that they felt the leaders of the firm thought were important and the characteristics that they personally thought were important. He was surprised to find that the two lists that emerged were quite different from each other. He told us that he learned a lot by even asking the question because it would have never occurred to him that the characteristics he was seeking in people were not characteristics that people really prioritized in their own business development styles. His analysis was that *"I don't want people to do it the way I did it, and I never stopped to think that they can do it very differently and get the same results, maybe even better results. But, don't tell them that I said that!"*

Another leader asked the partners/principals in his firm to get together to talk about this research so that they could better understand their own business development styles. *"You can't do better if you don't know what you are doing now,"* he said as he recounted how much he had learned in listening to people talk about their own styles and preferences.

Get to know the "one size" in your firm. Maybe you will agree with it and decide not to change it, but if you know it better, you can better articulate the behaviors that you want to see from the partners/principals in your firm. If you decide to expand approved sizes from the "one size" that is currently available, you can better articulate the ways in which you plan to expand the sizes.

CHAPTER 12

CHANGE WHAT YOU CHOOSE
(REFOCUS YOUR GOALS TO RESIZE BUSINESS DEVELOPMENT)

STRATEGIES FOR WOMEN (AND MOST MEN)

CHOOSE GOALS THAT YOU CAN GET EXCITED TO ACCOMPLISH, AND MAKE THEM COLLECTIVE GOALS IF POSSIBLE

Men in our study consistently reported being more excited than the women did to develop business and engage in the activities defined by the firm as business development activities. This enthusiasm fueled the men's activity levels while the lack of enthusiasm on the women's part depressed their activity levels. However, as demonstrated in the pilot program, when women chose goals that excited them—especially team goals that involved high levels of collaboration—the women's enthusiasm and business development activity levels significantly increased.

Based on the data from the surveys and interviews, women were most enthusiastic about choosing collective wins over individual wins, client satisfaction over monetary amounts, integrated work/family-life activities over additional time commitments in their calendars, and collaborative activities over individually focused activities.

Choosing goals that spark excitement was also the primary neutralizer of the *"I don't have time!"* challenge that was articulated by many women. The more collective, client-oriented, work/family-life integrated, and collaborative the business development activities were, the more likely the activities were to fit naturally into the women's calendars instead of taxing these calendars.

IF DISCOMFORT IS UNAVOIDABLE, CHOOSE THE DISCOMFORT OF CHALLENGING THE STATUS QUO OVER THE DISCOMFORT OF FAILING

One female partner adamantly told me that *"staying silent and feeling the pain of being passed over and unvalued is worse than speaking up and making the men in the firm uncomfortable. Staying silent guarantees that I won't get what I want. Speaking up may not get me what I want, but my chances are better than if I stayed silent. The problem for women is that we have been raised to think that internalizing pain is our job and it's never okay to make other people, especially men, uncomfortable. We have to fight that if we are going to change things."*

Women and men in the study frequently referred to the discomfort and vulnerability (personal, financial, reputational, etc.) of challenging the status quo in firms, but women who challenged the status quo collectively felt less discomfort and vulnerability than women who either did not have other women with whom they could forge a collective effort or chose to act in more individualized ways.

There is a high probability that there will be discomfort involved in maintaining a status quo that isn't working for you or in challenging the status quo. Choose the discomfort of challenging the status quo if possible—it will net you greater success in the long run and enable you to act from a position of choosing instead of reacting.

CHOOSE TO BE A VALUABLE TEAM PLAYER, NOT A GOOD TEAM PLAYER

In analyzing the conversations and survey narratives about teams and being a team player, I noticed an interesting pattern. When women were described as team players, they were described as good team players. When men were described as team players, they were described as valuable or necessary team players. We arranged a few informal follow-up interviews with partners/principals who had participated in our study to get their insights into being a valuable team player versus a good team player.

The conversations revealed that people saw good team players as people who did what their teammates asked of them and pitched in when needed to fill gaps. Valuable team players, on the other hand, did what was necessary to make the deal happen, to get the win. Good team players knew who the leaders were and deferred to them. Valuable team players were the leaders, and even when they weren't the leaders, they acted like the leaders. If valuable team players asked for business development credit, they got it. Good team players did not.

One partner summed it up this way: *"Good team players are replaceable . . . valuable team players are not replaceable."* Choose to be a valuable team player, not simply a good team player. If it's difficult to figure out exactly what that means in your specific firm, ask senior partners in your firm to describe the differences between the two.

Although a few partners/principals struggled with giving us a definitive answer, not a single partner/principal told us that there wasn't a difference between the two.

STRATEGIES FOR FIRMS AND FIRM LEADERS

CHOOSE CHANGE

If firms or firm leaders want to change the business generation differences between men and women, they have to be open to changing how business development is done. In my previous book, *The Next IQ*, I wrote about how strongly the status quo bias drives so much of the decision making in organizations even as these organizations tout their commitment to change. They want change (the noun), but they don't want to change (the verb).

In order to see change, firms have to first choose change and refocus their business development goals through the lens of changing how business development actually gets done. The following are three strongly recommended areas for change based on the input provided by the women (and men) in our study.

- Allow and encourage collective business development efforts to coexist alongside individual business development efforts as different equals instead of allowing the organizational culture to view individual business development efforts as superior to collective efforts.

- Decouple business development outcomes and leadership opportunities by creating different routes for women (and men) to advance into leadership. While it is more difficult to decouple business development outcomes and compensation schemes, allowing people to advance into leadership because of leadership capabilities instead of just business generational capabilities will allow for greater success for greater numbers of people in the firm and make the firm stronger in the process.
- Make the business development "credit systems" and consequent compensation processes more consistent and transparent.

CHOOSE TO CREATE SOLUTIONS, NOT FIND THEM

Professional service firms, regardless of industry, are in the business of solving problems. They solve problems for their clients with critical thinking, innovation, creativity, and determination, yet, when it comes to addressing gender differences in business development, they throw up their collective hands and say things like *It's not us, it's the industry* or *It has to do with work-life balance* or *We have tried everything, but nothing is really working.* If your firm approached any of your client's problems with these notions, you would not be in business for very long, so you have to ask yourself why failure in this arena is accepted when failure elsewhere is not.

Firms have implicitly colluded with other firms to give themselves permission to fail in this area, and change will happen when firms choose to no longer accept failure. One way to do this is to choose to create solutions instead of find them. In an environment where failure has been accepted as the status quo, there are no solutions that can be found; solutions have to be created, and they will probably have to be created from scratch without guidance from precedents or best practices.

If firms want to see more of the women in their ranks thrive as strong business developers, they will have to choose to create an environment in which that can happen. Choosing to create instead of find is not an easy choice, but given the dearth of comprehensive solutions that have been attempted, choosing to create solutions is the only path to change.

CHAPTER 13

CHANGE WHAT YOU SAY
(REVISE YOUR VOCABULARY TO RESIZE BUSINESS DEVELOPMENT)

STRATEGIES FOR WOMEN (AND MOST MEN)

CHANGE YOUR VOCABULARY TO REFLECT YOUR NEW PERSPECTIVES AND GOALS

A female partner contacted me after a group of women had met at her firm to talk about how to change their collective vocabulary. *"We realized that our vocabulary had somehow changed from succeeding to not failing. We were expecting failure and trying to avoid it instead of expecting success and trying to accomplish it."* They focused on changing their vocabulary to reflect a collective and collaborative process about which they were excited and confident.

A different group of women decided to change their vocabulary from reflecting dependence on men to being self-sufficient and independent. *"When we looked at what we were trying to accomplish, all of the stuff had to do with what we were going to get the men to do—recognize our efforts, include us in their marketing efforts, and so on. We decided to make our goals more independent of men and change our vocabulary to fit that."*

Of course, a change in vocabulary is not enough in itself, but it does offer a symbolic shift in how a situation is being experienced and what goals are being pursued. A change in vocabulary is a critical bridge from changing what you see and choose to changing what you actually do.

Examples of Vocabulary Shifts

1. CAN versus HOW CAN. One woman who was in a firm where she was the only female partner teamed up with a man who also "hated business development," and they decided to shift their vocabulary around business development from "can we successfully develop business" to "how can we successfully develop business." Where the former requires a yes/no answer, the latter encourages active problem solving. Most importantly, the former questions the possibility of success while the latter assumes the probability of success.

2. TRY NOT. DO. A group of women in a design firm made T-shirts for all the female partners that read TRY NOT. DO. One of the female partners was an avid *Star Wars* fan, and she felt that Yoda's famous advice was applicable to what the women were trying to accomplish together in her firm. To encourage Luke to use the powers of his mind, Yoda says, "No. Try not. Do. Or do not. There is no try." *"Many of us have said that we are trying to generate business, but either we are or we are not. Well, the truth is we are not. But, we keep saying we are trying like we are actually doing something. We use the quote to remind us that we either do or do not. We need to stop saying we are trying because that depresses us. When you keep trying and don't succeed, you feel bad. So, we will try not. We will do."*

STRATEGIES FOR FIRMS AND FIRM LEADERS

CHANGE YOUR "WHAT" VOCABULARY

What exactly are you trying to change when it comes to gender differences in business development in your firm? Are you trying to get more women to develop business as it is currently developed, or are you trying to get more women to develop business? Are you trying to fix something that's not working in women, or are you trying to fix something in the firm structure/culture that is not working for women?

Changing your "what" vocabulary is about revising your stated goals to accurately reflect what you have defined as the problem. It is also about recognizing that gender differences in business development are about how the current model of business development isn't working. Women aren't broken; the current model doesn't fit them. If you want to minimize the differences between men and women in business development, your vocabulary has to reflect an openness to changing the process, not just the women.

CHANGE YOUR "WHY" VOCABULARY

Why is it important for your firm to increase the numbers of women in your partnership and/or leadership? If you can answer this question with concrete reasons, the incentives for creating more sizes for business development become self-evident. Here are a few questions to consider as you think through and craft your why.

- Why is it important to achieve a better representation of women in leadership positions in the firm? What is something positive that will result from this achievement? What is something negative that will happen if greater inclusion is not achieved?
- Do you believe that business development is a good way (not necessarily the only way) to break down the barriers into partnership and leadership for women?
- How has your firm, its clients, and the market changed in the last 15 years? What role have women played in any or all of the changes? How could the firm be better positioned to meet those changes head-on if there were more female partners/leaders?
- What are some key ways in which the firm wants/plans to grow in the next ten years? How could that growth happen faster/better if more women were in your firm's leadership?

CHANGE YOUR "HOW" VOCABULARY

Changing your vocabulary around the "how" of change has to address the inherent resistance to change that is part of the human condition. The professional service firm leaders varied in their opinions on how the partners/principals in their firms would react to change, but none of the leaders felt that his or her partners/principals would welcome any changes in the business development system and its connections to the compensation system with open arms.

One leader told us that *"it's difficult to mention change of any kind in the firm, but some changes are easier to usher in than others . . . The closer the change gets to the partners'/principals' wallets, the harder it is to make the change happen . . . Client development and compensation? That's not just getting close to the wallet, it is the wallet."*

Another leader differentiated between changes in the business development system and changes in the connections between business development and compensation: *"No one would care if we changed how business development works. They care about how business development is connected to how much money they make. Firms have focused on business developers as the revenue engines for decades now. Changes in compensation because of changes in business development goes against everything we have done for so long. You have to tell the big dogs that they are not the big dogs anymore because we are changing the definition of who gets to be a dog."*

The difficulty with change was cited by every single leader as the biggest obstacle in reshaping business development protocols and practices, and many leaders emphasized that resistance to change is not unique to this issue but is a major challenge for leadership in general.

In order to get a better idea of how firms could prepare for and implement change—especially change in business development and compensation—we asked the leaders to reflect on changes that had been successfully implemented in the past ten years. They reflected on changes such as implementing past mergers with other firms, penetrating a new industry, getting out of a dying industry, reframing success after the loss of a major client, and other major changes that had impacted the infrastructure of their firms. We extracted and condensed the lessons they learned from these successful changes into a short and succinct list that can help in preparing your firm and people for changes to the business development and compensation systems. Basically, leaders need to prepare people for big change but ask them to make small changes.

- **Articulate a broad and comprehensive vision of where the change can lead the firm, but articulate the process of change in narrow and specific terms.** One of the leaders talked in detail about how people need something big and grand in order to motivate them to change, but the road to that big and grand needs to be explained in the smallest steps possible. *"People want to think big about where they want to go,* *but they won't take action and they won't let the leaders take action until the way to get there is explained in baby steps language. What will happen tomorrow? What will happen in a week?"*

- **Clearly describe (1) what is not working today and (2) what will work better after the change has occurred.** As James Belasco and Ralph Stayer discuss in *Flight of the Buffalo*, "[C]hange is hard because people overestimate the value of what they have—and underestimate the value of what they may gain by giving that up."[149] It is always harder to convince people of the future benefits of change if they are comfortable in the present; therefore, you have to articulate the ways in which the present is not as comfortable as people think it is. If people have a better idea of exactly what is not working right now (in quantitative, economic, personnel, etc., costs), they will be more open to seeing how potentially unstable or insecure the present is, thereby making them more open to change. After articulating what is not working now, the next step is to articulate in clear and concise detail what will work better if things change. The more specific the detail, the more people will be primed for the change you want to introduce.

- **Focus on how the firm will change, not on how the firm wants individuals to change.** From a cognitive perspective, people aren't necessarily resisting change in the environment. They are resisting changing themselves. The more change is framed as happening in the environment instead of as needing to happen in people, the more open people will be to that change.

- **Develop recognition and reward mechanisms that aren't solely rooted in compensation.** *"Money isn't just money in firms. It is feedback. It is winning. It is power because you scored more than someone else. In this firm and in other firms, money is the main way through which you get rewards, power, wins, and such. If you create other ways through which people can get those things, they aren't as attached to compensation."* The leader who shared that perspective with us implemented a leadership selection system in his firm that separated leadership qualifications from business development and/or compensation. He paved the way for this change by asking the top business generators in the firm to attend a private meeting where he explained how he was going to create a process through which the best business developers would be freed up to do what they did best instead of being bogged down with the administrative duties involved in leadership positions. He got them on board first and then slowly built support among the rest of the partners/principals for the idea that the people who were integrally involved with taking care of clients (even if they were not being given credit for the business) should be put into leadership roles because it would make the firm look good to the clients. Now, some partners/principals are being recognized for being business developers, and others are being recognized for being good leaders of client teams and departments. This leader plans to continue to expand the types of rewards and recognition that people can access so that the firm is not solely prioritizing business development. This method allows the change to feel more win-win instead of a zero-sum game.

CHAPTER 14

CHANGE WHAT YOU DO
(RESHAPE YOUR METHODS TO RESIZE BUSINESS DEVELOPMENT)

Changing what you see, choose, and say will jump-start the ways in which you see how the current size of business development in your firm may not be working for you, but changing what you do is where you actually start creating a different business development model for yourself. This next set of strategies is where you start experimenting with developing business differently . . . in ways that will work for you.

STRATEGIES FOR WOMEN (AND MOST MEN)

When developing business is not an option, you can either create a size that specifically fits you or you can take the existing size and try to fit into it. The former challenges the status quo and takes more work initially, but it will lead to business development activities that work for you. The latter does not challenge the status quo and takes less work initially, but trying to fit into a size not created for you is ineffective—and painful—in the long run.

The following are ideas to get you creating your own size of business development. While some of the macro strategies that we have discussed thus far such as team-based business development are powerful ones to create big change, the micro strategies discussed here are great for creating many small changes that can add up to equally big change.

CREATE A "FIT LIST"

When do you feel most like you are being yourself? Create a list of places, activities, and people that inspire and allow you to be yourself. People who are being themselves are more successful at business development; they actually enjoy it, which makes them do it more, and they become even more successful. In order to get this virtuous cycle working for you, you have to first really understand when, where, and around whom you feel most comfortable being yourself. Once you have this list, brainstorm business development activities based on your "fit list."

If there is a significant divergence between your ideas for activities and the usual business development activities for your firm, get your game face on. It will take some courage to break out of the mold with which other people are comfortable. If courage eludes you, remind yourself that the pain of walking in shoes that don't fit is far greater than the pain of answering the questions that will be asked of you about the new, funky shoes that you made for yourself. Refer to Caroline's story for inspiration!

Create a fit list. Then, work it.

CREATE A "MISFIT LIST"

This is the reverse of the preceding strategy. When do you feel most like you are *not* being yourself? Create a "misfit list" of places, activities, and people that prevent you from or punish you for being yourself. People who are not being themselves do miserably in business development, are less engaged at work, and are at higher risk for voluntary and involuntary attrition. In order to keep this vicious cycle from working against you, you have to really understand when, where, and around whom you feel most uncomfortable being yourself. Once you have this list, avoid everything on it as much as possible!

If there is a significant convergence between what you need to avoid and the usual business development activities for the firm, get your game face on again because you will need some more courage. Buy a pair of shoes that are at least one size too small and walk in them whenever you need a reminder of how painful a misfit really is.

Create a misfit list. Then, actively avoid what's on it.

GET TO KNOW YOUR STRENGTHS AND START WORKING YOUR STRENGTHS

When we asked about strengths and weaknesses in our interviews, we found that men primarily talked about their strengths and how their business development styles aligned with those strengths. Women, on the other hand, mostly talked about their weaknesses, areas of their professional and personal lives that they needed to improve and fix in order to be better business developers. Men focused on leveraging their strengths while women focused on neutralizing their weaknesses. The result—the focus on strengths made men feel positive and enthusiastic about their abilities to develop business, and the focus on weaknesses made women hypercritical about themselves and depressed about their abilities to develop business.

Research has consistently shown that women are more likely to attribute their successes to external sources and their failures to internal weaknesses.[150] In our work, we found that when women actively become aware of their strengths, they are more likely to feel like they achieved success instead of thinking success happened to them.

Personal assessments are invaluable tools for helping you focus directly on better understanding your communication, relationship, conflict management, and decision-making styles so that you can build a business development model that identifies and leverages yours strengths to fit who you are. Popular assessments include the MBTI (Myers-Briggs Type Indicator) for communication and information processing preferences, the FIRO-B (Fundamental Interpersonal Relations Orientation—Behavior) for interpersonal relational styles, the TKI (Thomas-Kilmann Conflict Mode Instrument) for conflict resolution styles, and the StrengthsFinder to discover the strengths that drive your choices and behaviors.

Use your strengths to drive your business development efforts. You do not have to neutralize your weaknesses in order to leverage your strengths; you just have to know what your weaknesses are so that you can accommodate them. A male firm leader explained his philosophy on strengths and weaknesses in this way: *"I operate on my strengths and I outsource my weaknesses. I don't try to get better at what I'm weak at . . . I find people that are good at the stuff I'm bad at and make sure that they are a part of my team. Not only does it make no sense to try and get good at what you are not good at, it makes for a bad day. It's fun to do what you are good at."*

GET A GHOSTWRITER OR A BLACK BOX
SUBLIMINAL NOISE GENERATOR

Jessi Smith, Professor of Psychology at Montana State University, did an interesting study involving women's ability to toot their own horn.[151] Smith told a group of female subjects that a panel of judges would award scholarship money based on the recommendation letters written for various students. Each woman was then tasked to write two letters of recommendation, one for herself and one for a friend. The letters that women wrote for their friends were judged to be better in quality, more descriptive of accomplishments, and more effusive with praise than were the letters that the women wrote for themselves.

Women will generally not be surprised by this result. As a matter of fact, every woman with whom I've discussed this research has agreed in an almost *"did you expect something different"* tone. One female partner in our study even said to me how surprised she was that *"researchers had to research the obvious to make the obvious make sense to people."* Women agreed wholeheartedly that they would have done the same thing, while many men, in a more objective tone, stressed that they would write better letters for friends who deserved better letters, and they would write very fair letters for themselves because of the financial reward involved.

That got me thinking that women would be better served if they had friends of theirs write their bios, professional profiles, and résumés. I asked a few female partners/principals who knew each other to write their own bios/résumés and a bio/résumé for one of the other partners/principals. When the women compared what they had written for themselves with what the other women had written about them, they were astounded. One of the female partners/principals who participated in this exercise was crying when she called me. She told me that she was *proud of the woman in that bio that I did not write. She sounded amazing and accomplished. I wish I saw myself that way. I know I am that person, but I don't live my life as that person. I should though because she is pretty amazing.*

Get a ghostwriter to write your bio, professional profile, résumé, and anything else that describes you to the world. In one midsize firm, the female partners/principals got together to discuss how none of them had been submitting any updates or news articles for the firm's newsletter. They talked in detail about how they knew they were being too self-effacing but they couldn't help themselves, so each woman became another woman's ghost-writer for public relations–type materials for the firm's website, newsletter, and other communications, especially to clients. Each woman would call her ghostwriter as soon as something of note occurred, and the ghostwriter would compile the data and send an e-mail about how fabulous the partner was and all that she had accomplished. The women's stories were heard with-out them having to tout their own accomplishments.

If you don't want to go the ghostwriter route, you should invest in a Black Box Subliminal Noise Generator, but these boxes may be a tad difficult to acquire. When Smith did her research on how women wrote recommenda-tions for themselves in comparison to their friends, she wondered what would happen if women were tricked into thinking they weren't really feeling bad about advocating for themselves.

Smith divided her subjects into two groups and informed one group that there was a Black Box Subliminal Noise Generator in the room that would cause them anxiety through subliminal brain waves. When women sat down in the room with the Black Box Subliminal Noise Generator to write the rec-ommendation letters for themselves, they felt the anxiety that most women feel in considering the norm-violative behavior of self-promotion. However, this time, they had something else to which they could attribute their anxi-ety—the "black box subliminal noise generator."

This was an exercise in deliberate misattribution—an attribution of a feel-ing/thought to something other than what actually caused it. In other words, if women could attribute their anxiety to something other than themselves, would they be less likely to be influenced by the anxiety?

By now, you may have guessed that there is no such black box thing. Nonetheless, the women in the room did not know that; therefore, the abil-ity to attribute their anxiety to this thing outside themselves allowed them to ignore the anxiety of self-promotion and write letters for themselves that were more effective and more accurate. The black box—albeit an illusion—gave the women a respite from their anxiety about violating the norms of self-promotion, a respite that resulted in a more accurate self-description and depiction.

What would you say about yourself if you didn't have to worry about how you came across to others? What would you identify as strengths and accomplishments that you are most proud of, and do you feel comfortable talking about these things with others in your firm? Not only should you focus on these questions as you think about developing business externally, but the impressions that you create within the firm impact referrals within the firm, enthusiastic invitations to develop and participate in pitches and lead client teams.

Here are some "black boxes" that some female partners/principals were able to create for themselves:

I asked one of the senior partners to help me with my end of the year self-evaluation. That way, I could tell him everything I did and be very candid about it, but because I was doing it in an "I need your help" kind of context, I wasn't uncomfortable. He helped me put together my self-evaluation, and I didn't always listen to all his suggestions, but he was in the club . . . and he knew everything I did even if I didn't write it down. That was my work-around as they call it.

Instead of writing a narrative, I wrote a Q&A format. To be extra focused, I asked several leaders what kinds of questions they would want to see answered, and I listed the questions and wrote my answers to them. The "tell me your story" format didn't work for me.

I got better at asking my clients, in a joking sort of way, to "put it in writing" if they ever complimented me . . . I saved the e-mails and attached them to my end of the year development plan.

STRIKE A POSE . . . A POWER POSE

This strategy doesn't quite fit in with the rest of the strategies, but when tested, it actually showed enough of a success rate to warrant its inclusion.

We are all aware that we can tell a lot about how people are feeling or what they are thinking through the body language that they exhibit. While our abilities to read these cues vary from person to person, almost all of our body language is actually unconscious. We don't often realize that we just crossed our arms because we felt threatened by someone's statement, or we may not realize that our hunched shoulders just relaxed because someone we trust just walked into the room. There has been a lot of research and insight about how we can become more aware of our body language, but Amy Cuddy from Harvard Business School is shaking up that research with a radical new notion: not only does our body language reflect our inner state of mind but consciously changing our body posture can actually change our inner state of mind.

Cuddy explains that previous research has proven that "[i]n both human and non-human primates, expansive, open postures reflect high power, whereas contractive, closed postures reflect low power."[152] Then, she expands on that to assert that "[n]ot only do these postures reflect power, they also *produce* it; in contrast to adopting low power poses, adopting high power poses increases explicit and implicit feelings of power and dominance, risk-taking behavior, action orientation, pain tolerance, and testosterone (the dominance hormone), while reducing stress, anxiety, and cortisol."[153] (She explains her research in a phenomenal TED Talk that I highly recommend.[154])

Your body language doesn't just reflect what you are feeling; it can actually shape what you are feeling. And, feeling powerful is a state of mind, which you can access simply by consciously changing your posture.

When you are meeting with a potential client, confronting a partner who should have shared more credit for the client you brought in together, or closing out a deal in a way that ensures future referrals from your current client, strike the right pose. If you are conscious about how you sit, stand, or just be, maybe you won't have to toot your own horn. Your body will do it for you.

STRATEGIES FOR FIRMS AND FIRM LEADERS

ADD ADDITIONAL SIZES TO THE MODEL FOR OPTIMAL SUCCESS

Every firm that participated in our study in any way talked about business development as a key strategic business challenge currently facing the firm. Whether it was the fickleness of clients, the changing dynamics in their industry, or the client pressures regarding fee structures and billing processes, every firm was intensely focused on how to become better at collectively getting and keeping good clients.

It's one thing to have this challenge. It's another thing to have this challenge year after year (as many firms said they did) without doing anything differently. The author Israelmore Ayivor summed up this leadership lesson nicely when he wrote, "If the problems you have this year are the same problems you had last year, then you are not a leader. You are rather a problem on your own that must be solved."

While no professional service firm leader agreed with the statement that there is only one way to develop business, most of them had not proactively tried to integrate different business development models into the firm's overall strategy. A good place to begin figuring out new models to encourage in your firm is to identify what may already exist in your firm that is currently going unrecognized and/or unrewarded.

Ask the men and women (at all levels in the firm) to identify which characteristics of the 24 listed in Chapter 6 they think best describe their styles of communication and business development. See if there are gender differences in your firm. If there are differences, look at those differences not from the perspective of erasing them but of using them to expand how success is attained.

Despite how provocative this step is in evoking the paradox of generalizing to individualize, conducting a comparative gender analysis of which characteristics are reported by men and which are reported by women will provide some insights into how women are performing in comparison to men. More importantly, this analysis can serve as a guide to help you create frameworks that enhance women's chances of succeeding because there is not a firm leader who cares about his or her firm who would say that fewer people successfully developing business in the firm is better than more.

This is not *"as easy as it sounds,"* warned one firm leader. *"The idea that women may do this differently feels to a lot of people like we are making excuses for women. That we are saying we have to soften the standards so that we can accommodate women's styles. It's hard to help people see that it's not softening the standards but kind of changing them. They are not less than they were before . . . they are just different."*

It is, as this leader warns, definitely not easy for reasons that have been covered in detail in the preceding chapters. That said, it is also not a choice for any firm that wants to not just survive but win.

GOOGLE IT, SORT OF

Data is everything at Google, so it's not surprising that the company would approach a question about women at Google using lots of data and complex algorithms to analyze that data. With women comprising about a third of

Google's global workforce, the tech giant has had its ups and downs with hiring, retaining, and advancing women.

As reported in the *New York Times*, the algorithms helped Google pinpoint two specific areas where the numbers of women were not what they should be: (1) potential female hires were disproportionately not making it past the telephone interview, and (2) women were disproportionately not being considered for promotions in technical areas.[155] A deeper dive into the data revealed the commonality between these two areas: women were not promoting themselves as much as their male counterparts were.

In the telephone interviews, women were not as expressive of their accomplishments as the men were, thereby leaving the interviewers with the impression that the women were not as accomplished or experienced as their male counterparts. Tweaking the way that the interviewers asked the questions and reported the answers minimized the impact of self-promotion (or the lack thereof), and the result was that more women started getting hired.

In technical areas, employees at Google have to nominate themselves in order to be evaluated for a promotion. Women were not nominating themselves as much as their male counterparts were, so they were not being considered for promotions. Google started hosting workshops for women on the importance of nominating themselves and creating support systems to help them nominate themselves. The numbers of promotions of women increased.

Google is far from perfect when it comes to full representation of women throughout its employee and leadership ranks, but these two tweaks to the system in order to neutralize the self-promotion differentials between men and women demonstrated ways in which differences between men and women don't have to be erased—they can just be taken out of the evaluative process in understanding talent and potential.

Many professional service firms have end-of-year self-evaluations in which partners/principals have to articulate what they accomplished that year. Women's self-evaluations tend to be very understated and modest, and many men's self-evaluations are actually overstated and their roles in projects exaggerated. When we reviewed these self-evaluations in various types of professional service firms, we found that men used "I" more than women and women used "we" more than men,[156] and that men wrote about leading teams and projects while women talked about being on teams and projects. Any reasonable person who read many of these self-evaluations would pick the men over the women because they looked more experienced, accomplished, and stronger, at least on paper.

Nonetheless, we noticed that in some firms, the difference between men and women was less than in other firms. The difference was that the more specific the questions were on the self-evaluation form, the fewer differences there were between the men and the women. The more open ended the questions, the more differences between men and women. The specificity of the questions made it feel more to women like they were responding to a request for information instead of promoting themselves. The differentials between men and women were nearly indiscernible in firms where the form asked very specific questions and offered several multiple-choice questions.

Google it, as in do what Google did. Get specific in the requests for information. Ask for details instead of assuming a lack of details when none is offered. Recognize that men and women may express their accomplishments differently, so ask more questions of women. Google has crunched the data and extracted the lessons. All you need to do is implement the lessons in a way that makes sense for you.

CREATE NEW IN-GROUPS TO NEUTRALIZE OUTMODED OUT-GROUPS

A lot has been written about in-groups and out-groups in the last couple of decades, and we have learned a lot not just about what these concepts mean in terms of how people see themselves in relation to others but also about how we can manage these concepts to create relationships where none existed before.

Fundamentally, an in-group is a social group of some sort that a person feels connected to on a deep level. The social group can be a gender, racial/ethnic, sexual orientation, national, or other group that focuses on one's identity, but the group can just as easily be an alma mater, athletic team, interest group, religious, or other affiliation. In-groups, in our minds, are people who are like us in some way that is really important to us. Out-groups, conversely, are social groups with whom an individual does not feel connected. Most often out-groups are defined in direct inverse relation to the in-groups to which the individual belongs. For example, a Boston Red Sox fan would consider other Red Sox fans part of his in-group and Yankees fans as part of his out-group, but he wouldn't think twice about Chicago Cubs fans because he wouldn't necessarily sense a feeling of competition from them. Most people's out-groups are closely connected to their in-groups through a sense of competition, dislike, historical animosity, and so forth.

Naturally, we are nice to people in our in-groups, and we are not nice to people in our out-groups, but our in-groups and out-groups are not as organic or stable as we think. In fact, it is very easy for in-group/out-group parameters to be erased and redrawn, especially by people in positions of power.

One of the most powerful examples of this was the exercise conducted by Jane Elliott in her third-grade class in 1968 following the assassination of Dr. Martin Luther King Jr.[157] Elliott wanted to teach her students about difference and privilege, so she divided her class into blue-eyed kids and brown-eyed kids and created rules about who were the superior kids. On the first day, she made the blue-eyed kids the superior kids, and she had them tie brown collars around the necks of the brown-eyed kids so that they could be identified easily. On that day, the blue-eyed kids got all the privileges that third graders value so very highly like five extra minutes for recess, restricted access to playground favorites, and extra food at lunch. She added many more layers to this experience such as having the kids drink from separate water fountains and sit in different locations in the classroom. By the end of the day, the blue-eyed kids were being quite mean to their brown-eyed classmates, even to the ones who had been their friends just earlier that day. The blue-eyed kids talked more in class and were more confident about their schoolwork while the brown-eyed kids got more and more quiet and became insecure about their abilities to do their classwork.

If Elliott had stopped there, she would have had adequate evidence to prove her point about in-groups and out-groups, but the next day, she switched the roles, telling the kids that there had been a mistake and making the brown-eyed kids the superior kids. The mean behaviors were now exhibited by the brown-eyed kids, and the blue-eyed kids exhibited none of the aggressive behaviors from the day before.

The reaction from the public was swift, intense, and deeply divided. While some people felt that the children learned an important lesson, others felt that the children had been manipulated for political means. The controversy faded, but the impact remained. Since Elliott's exercise in 1968, we have seen the research on in-groups and out-groups grow into a robust arena of learning, experimentation, and behavioral modification with insights that have great value and application in many areas where gender has become the source of in-group and out-group identification.

In almost every firm involved in our study, we found that gender was an axis along which people identified either their in-group, their out-group, or both. Even if men did not see other male partners/principals as their in-group, they referred to female partners/principals as their out-group, a group with which they had little or no connection. Women were highly likely to see themselves as belonging to the female partner in-group (even if they didn't personally connect with all of the other female partners/principals) and see their experiences as a contrast to those of the male partners/principals.

Interestingly, in firms that had high levels of interdepartment competition, the male and female partners/principals had less connection to the gender-based in-group/out-group identity. The strength of another identity within the firm weakened the focus on gender identity and created stronger relationships between men and women, which led to more joint business development activities. While we did not have the time or resources to experiment more fully in this area, we tried a few micro experiments involving the strengthening of a new in-group to fade the focus on gender identity, and we saw good results.

In one medium-size firm, the leaders decided to focus on intensifying the in-group firm identity by casting their main competitor as the out-group. Borrowing from Nike's mission statement in the 1980s—"Crush Reebok"—this firm created an internal in-group mission statement that sought to outperform their competitor. (The firm's actual mission statement was quite powerful, expletives and all.) One of the partners/principals had worked at Nike during the 1980s and remembered that *"you knew you were Nike if you were working to crush Reebok . . . with us or against us . . . no career development type stuff . . . if someone from Nike went to Reebok, no one from Nike would talk to you . . . possibly ever."* This intense focus on firm identity in relation to an external competitor reduced the intrafirm competition dramatically. More people started helping each other develop business because the out-group was clear.

Create new in-groups. They can be by department, against an external competitor, or toward a clear internal goal. Women compete well and hard when they are part of a team. Create an in-group for them to compete on behalf of, and the out-group they face off against will not know what hit them!

CREATE NEW COLLABORATIVE SIZES TO FIT PEOPLE'S COLLABORATIVE STYLES

Trying to fit the collaborative style into competitive shoes does not work, and continuing to try and make it work embodies the cliché that insanity is the doing of the same thing over and over and expecting different results. One professional service firm leader opposed a collaborative business development style so vehemently that when I asked him whether his firm's goal was to adhere to the competitive style or get more business in the door, he had to think about his answer for a while before he reluctantly settled on the latter as the goal.

Making new sizes does not mean that the competitive size will be replaced; it means that there will be more options through which people can maximize their contributions to their firms. You can pilot a collaborative strategy as discussed in Chapter 10. You can also just simply let people know that the firm is open to recognizing and rewarding collaborative alternatives to business development and see what bubbles up organically . . . and be open to surprises. It may not just be women who take you up on the offer!

PROFILE THE FINDERS; EXPAND THE PROFILES

When we asked leaders in firms to quickly name the finders in their firms, they were able to immediately start rattling off names. When we asked the leaders to tell us what these top finders had in common, most of them couldn't come up with more than two or three commonalities in the group. (There were fewer finders in smaller firms and more depth of connection, so the number of commonalities increased as the size of the firm decreased.)

We created an inventory of 15 demographic / social interest / personality / life experience characteristics and asked leaders to see what common profiles emerged from the inventory. The inventory is not meant to be exhaustive; it was designed primarily to execute a quick experiment with firm leaders. The inventory included race/ethnicity, gender, alma mater(s), parents' occupations, place of birth, place of current residence, whether at least 25 percent of the finders' clients were family and friends before they became clients, membership affiliations and board service, tenure at the firm, tenure in the profession overall, introversion versus extroversion, profession of spouse, personal recreational interests, levels of interest in mentoring younger professionals, and a general tendency to share the credit for bringing in clients.

For the purposes of our quick experiment, we asked the leaders to fill out this inventory list for the top finders in their firms from their own knowledge of the finders. A general profile of a finder slowly emerged across all the different firms represented by the leaders: an extroverted white male who had a spouse who did not work outside the home, had at least 25 percent of his business from friends and family, served on two to three large civic/not-for-profit boards, played golf, and traveled. While these were common characteristics among finders across firms, industries, and geographical locations, finders in the same city tended to live in the same or similar neighborhoods. There was no consistency among the other criteria.

While firm leaders had known these facts about their finders prior to the exercise, the quick creation of a general profile helped them understand that finders had a type, and women and people of color were most likely to not possess the majority of characteristics that comprised this general profile.

Profile the finders. Then, expand the profile to create more finders.

CREATE A FIRMWIDE BUSINESS DEVELOPMENT ACTIVITY LIST

One of the firms in our study had created an internal database of all the business development activities in which the partners/principals were engaging. Instead of asking the partners/principals to contribute this information (they tried that with very little success), the firm compiled the list from the reimbursement receipts. This one small act of transparency had a huge impact on partners'/principals' understanding of the full breadth of activities that were being reimbursed by the firm, and it encouraged more women to submit activities that they had not previously thought of as reimbursable. One of the leaders of the firm had cautious optimism for the success: *"Not sure if they got business out of them [the activities], but an increase in doing something is the start of getting something, so I would say it worked."*

DON'T ASSUME THAT KNOWING LEADS TO DOING.

Imagine a scenario in which you tell someone that the shoes he wants you to wear to work are too small for you. He responds by describing how shoes work and articulating the steps that you need to take to put on the shoes. You tell him that you know and understand how shoes work and how to put them on; you just cannot wear the shoes that he wants you to wear because they don't fit you. He tells you how important it is to wear shoes. You sigh and try to explain again that you understand the issues around wearing shoes; you just cannot wear the shoes he wants you to wear because they hurt your feet. You ask about getting a different size of shoes, and he suggests that you attend a training on how to put on shoes.

When the story is told this way, it has a humorous and slightly absurd feel, but this dialogue is occurring every day about business development between firm leaders and female partners/principals.

- Remember that not doing is not the same thing as not knowing or not understanding.
- Don't equate knowing and doing or assume that knowing leads to doing. Success in business development is rooted in attaching the development activities to existing interests, not twisting behaviors to fit interests that are not organic to an individual.
- Drop the assumptions and develop more sizes that fit. You will be surprised how many more people will do what you want them to if you ask them to do things they actually want to do.

GET OVER (OR DIFFUSE) THE "GENDER AWKWARDNESS" TENSION

One of the thorniest areas in exploring gender differences in business development is an individual's ability to navigate waters that are charged with gender norms and expectations without violating those norms and expectations. This is a delicate skill, and many choose to avoid the other gender instead of figuring out how to navigate these waters professionally and elegantly. It is especially critical for leaders and other senior people to be unafraid in navigating these waters because if the leaders in a firm are not mentoring women to the same extent as they are mentoring men, they are withholding key information, resources, relationships, and advocacy from the women.

One firm termed these waters "gender awkwardness," and the partners/principals talked openly about what it was, how real it was, and what they could do to neutralize it so that the partners/principals—especially the male ones since they were in the overwhelming majority—could invest equally in younger male and female professionals. As one female partner asserted, *"It is difficult to talk about business development once you are partner when you were not similarly invested in as an associate. That investment in you is what has groomed you. And the men are hesitant to invest in the young women like they invest in the young men."*

Researchers from the Center for Talent Innovation reported in 2010 that male executives admit to being more nervous about the social implications of being seen at dinners or at networking events with young women than with young men.[158] This research led to a few attention-grabbing headlines such as "The Lolita Effect: Are Male Execs Too Nervous to Mentor Young Women?"[159] but it didn't create enough of a dialogue in workplaces to make this topic easier to talk about or address.

Many of the senior male partners/principals in our study talked about this "gender awkwardness" and specifically mentioned that it was a difficult topic for them to raise in their firms. One partner talked at length about the lack of opportunities and/or resources for a senior male to be able to talk about this issue candidly and productively: *"If you say something, you are the old creepy guy. If you don't say anything, you are the clueless guy. I talk about it sometimes with other guys like me, but none of us know what to do. Somebody brings this up, and the subject gets changed pretty quickly. I don't like not investing in my female associates. Truth be told, they are my smarter ones. But, the tension around this topic makes it difficult."* Another partner directly asked us to give him suggestions as part of this research study, *"Put a list in your book . . . a list of things I can do to diffuse this tension because I want to be a better mentor."* Sir, the list follows. (I use the word "mentor" to generally mean a colleague who could benefit from your investment of time and resources, not a relationship in any formal mentoring program.)

- **Other people's perceptions often follow your own perceptions.** When you get comfortable, others will too. If you project discomfort or awkwardness, misperceptions are more likely to occur.
- **Mentor people in small, mixed-gender groups of two or three people.** Asking a group of young people to a mentoring lunch, cocktails after work, dinner, and the like does not trigger the same awkwardness that one-on-one events do. It's more comfortable to ask, to execute, and to repeat. This strategy also creates better bonds among the people you are mentoring, and they are more likely to see each other as sources for ideas, resources, and support.

- **Breakfast and lunch are less awkward than after-work cocktails and/or dinner.** Grabbing a coffee may be even better than breakfast and lunch in regard to bypassing people's stereotype triggers.
- **Use common spaces in and around the firm instead of going "off-site."** The firm's lunchroom or even a conference room reduces the awkwardness with logistics (will you meet there, will you drive together or separately, etc.), venue, length of the meeting especially if you all are headed back to work afterward, and so on.
- **Create opportunities to get to know the mentee's significant other/ family and for your mentee to get to know your significant other/ family.** As you get to know a mentee's significant other, the awkwardness dissipates because discussion of family can be a great starting point into a conversation in the "awkwardness-free zone."
- **Travel is tough and requires deliberate effort to reduce awkwardness.** It's one thing to have gender awkwardness when you are going home every night, but travel—being away from family and working long hours and staying at the same hotel—was mentioned by many people as a particularly tough challenge. It is a tough challenge, but it's important to remember that diffusing awkwardness around gender issues is primarily about the management of other people's perceptions. Identify the areas where you feel the perceptions are most likely to get triggered in the negative direction and use other strategies in this list to deliberately create a safety net for travel.
- **Be consistent.** Nothing triggers rumors like a lack of consistency. If women are underrepresented in your firm, the socialized experiences in areas such as the avoidance of gender awkwardness are more difficult to navigate. If you choose who you mentor, unconscious questions will arise in people's minds about the reasons why you selected those one or two people out of an already small group.

CHAPTER 15

CHANGE WHAT ISN'T WORKING
(REVIEW AND REPEAT YOUR SUCCESSES TO RESIZE BUSINESS DEVELOPMENT)

STRATEGIES FOR WOMEN (AND MOST MEN)

In order to truly be successful in your business development efforts, you have to begin with knowing exactly what success is. Earlier, you explored ways in which you can see yourself differently, choose your goals and vocabulary deliberately, and engage in activities that are enjoyable for you. This last set of strategies is about engaging in frequent reviews of what you are doing and what you are getting done. It's about analyzing the activity and the results to ensure that you are accomplishing what you want to accomplish so that you can change what isn't working. The number of people in our study who did not review their efforts and focused on doing more of what wasn't working was surprisingly high. When you review your successes, your fit list and misfit list are great lenses to help you focus on how you evaluate your successes.

CHASE THE GOALS YOU HAVE CHOSEN

It is impossible to create a new size for yourself if you are defining success based on the current size. In the pilot program, the women discovered that while chasing a dollar amount did not incentivize them, chasing a great client experience did. This did not mean that the women were not focused on generating revenue, but the immediate achievement that they were measuring was client satisfaction, not revenues generated. The women focused on the client experience as their deliverable, and the revenue was a product of that deliverable.

One of the leaders in the firm where the pilot program was implemented felt that this difference was a semantic one: *"If the end goal is still the business generated, I don't understand the difference."* A female partner's response was that *"the ways in which you define the goal do matter because monetary goals don't move me, but people goals do . . . for others, people goals don't move them but monetary goals do . . . I don't understand why it should be seen as odd to want to see business development goals as people goals . . . It's the first time I'm excited to think about business development."*

KEEP TEAM STATS...EVEN IF YOUR FIRM DOESN'T

If your firm only keeps individual statistics around business development, client successes, or any other key measures of success, identify the teams in which you work and keep team stats. For example, one partner who worked in a large firm kept track of her team's client development and client service successes regardless of which senior partner was leading a particular pitch or deal. The team had a very high success percentage, and she mentioned it—somewhat tongue in cheek—to one of the firm leaders one day when she told him that if there were senior partners/principals struggling for some wins, her team would be happy to take them on. She did it with humor, but she got the point across, and her team's success was now on the leaders' radar screens even though the firm had never measured success by team.

Henry Ford once said that if he asked the people what they wanted, they would have asked for faster horses. People couldn't have asked for cars before they knew how much better cars would be in comparison to horses, so they would have just asked for faster horses. If your firm is stuck in trying to improve individual statistics, it may very well be because the leaders can't even imagine what team statistics would look like and how those statistics would assist them in driving performance.

So, keep team stats and share them, because once the leaders can see them and use them, they will adopt them.

CREATE A STRATEGIC BUSINESS DEVELOPMENT BOARD OF ADVISORS

A strategic Board of Advisors for business development purposes accomplishes several things that assist women (and many men) with their business development efforts. I stress the word "strategic," because putting together a board of people you know and like is not strategic.

Creating a strategic business development Board of Advisors requires knowing your strengths and challenges in business development and identifying key people in your personal and professional lives who will help you leverage your strengths and neutralize your weaknesses. Potential clients make great advisors because they can tell you what people like them are looking for from you. Current clients make great advisors because they can tell you why they picked you and the areas in which you hold an edge or advantage over your peers. A marketing / public relations professional may make a great advisor as would an expert in the type of work you do.

You should deliberately create a diverse Board of Advisors who don't know each other, don't always agree with each other, and are committed to investing in your business development on a short-term or long-term basis. The following are tips submitted by women who created and are effectively using their Boards of Advisors:

- You can name this group anything you want. Board of Directors. Success Board. Board of Advisors. Advisory Board. The more the name fits how you see it, the more you will think about it and talk about it and the more successful it will be.
- Be very specific about why you want someone to be your advisor and what you want her or him to do. When you are too general in asking for help or advice, you actually make it hard for people to help you.
- Use specific time frames when you ask people to be your advisors. You might say, "I'm trying to accomplish this specific thing in the next year

so it would be great if you would be my advisor for the next 12 to 18 months." Indefinite time frames are scary for people, so make it specific and tell them why the time frame is what it is.

- Get all of your advisors together once a year or so if possible. They will love meeting each other because they have you and your success in common. You can use this as an opportunity to have them collectively help you set some goals, and some personal and professional connections might be made between your advisors for their own networking purposes.

- Tell your advisors your specific goals and have them evaluate your progress toward your goals. The accountability will keep you on track and will keep them invested as well.

- Be honest with them about your challenges and boundaries. You are asking them to help you achieve something given who you really are. If you just hate asking for business, tell them so they can help you figure out alternatives.

- Don't aim low when you are trying to find advisors. Try to find people who will push you and help you grow.

- Don't take a "no" personally. Expect a "no," ask anyway, and celebrate when you get a "yes." Remember that you are asking for help. People actually really love to say yes to helping someone.

- Send individualized thank-you cards and gifts twice a year.

STRATEGIES FOR FIRMS AND FIRM LEADERS

MAKE THE CONVERSATION ABOUT DIFFERENT SIZES AN ONGOING DIALOGUE

The conversation on creating new sizes is a difficult conversation that is still in its infancy in many firms. Conversations on this topic are uncomfortable and awkward, but robust and productive aspects of the conversation cannot be activated until you go through the initial discomfort and awkwardness. The best way to start this conversation is to create a mosaic of ongoing, small discussions with and between various groups of people that do not need to be completed or resolved in any one setting. This collection of conversations should be used by firm leaders as an opportunity to learn about gender differences in business development, the impact of these differences on women's advancement in the firm, and possible alternatives—different sizes—that can be created to benefit women and the firm's overall economic and competitive health.

Ongoing dialogues focus on achieving increased understanding and progress, not answers and decisive resolutions. If leaders start this cluster of conversations as an ongoing dialogue, all participants will have the opportunity to digest the research and reframe their perspectives, refocus their goals, revise their vocabulary, reshape their methods, and review alternatives with collaborative intent.

FOCUS ON RESULTS, NOT PROCESSES

When one female partner in an engineering services firm approached the head of her department to explore the idea of team-based business development, the department head's immediate reaction was that it would not work because the system was structured to measure individual generations, not collective generations. The female partner persevered by appealing to the leader's logic and asked him why collective efforts would not work if the people in the collective were willing to report it in equally divisible individual parts. He thought about it for a few moments and responded that he did not think anyone in a collective would actually agree to divide the revenue numbers equally.

The female partner realized that the leader was not fighting the implementation of the process; he was fighting to imagine what the process actually looked like. After this conversation, the female partner also realized that the women who wanted to engage in this collective effort did not need anyone's permission to do so as long as they reported the revenue generation individually.

"They can't support it because they cannot even see it," she told me. *"It's like you are asking them if they will support ordering pizza for dinner when they have only ordered hamburgers before, and they don't know what a pizza looks like, and they don't know how it tastes. Of course, they will say that they would rather order hamburgers again, but if you order the pizza and have it there and they see that they like it, they will order it the next time you suggest it."*

Focusing on the process requires a concentrated effort to understand something that looks and feels very different from what you are used to.

Focusing on the results is, in comparison, much easier because the need for controlling the process can be replaced by the trust that different processes can still lead to the same desirable goals.

If you focus on the results, your ability to be comfortable with and even support different methods of getting those results is enhanced. Team-based business development, different types of development events and activities, and so forth don't trigger discomfort because the goal is still the same.

CONCLUSION

⚹ ANITA

Anita was elected into her firm's partnership at the end of 2013. She is excited, relieved, overwhelmed, and proud, and, above all, she is prepared to thrive as a partner. *"I know that it's all about getting the business, and I'm ready. I've already started seeing some bullying from a few members of the 'old boys club' here, but I have an advantage in this game . . . I know exactly who I'm dealing with, but they have no idea who they are dealing with . . . They see a young female partner who doesn't have business and they see weakness, but I know the game and while they are underestimating me, I will be playing the game my way."*

Anita has been learning the game since she was a young girl. Her mother was a partner at a professional service firm, and Anita grew up listening to her mother and father talk about what her mother had experienced in the firm. *"I heard her stories and I saw what they did to her. She is brilliant, but she did not bring in any business of her own. Of course, the people who were given credit for bringing in the business were selling her skills and her reputation because people wanted her to work on their stuff, but she was treated like the hired help and the guys who brought in the business were treated like royalty."*

Anita's mother did not want Anita to go into a firm, but when Anita insisted that it was what she wanted to do, her mother told her that the three nonnegotiable rules for female partners were *"One, do not trust anyone else to take care of your career, no matter what they say or what promises they make. Two, know what you are worth to yourself and in the marketplace, and do not let anyone else persuade you to downgrade your worth. Three, people always act in their own self-interest, and if you can figure out what that self-interest is, you can make anyone into an ally."* Anita talks to her mother a couple of times every week, and her mother continues to repeat these rules to her. *"I know that she is being protective because of what she went through, and I think it's healing for her to be able to mentor me through the process."*

Immediately after her election to partnership was announced, Anita sent personalized thank-you notes to a few people and asked them to be on her Advisory Board. *"I'm not comfortable asking for business, but I am comfortable asking for help. There are three potential clients who have agreed to serve on my Board, and these are people that I would have never called to ask for business directly. I have meetings set up with each of them in their offices to ask for their advice and insights on how to develop business. One of them is shopping for a new firm to do some niche work, and that is on the agenda for our conversation."* She has also started implementing a few other strategies from this book including writing a story and creating a misfit list. *"I will keep trying things until I find what really works for me. What I will not do is wait for anyone at the firm to help me or do things in a way that feels uncomfortable for me."*

In my last conversation with Anita, she told me how much she enjoyed participating in this study not just because it helped crystallize her thinking on the issue but because it gave her the ability to formally recognize her mother's experiences. *"My mom doesn't want me to lose myself as I strive for success in the firm. She wants me to be successful but in a way that makes me happy. That's the challenge for my generation . . . to play the game well and win while changing the game as we do it."*

Alice Paul, one of the key architects of the women's suffrage movement in the United States, described the women's movement as "a sort of mosaic. Each of us puts in one little stone, and then you get a great mosaic at the end." Her words, as valid today as they were then, remind us that no one voice, one story, one study, or one set of perspectives can capture the full landscape of women's full equality, but all voices, stories, studies, and perspectives are necessary in order for the landscape to exist. Each stone is unique, and each stone is essential to the mosaic. We—women and men—all add our individual insights, experiences, and efforts to this mosaic one stone at a time, and the image that emerges is one that none of us could have created on our own but one that we all helped to shape.

This book is one stone in the great mosaic. It is about gender differences in business development within professional service firms; it is about what these gender differences look like, how they affect women (and men) in these firms, and what women (and men) can do to neutralize the differences to enhance the success of women, men, and the firms in which they work. This stone builds on the stones already present like women's participation and success in higher education, gender differences in neurobehavioral patterns, the unique histories and cultures of professional service firms, our socialized perspectives on competition and selling, gender differences in leadership, and intersectionality dynamics. Equally importantly, this stone builds on the stones added by the experiences of women like Patricia, Elizabeth, Terri, Caroline, Marie, Lisa, Susan, Anita, her mother, and the dozens of other women whose stories comprise the heart and soul of this research.

This book—this stone—is about the reality that there is currently only one size available in business development within professional service firms, and this size does not fit women (or all men). If women want to succeed in these firms today, they endure the pain of the misfit, but not enough women can or want to endure the pain for very long, and they leave. The void they leave in their wake is a void that hurts them, the firms they are leaving, and all of us who want to see greater gender equality in workplaces.

This book brings together the individual voices of the professionals and the leaders in these firms in an objectively collective way to illustrate the realities behind the numbers, the dearth of female leaders in these firms, and the inertia around creating change. Of course, the narratives of the voices included in this book are not reflective of all the men and women in professional service firms, and more stones on this topic are needed before a more comprehensive picture emerges. I do believe, however, that this one stone gives us enough of what we need to catalyze change—to stop doing what we are currently doing and start doing what actually works.

I have spent the last 15 years working closely with professional service firms in the area of inclusion and equality for those who are culturally not included and therefore not advanced into leadership in these firms. We are missing out on so much brilliance, creativity, innovation, and leadership because we are not hearing their voices. And, we cannot afford to!

While the inclusion of all marginalized people is critical to the success of these firms, our country, and the world, the gender disparities are especially troubling because we are talking about the majority of our population. Fifty-one percent of our population is female. Almost 60 percent of students in colleges and universities are female. It doesn't make sense that firms are not able to capitalize on the majority of the talent available to them because they want to hang on to the status quo in business development practices.

Changing business development in professional service firms may seem like a mammoth task with a low probability of immediate success. That is not just my opinion—I was told directly by many of the professionals and leaders in this study that this research may better illuminate some issues but will do nothing to change anything. One firm leader gently told me at the end of his interview, *"I think the research is important too, but I wouldn't get my hopes up about changing things . . . money and power . . . people won't give that up without a fight."*

I agree that people who want to maintain the status quo will not give up without a fight, but I also know that people who want to see change won't give up without a fight either. The hundreds of men and women who participated in this research invested their time and energy to question the status quo and engage in experiments that test-drove the change. And, we have learned throughout history that change is ironically a greater constant than the status quo.

The women who piloted a team-based business development program in their firm were told that they were crazy. They were told that they would have conflicts within the team and that they would never be able to *"get it together to actually get business in the door."* They did it anyway, and it worked for them. Moreover, once firm leaders saw that it worked, the team-based approach went from being seen as insane to being rearticulated as innovative. The status quo tried to hang on, but the change won.

There are strategies in this book for individual women (and men) who want to create new business development sizes for themselves. There are also strategies for firms and firm leaders who want to introduce new sizes—innovations—into their firms. The strategies in this book work. We have seen them work, but they will only work if you act on them and tailor them for your unique contexts and experiences.

This book is one stone that I add to the larger mosaic of gender equality in our workplaces and in our world, and I hope this stone inspires and empowers you to create and add your own unique stone to the mosaic.

The mosaic will be incomplete without your contribution.

NOTES

1. Karen M. Richardson, "200 Largest U.S. Law Firms Report Only 17 Percent of Equity Partners Are Women, According to National Association of Women Lawyers Annual Survey," *NAWL Blog*, February 25, 2014, http://www.nawl.org/p/bl/et/blogaid=56.

2. ABA Commission on Women in the Profession, *From Visible Invisibility to Visibly Successful: Success Strategies for Law Firms and Women of Color in Law Firms* (Chicago: American Bar Association, 2008); ABA Commission on Women in the Profession, *Visible Invisibility: Women of Color in Law Firms* (Chicago: American Bar Association, 2006); Minority Corporate Counsel Association, *Sustaining Pathways to Diversity:® The Next Steps in Understanding and Increasing Diversity and Inclusion in Large Law Firms* (Washington, DC: MCCA, 2009).

3. Lee Drutman, "The Political 1% of the 1% in 2012," *Sunlight Foundation* (blog), June 24, 2013 (9:00 a.m.), http://sunlightfoundation.com/blog/2013/06/24/1pct_of_the_1pct/.

4. Ibid.

5. Sarah Bryner and Doug Weber, "Sex, Money and Politics," Center for Responsive Politics, September 26, 2013, http://www.opensecrets.org/downloads/CRP_Gender_Report_2013.pdf.

6. "Explore the Data: The State of Women in America," Center for American Progress, accessed January 3, 2014, http://interactives.americanprogress.org/projects/tp/2013/women/.

7. Mary Ann Keogh Hoss, Paula Bobrowski, Kathryn J. McDonagh, and Nancy M. Paris, "How Gender Disparities Drive Imbalances in Health Care Leadership," *Journal of Healthcare Leadership* 3 (2011): 59–68, www.dovepress.com/getfile.php?fileID=11397.

8. Caroline J. Tolbert and Gertrude A. Steuernagel, "Women Lawmakers, State Mandates and Women's Health," *Women and Politics* 22, no. 2 (2001): 1–39.

9. Kathlene Lyn, "Alternative Views of Crime: Legislative Policymaking in Gendered Terms," *Journal of Politics* 57, no. 3 (1995): 696–723.

10. Lonna Rae Atkeson, "Not All Cues Are Created Equal: The Conditional Impact of Female Candidates on Political Engagement," *Journal of Politics* 65, no. 4 (2003): 1040–61.

11. Selwyn Duke, "Enough Already with the Women-Get-Paid-Less Nonsense," *New American*, October 19, 2012, http://www.thenewamerican.com/reviews/opinion/item/13290-enough-already-with-the-women-get-paid-less-nonsense; Sabrina Schaeffer, "Business Must

Stop Coddling Women in the Workplace," *Forbes*, December 4, 2013, accessed February 27, 2014, http://www.forbes.com/sites/sabrinaschaeffer/2013/12/04/business-must-stop-coddling-women-in-the-workplace/; Carey Roberts, "McCain Lampoons the Gender Wage Gap Myth," *RenewAmerica*, May 15, 2008, accessed February 27, 2014, http://www.renewamerica.com/columns/roberts/080515.

12. United Nations Development Programme, UN Millennium Project, "United Nations Millennium Development Goals," accessed February 27, 2014, http://www.un.org/millenniumgoals/.

13. United Nations Development Programme, "How Is the GII Calculated, and What Are Its Main Findings in Terms of National and Regional Patterns of Inequality?," *Human Development Reports FAQ* (blog), http://hdr.undp.org/en/content/how-gii-calculated-and-what-are-its-main-findings-terms-national-and-regional-patterns.

14. Ibid.

15. Mayra Buvinic, "Gender Equality and Poverty Reduction," *Closing the Gender Gap: The Business Case for Organizations, Politics and Society*, held at the Harvard John F. Kennedy School of Government, http://www.hks.harvard.edu/var/ezp_site/storage/fckeditor/file/pdfs/centers-programs/centers/wappp/events/business-case-conference-2010/Gender_Equality_and_Poverty_Reduction_Mayra_Buvinic.pdf.

16. DeAnne Aguirre, Leila Hoteit, Christine Rupp, and Karim Sabbagh, *Empowering the Third Billion: Women and the World of Work in 2012* (Booz & Company Inc., 2012), http://www.booz.com/global/home/what-we-think/reports-white-papers/article-display/empowering-third-billion-women-world, 5.

17. Joanna Barsh and Lareina Yee, *Unlocking the Full Potential of Women at Work* (McKinsey & Company, 2012), http://www.mckinsey.com/client_service/organization/latest_thinking/women_at_work.

18. Cristian L. Dezso and David Gaddis Ross, "Does Female Representation in Top Management Improve Firm Performance? A Panel Data Investigation" (working paper, Robert H. Smith School of Business Research, 2011), Social Science Research Network.

19. André Chanavat, *Women in the Workplace: Latest Workforce Trends in Gender Equality* (Thomson Reuters Special Report, 2012), http://alphanow.thomsonreuters.com/ebooks/women-in-the-workplace/.

20. Catalyst, "Statistical Overview of Women in the Workplace," last modified December 10, 2013, accessed January 4, 2014, http://www.catalyst.org/knowledge/statistical-overview-women-workplace.

21. Ibid.

22. Bureau of Labor Statistics, "Labor Force Statistics from the Current Population Survey, Table 11: Employed Persons by Detailed Occupation, Sex, Race, and Hispanic or Latino Ethnicity, *Annual Averages 2012*," last modified February 5, 2013, http://www.bls.gov/cps/cpsaat11.htm.

23. Kat Gordon, The 3% Conference, "Building the Business Case for More Female CDs," accessed February 27, 2014, http://3percentconf.com/index.php/about/history.

24. Richard Lapchick, Djuan Bragg, Wayne Clark, Demetrius Frazier, Aaron J. Gearlds, Tavia Record, and Christopher D. Sarpy, *White Men Continue to Dominate Advertising Agencies: A Study of the Super Bowl 2011 Ads* (Florida: The Institute for Diversity and Ethics in Sport, 2011), accessed February 27, 2014, http://www.tidesport.org/MadAve/MadisonAvenue2011_FINAL.pdf.

25. Amanda Kolson Hurley, "Double Whammy: Would There Be More Women in Architecture if There Were More Women in Development?," *Architect Magazine* (blog), September 17, 2012, http://www.architectmagazine.com/architects/would-there-be-more-women-architects-if-there-wer.aspx.

26. Catalyst, "Quick Take: Women in Accounting," last modified December 10, 2013, accessed January 30, 2014, http://www.catalyst.org/knowledge/women-accounting.

27. NALP, *Representation of Women Associates Falls for Fourth Straight Year as Minority Associates Continue to Make Gains—Women and Minority Partners Continue to Make Small Gains* (Washington, DC: NALP, 2013), accessed January 30, 2014, http://www.nalp.org/lawfirmdiversity_2013.

28. Giulia Tongnini, "Gender Diversity in Professional Service Firms: Female Representation Boosts Performance," *PwC* (blog), September 4, 2012, http://pwc.blogs.com/gender_agenda/2012/09/gender-diversity-in-professional-service-firms-female-representation-boosts-performance-.html.

29. Lisa Bertagnoli, "Venture Capital: A 'Relationships Business' That's Stayed Clubby," *Crain's Chicago Business* (blog), January 27, 2014, http://www.chicagobusiness.com/article/20140125/ISSUE02/301259992/venture-capital-a-relationships-business-thats-stayed-clubby.

30. The National Council for Research on Women, *Women in Fund Management Report: A Road Map for Achieving Critical Mass—and Why It Matters* (New York: New York City, 2009).

31. Ibid.

32. Mindi Rosser, "Researching Female Creative Directors with Professor Ashley Shoval," *The 3% Conference Blog*, November 11, 2013, http://3percentconf.com/blog/2013/11/ashley-shoval-female-creative-directors-research/.

33. U.S. Department of Labor, "Women Still Underrepresented among Highest Earners," *Issues in Labor Statistics,* Summary 06-03 (2006), accessed January 10, 2014, http://www.bls.gov/opub/ils/pdf/opbils55.pdf.

34. Ibid.

35. Mark Galanter and William Henderson, "The Elastic Tournament: The Second Transformation of the Big Law Firm," *Stanford Law Review* 60, no. 6 (2008): 1867–1930.

36. Ibid.

37. Amelia J. Uelmen, "The Evils of 'Elasticity': Reflections on the Rhetoric of Professionalism and the Part-time Paradox in Large Firm Practice," *Fordham Urban Law Journal* 33, no. 1 (2005): 101–36.

38. Sandrine Devillard, Sandra Sancier-Sultan, and Charlotte Werner, *Moving Mindsets on Gender Diversity: McKinsey Global Survey Results* (McKinsey, 2014), accessed February 27, 2014, http://www.mckinsey.com/insights/organization/moving_mind-sets_on_gender_diversity_mckinsey_global_survey_results.

39. Ibid.

40. Ibid.

41. Even though men and women are leaving organizations for work-life balance reasons, we acknowledge that the perceptions, expectations, and experiences of work-life balance are different for men and women. There is a considerable body of research that illustrates how women are making decisions about their careers for work-life reasons before they even have work-life conflict because of socialized expectations of themselves and their workplaces. You will find more research and coverage of these issues in the following resources: *Harvard Business Review on Work and Life Balance* (Boston, MA: Harvard Business School Press, 2000); Anne Bogel, *Work Shift: How to Create a Better Blend of Work, Life, and Family,* (Kindle [self-published], 2012); A. Roger Merrill and Rebecca Merrill, *Life Matters: Creating a Dynamic Balance of Work, Family, Time, and Money* (New York: Franklin Covey, 2003); Matthew Kelly, *Off Balance: Getting Beyond the Work-Life Balance Myth to Personal and Professional Satisfaction* (New York: Penguin Group, 2011); Sharon Lerner, *The War on Moms: On Life in a Family-Unfriendly Nation* (Hoboken, NJ: John Wiley, 2010); Cathy L. Greenberg and Barrett S. Avigdor, *What Happy Working Mothers Know: How New Findings in Positive Psychology Can Lead to a Healthy and Happy Work/Life Balance* (Hoboken, NJ: John Wiley, 2009).

42. Arin N. Reeves, "Diversity in Practice: The Last 6.2 Miles," *Chicago Lawyer Magazine,* November 1, 2013, accessed January 10, 2014, http://www.chicagolawyermagazine.com/Archives/2013/11/Diversity-in-Practice-ArinReeves.aspx.

43. Galanter and Henderson, "The Elastic Tournament."

44. http://www.americanbar.org/content/dam/aba/administrative/women/closing_the_gap.authcheckdam.pdf.

45. Stephanie N. Mehta, "The Best Advice I Ever Got: Robbie Kaplan & Christie Smith," *Fortune*, November 18, 2013, 126.

46. James B. Stewart, "A Lawyer and Partner, and Also Bankrupt," *New York Times*, sec. Business Day: Common Sense, January 24, 2014, accessed January 30, 2014, http://www.nytimes.com/2014/01/25/business/partner-in-a-prestigious-law-firm-and-bankrupt.html?_r=1.

47. Cynthia Fuchs Epstein, Robert Sauté, Bonnie Oglensky, and Martha Gever, "Glass Ceilings and Open Doors: Women's Advancement in the Legal Profession," *Fordham Law Review* 64, no. 2 (1995): 291–449, accessed January 19, 2014, http://ir.lawnet.fordham.edu/flr/vol64/iss2/2.

48. Scott Pollack, "What, Exactly, Is Business Development?," *Forbes: Entrepreneurs* (blog), March 21, 2012, http://www.forbes.com/sites/scottpollack/2012/03/21/what-exactly-is-business-development/.

49. Ibid.

50. Lauren A. Rivera, "Hiring as Cultural Matching: The Case of Elite Professional Service Firms," *American Sociological Review* 77, no. 6 (2012): 999–1022.

51. Ibid.

52. Ibid.

53. Andrew Von Nordenflycht, "What Is a Professional Service Firm? Towards a Theory and Taxonomy of Knowledge Intensive Firms," *Academy of Management Review* 35, no. 1 (2010): 155–74.

54. Ibid.

55. William H. Starbuck, "Learning by Knowledge-Intensive Firms," *Journal of Management Studies* 29, no. 6 (1992): 713–40.

56. Robin Tolmach Lakoff, *Language and Women's Place: Text and Commentaries*, ed. Mary Bucholtz (New York: Oxford University Press, 2004); Matthew L. Newman, Carla J. Groom, Lori D. Handelman, and James W. Pennebaker, "Gender Differences in Language Use: An Analysis of 14,000 Text Samples," *Discourse Processes* 45, no. 3 (2008): 211–36.

57. Ibid.

58. I would like to thank the following coaches for the amazing work that they do and for their invaluable contributions to this research: Cordell Parvin, Cordell Parvin LLC; Patrick Pruett, The Rainmaker Companies; Precious Williams Owodunni, Mountaintop Consulting; Rani Monson, RainMaking Marketing; Roy Ginsburg, Independent Consultant; Sylvia Lafair, Creative Energy Options; Veronika Powlis, Independent Consultant.

59. "Pols Told to Be Wary of Female Lobbyists," *Pagesix.com*, last modified July 21, 2010, accessed January 19, 2014, http://pagesix.com/2010/07/21/pols-told-to-be-wary-of-female-lobbyists/.

60. Ibid.

61. Susan Crabtree, "Female Lobbyists Cry Foul as Republican Lawmakers Keep Their Distance on the Hill," *TheHill.com*, last modified October 5, 2010, accessed January 19, 2014, http://thehill.com/homenews/house/122509-k-street-women-crying-foul-as-lawmakers-keep-distance-.

62. Cynthia Fuchs Epstein, Robert Sauté, Bonnie Oglensky, and Martha Gever, "Glass Ceilings and Open Doors: Women's Advancement in the Legal Profession," *Fordham Law Review* 64, no. 2 (1995): 331, accessed January 19, 2014, http://ir.lawnet.fordham.edu/flr/vol64/iss2/2.

63. Ibid., 332.

64. David Dupree, "U.S. Men's Basketball Falls Flat on World Stage," *usatoday30.usatoday.com*, last modified August 16, 2004, accessed January 19, 2014, http://usatoday30.usatoday.com/sports/olympics/athens/basketball/2004-08-15-us-puerto-rico_x.htm.

65. Ibid.

66. "USA Basketball Names Jerry Colangelo USA Men's Sr. Team Managing Director," *nba.com*, last modified April 27, 2005, accessed January 19, 2014, http://www.nba.com/suns/news/colangelo_usab_050427.html.

67. Eric Williams, "Jerry Colangelo Is Making the Right Selections for the U.S. Team," *Voices.yahoo.com*, last modified March 25, 2006, accessed January 19, 2014, http://voices.yahoo.com/jerry-colangelo-making-right-selections-for-27021.html?cat=14.

68. Brent Adamson, Matthew Dixon, and Nicholas Toman, "Why Individuals No Longer Rule on Sales Teams," *HBR Blog*, January 9, 2014, accessed January 19, 2014, http://blogs.hbr.org/2014/01/why-the-individual-no-longer-rules-in-sales/?utm_source=feedburner.

69. Michael Lewis, *Moneyball: The Art of Winning an Unfair Game* (New York: W.W. Norton, 2003).

70. Sian Beilock, "The Best Players Rarely Make the Best Coaches: Why Those Who Do Can't Teach," *Psychology Today: Choke* (blog), August 16, 2010, http://www.psychologytoday.com/blog/choke/201008/the-best-players-rarely-make-the-best-coaches.

71. Andris A. Zoltners, P. K. Sinha, and Sally E. Lorimer, "Think Twice Before Promoting Your Best Salesperson," *HBR Blog*, July 6, 2012, accessed January 19, 2014, http://blogs.hbr.org/2012/07/think-twice-before-promoting-your-best/.

72. This list of 35 characteristics is a combined list of characteristics submitted by these leaders and 35 additional partners from professional service firms.

73. Claire Damken Brown and Audrey Nelson, *The Gender Communication Handbook: Conquering Conversational Collisions between Men and Women* (San Francisco, CA: Pfeiffer, 2012); Diana K. Ivy, *GenderSpeak: Personal Effectiveness in Gender Communication*, 5th ed. (New Jer-

sey: Pearson Education, 2012); *Sex Differences and Similarities in Communication*, 2nd ed., ed. Daniel J. Canary and Kathryn Dindia (New York: Taylor, 2006); Janet Holmes, *Gendered Talk at Work: Constructing Gender Identity through Workplace Discourse* (Malden, MA: Blackwell, 2006).

74. Aggressive (Men); Determined (Both); Effective (Men); Friendly (Women); Helpful (Women); Loyal (Both); Reluctant (Women); Strong (Men); Tenacious (Men)

75. *Merriam-Webster OnLine*, s.v. "compete," accessed January 25, 2014, http://www.merriam-webster.com/dictionary/compete.

76. *Merriam-Webster OnLine*, s.v. "collaborate," accessed January 25, 2014, http://www.merriam-webster.com/dictionary/collaborate.

77. See, for example, Melissa Hines, *Brain Gender* (New York: Oxford University Press, 2004); Louann Brizendine, *The Male Brain* (New York: Broadway Books, 2010).

78. John Coates, *The Hour between Dog and Wolf: Risk-Taking, Gut Feelings and the Biology of Boom and Bust* (New York: Penguin Press, 2012).

79. Ibid., 21.

80. Re:Gender (formerly National Council for Research on Women), *Women in Fund Management: A Road Map for Achieving Critical Mass—and Why It Matters* (New York: NCRW, 2009).

81. Ibid.

82. William H. Alden, "Want Better Hedge Fund Returns? Try One Led by a Woman," *New York Times: Dealbook Blog*, January 15, 2014, http://dealbook.nytimes.com/2014/01/15/want-better-hedge-fund-returns-try-one-led-by-a-woman/?_php=true; Rothstein Kass Institute, *Women in Alternative Investments: A Marathon, Not a Sprint—For Women Fund Managers, Endurance Trumps Pace* (New York: Rothstein Kass, 2013).

83. Re:Gender, *Women in Fund Management.*

84. Jane Goodman-Delahunty, Par Anders Granhag, Maria Hartwig, and Elizabeth F. Loftus, "INSIGHTFUL OR WISHFUL: Lawyers' Ability to Predict Case Outcomes," *Psychology, Public Policy, and Law* 16, no. 2 (2010): 133–57.

85. Abhijit Barua, Lewis F. Davidson, Dasaratha V. Rama, and Sheela Thiruvadi, "CFO Gender and Accruals Quality," *Accounting Horizons* 24, no. 1 (2012): 25–39.

86. Ibid.

87. Walter B. Cannon, *The Wisdom of the Body* (The United States of America: W.W. Norton, 1932); Walter B. Cannon, *Bodily Changes in Pain, Hunger, Fear and Rage* (New York: Appleton-Century-Crofts, 1929).

88. Shelley E. Taylor, Laura Cousino Klein, Brian P. Lewis, Tara L. Gruenewald, Regan A. R. Gurung, and John A. Updegraff, "Biobehavioral Responses to Stress in Females: Tend-and-Befriend, Not Fight-or-Flight," *Psychological Review* 107, no. 3 (2000): 411–29; Shelley E.

Taylor, *The Tending Instinct: How Nurturing Is Essential to Who We Are and How We Live* (New York: Henry Holt, 2002).

89. Coates, *The Hour between Dog and Wolf*, 271.

90. Anita Williams Woolley, Christopher F. Chabris, Alex Pentland, Nada Hashmi, and Thomas W. Malone, "Evidence for a Collective Intelligence Factor in the Performance of Human Groups," *Science* 330, no. 6004 (2010): 686.

91. Ibid., 688.

92. George Bush, Phan Luu, and Michael I. Posner, "Cognitive and Emotional Influences in Anterior Cingulate Cortex," *Trends in Cognitive Sciences* 4, no. 6 (2000): 215–22; Michael I. Posner and Gregory J. DiGirolamo, "Executive Attention: Conflict, Target Detection, and Cognitive Control," in *The Attentive Brain*, ed. Raja Parasuraman (Cambridge, MA: MIT Press, 1998).

93. Julie A. Markham and William T. Greenough, "Experience-Driven Brain Plasticity: Beyond the Synapse," *Neuron Glia Biology* 1, no. 4 (2004): 351–63, accessed January 25, 2014, http://dx.doi.org/10.1017/s1740925x05000219.

94. Uri Gneezy, Kenneth L. Leonard, and John A. List, "Gender Differences in Competition: Evidence from a Matrilineal and a Patriarchal Society," *Econometric Society* 77, no. 5 (2009): 1637–64.

95. Ibid.

96. Muriel Niederle and Lise Vesterlund, "Do Women Shy Away from Competition? Do Men Compete Too Much?," *Quarterly Journal of Economics* 122, no. 3 (2007): 1067–1101.

97. Uri Gneezy, Muriel Niederle, and Aldo Rustichini, "Performance in Competitive Environments: Gender Differences," *Quarterly Journal of Economics* 118, no. 3 (2003): 1049–74.

98. Peter J. Kuhn and Marie Claire Villeval, "Are Women More Attracted to Cooperation than Men?" (working paper, National Bureau of Economic Research, No. w19277, 2013).

99. Ibid.

100. Evren Ors, Frédéric Palomino, and Eloic Peyrache, "Performance Gender Gap: Does Competition Matter?," *Journal of Labor Economics* 31, no. 3 (2013): 443–99.

101. Ibid.

102. Ibid.

103. Radosveta Ivanova-Stenzel and Dorothea Kübler, "Courtesy and Idleness: Gender Differences in Team Work and Team Competition" (working paper, Humboldt University, Collaborative Research Center, 649, 2005).

104. Ibid.

105. Muriel Niederle and Lise Vesterlund, "Gender Differences in Competition: Evidence from a Matrilineal and a Patriarchal Society," *Negotiation Journal* (October 2008): 447, accessed January 25, 2014, http://www.pitt.edu/~vester/NJ2008.pdf.

106. George Ritzer and Douglas J. Goodman, eds., *Sociological Theory*, 6th ed., s.v. "Agency-Structure Integration" (New York: McGraw-Hill, 2003).

107. Ibid.

108. Sheryl Sandberg , *Lean In: Women, Work, and the Will to Lead* (New York: Knopf, 2013), 42.

109. Kathleen L. McGinn and Nicole Tempest, "Heidi Roizen" (case study, Harvard Business School, HBS Case Collection 800-228, 2010, http://www.hbs.edu/faculty/Pages/item.aspx?num=26880.

110. Ibid.

111. Laurie A. Rudman and Peter Glick, "Feminized Management and Backlash toward Agentic Women: The Hidden Costs to Women of a Kinder, Gentler Image of Middle Managers," *Journal of Personality and Social Psychology* 77, no. 5 (1999): 1004–10.

112. For a good summary of this research, see the PBS documentary on connection and happiness at http://www.pbs.org/thisemotionallife/topic/connecting/connection-happiness.

113. Gail Collins, *When Everything Changed: The Amazing Journey of American Women from 1960 to the Present* (New York: Little, Brown, 2009).

114. Lilly J. Goren, *You've Come a Long Way, Baby: Women, Politics, and Popular Culture* (Lexington: University Press of Kentucky, 2009), 139.

115. Jere Longman and Juliet Macur, "For Women's Road Records, No Men Allowed." *New York Times*, sec. Sports, September 21, 2011, accessed January 26, 2014, http://www.nytimes.com/2011/09/22/sports/for-womens-road-records-only-women-only-races-will-count.html?_r=2&.

116. Scott Pollack, "What, Exactly, Is Business Development?," *Forbes: Entrepreneurs* (blog), March 21, 2012, http://www.forbes.com/sites/scottpollack/2012/03/21/what-exactly-is-business-development/.

117. Neal Kielar, "Sales vs. Business Development: Match the Toolkit to the Business Model for the Right Results," *Agency Babylon* (blog), May 18, 2012, http://agencybabylon.com/2010/05/18/sales-vs-business-development-similar-objectives-but-different-approaches-measurement/.

118. Scott Pollack, "What Does a Biz Dev Person Actually Do?," *Forbes: Entrepreneurs* (blog), March 28, 2012, http://www.forbes.com/sites/scottpollack/2012/03/28/what-does-a-biz-dev-person-actually-do/.

119. Cathy Benko and Bill Pelster, "How Women Decide," *Harvard Business Review*, September 2013.

120. Trulia Trends Team, *Is Real Estate a Man's or Woman's World?* (2011), accessed January 26, 2014, http://trends.truliablog.com/2011/10/is-real-estate-a-mans-or-womans-world/.

121. Ibid.

122. Daniel H. Pink, *To Sell Is Human: The Surprising Truth about Moving Others* (New York: Penguin Group, 2012).

123. Jim Collins, *Good to Great: Why Some Companies Make the Leap . . . and Others Don't* (New York: HarperCollins, 2001).

124. Laurie A. Rudman, "Self-Promotion as a Risk Factor for Women: The Costs and Benefits of Counterstereotypical Impression Management," *Journal of Personality and Social Psychology* 74, no. 3 (1998): 629–45.

125. Sophia Dembling, "Are Men Better at Selling Themselves?," *gradPSYCH Magazine*, November 2011, accessed January 26, 2014, http://www.apa.org/gradpsych/2011/11/cover-men.aspx.

126. Ibid.

127. Ibid.

128. Ibid.

129. Laurel Bellows (American Bar Association President), interview by Sue Tomchin, "The Largest Voluntary Professional Association's Leader Explains Why She's Making Combating Human Trafficking the Priority of Her Administration. Q&A: Laurel Bellows, American Bar Association President," *Jewish Woman Magazine*, Fall 2012, http://www.jwmag.org/page.aspx?pid=3408.

130. Debra Cassens Weiss, "'Talking about Work-Life Balance Is Fraud' Says ABA President Laurel Bellows," *ABA Journal: Women in the Law* (blog), April 8, 2013, http://www.abajournal.com/news/article/aba_president_laurel_bellows_talking_about_work-life_balance_is_fraud/.

131. Victoria Pynchon, "ABA President, Scorning 'Work-Life' Balance, Abandons the Profession's Women," *Negotiation Law Blog*, April 11, 2013, http://www.negotiationlawblog.com/american-bar-association-president-scorns-idea-of-work-life-balance/.

132. Susan T. Fisk, Steven L. Neuberg, and Mark P. Zanna, "A Continuum of Impression Formation, from Category-Based to Individuating Processes: Influences of Information and Motivation on Attention and Interpretation," *Advances in Experimental Social Psychology* 23 (1990): 1–74, http://www.sciencedirect.com/science/article/B7J09-4S86G6G-5/2/f6761d92f23b3d1c3ab8b598289efe48.

133. Corinne A. Moss-Racusin and Laurie A. Rudman, "Disruptions in Women's Self-Promotion: The Backlash Avoidance Model," *Psychology of Women Quarterly* 34, no. 2 (2010): 186–202.

134. James L. Hilton and John M. Darley, "The Effects of Interaction Goals on Person Perception," *Advances in Experimental Social Psychology* 24 (1991): 235–67.

135. IAB and TA editorial, "Top Female Accounting Leaders Share Their Views on Gender," *The Accountant* (blog), March 8, 2013, http://www.theaccountant-online.com/news/iabta-exclusive-top-female-accounting-leaders-share-their-views-on-gender/.

136. Ibid.

137. Paolo Rossetti, "Gender Differences in E-mail Communication," *Internet TESL Journal* 4, no. 7 (July 1998): n.p., accessed March 2014, http://iteslj.org/Articles/Rossetti-GenderDif.html.

138. Warren Buffett, "Warren Buffett Is Bullish . . . on Women," *Fortune*, May 2, 2013, http://money.cnn.com/2013/05/02/leadership/warren-buffett-women.pr.fortune/index.html.

139. Ibid.

140. Mike Schultz, John E. Doerr, and Lee Frederiksen, *Professional Services Marketing: How the Best Firms Build Premier Brands, Thriving Lead Generation Engines, and Cultures of Business Development Success*, 2nd ed. (Hoboken, NJ: RAIN Group, LLC, 2013); Michael W. McLaughlin, *Winning the Professional Services Sale: Unconventional Strategies to Reach More Clients, Land Profitable Work, and Maintain Your Sanity* (Hoboken, NJ: John Wiley, 2009); Mike Schultz and John E. Doerr, *Rainmaking Conversations: Influence, Persuade, and Sell in Any Situation* (Hoboken, NJ: John Wiley, 2011); Andrew Sobel and Jerold Panas, *Power Questions: Build Relationships, Win New Business, and Influence Others* (Hoboken, NJ: John Wiley, 2012).

141. Many resources are available for women (and men) who want to become more empowered to negotiate on their own behalf or learn more about focused business development activities: Sara Holtz, *Bringing in the Rain: A Woman Lawyer's Guide to Business Development* (Kindle [self-published]: 2008), a great step-by-step guide to business development that is specifically written for female lawyers but is useful for women in other professional service industries as well; Linda Babcock and Sara Laschever, *Ask for It: How Women Can Use the Power of Negotiation to Get What They Really Want* (Kindle [self-published], 2008); Lois P. Frankel, *Nice Girls Don't Get the Corner Office: 101 Unconscious Mistakes Women Make That Sabotage Their Careers* (New York: Warren Business Books, 2004). These are all great resources for women who want to learn more practical tips to enhance their skills in asking for what they want.

142. C. M. Steele and J. Aronson, "Stereotype Threat and the Intellectual Test Performance of African-Americans," *Journal of Personality and Social Psychology* 69 (1995): 797–811; C. M. Steele, S. J. Spencer, and J. Aronson, "Contending with Images of One's Group: The Psychology of Stereotype and Social Identity Threat," in *Advances in Experimental Social Psychology*, ed. M. Zanna (San Diego, CA: Academic Press, 2002).

143. Steven J. Spencer, Claude M. Steele, and Diane M. Quinn, "Stereotype Threat and Women's Math Performance," *Journal of Experimental Social Psychology* 25 (1998): 4–28.

144. C. Good, J. Aronson, and J. A. Harder, "Problems in the Pipeline: Stereotype Threat and Women's Achievement in High-Level Math Courses," *Journal of Applied Developmental Psychology* 29 (2008): 17–28.

145. Lee W. Frederiksen, *Professional Services: How Buyers Buy* (Reston, VA: Hinge, 2009), accessed January 19, 2014, http://www.hingemarketing.com/uploads/How-Buyers-Buy.pdf.

146. Das Narayandas and Robert G. Eccles, *Building Client Management Capabilities in Professional Service Firms: Q&A with HBS Professors Das Narayandas and Robert G. Eccles* (Boston, MA: Harvard Business School Executive Education, 2009), accessed February 27, 2014, http://www.exed.hbs.edu/assets/Documents/facultyqabcmc09.pdf.

147. Interestingly, the ostrich has always been falsely accused of burying its head in the sand. It actually pokes its head into the sand to make sure that its eggs are okay and to turn the eggs for better maturation, but while it is doing this, it is clearly unaware of the approach of potential predators.

148. United States v. Jewell, 532 F.2d 697 (9th Cir. 1976).

149. James A. Belasco and Ralph C. Stayer, *Flight of the Buffalo: Soaring to Excellence, Learning to Let Employees Lead* (New York: Warner Books, 1993).

150. Esther D. Rothblum, "Leaving the Ivory Tower: Factors Contributing to Women's Voluntary Resignation from Academia," *Frontiers* 10, no. 2 (1988): 14–17.

151. Carol Schmidt, "Bragging Rights: MSU Study Shows That Interventions Help Women's Reluctance to Discuss Accomplishments," *Montana State University News* (blog), January 10, 2014, http://www.montana.edu/news/12368/bragging-rights-msu-study-shows-that-interventions-help-women-s-reluctance-to-discuss-accomplishments.

152. Amy Cuddy, Caroline A. Wilmuth, and Dana R. Carney, "The Benefit of Power Posing before a High-Stakes Social Evaluation," Harvard Business School Working Paper No. 13-027 (September 2012), p. 3, http://dash.harvard.edu/bitstream/handle/1/9547823/13-027.pdf?sequence=1.

153. Ibid.

154. Amy Cuddy, "Your Body Language Shapes Who You Are," *TEDGlobal 2012*, http://www.ted.com/talks/amy_cuddy_your_body_language_shapes_who_you_are.html.

155. Claire Cain Miller, "In Google's Inner Circle, a Falling Number of Women," *New York Times*, sec. Business Day: Technology, August 22, 2012, accessed February 27, 2014, http://www.nytimes.com/2012/08/23/technology/in-googles-inner-circle-a-falling-number-of-women.html?pagewanted=all&_r=0.

156. Arin N. Reeves, "Diversity in Practice: The Power of the Pronoun," *Chicago Lawyer*, April 1, 2011, accessed February 27, 2014, http://www.chicagolawyermagazine.com/ Archives/2011/04/The-power-of-the-pronoun.aspx.

157. For more coverage of this story, see "A Class Divided," *Frontline*, PBS, http://www.pbs. org/wgbh/pages/frontline/shows/divided/.

158. Sylvia Ann Hewlett, Kerrie Peraino, Laura Sherbin, and Karen Sumberg, *The Sponsor Effect: Breaking Through the Last Glass Ceiling* (Harvard Business Review and Center for Work-Life Policy, 2010).

159. Kate Ashford, "The Lolita Effect: Are Male Execs Too Nervous to Mentor Young Women?," *LearnVe$t* (blog), May 2, 2013, http://www.learnvest.com/2013/05/ are-male-executives-too-nervous-to-mentor-younger-women/.

ACKNOWLEDGMENTS

"In the end, though, maybe we must all give up trying to pay back the people in this world who sustain our lives. In the end, maybe it's wiser to surrender before the miraculous scope of human generosity and to just keep saying thank you, forever and sincerely, for as long as we have voices."
—Elizabeth Gilbert (Eat, Pray, Love:
One Woman's Search for Everything
Across Italy, India and Indonesia)

I have, without a doubt, been a beneficiary of what Elizabeth Gilbert calls the *miraculous scope of human generosity*, and I have learned and realized that this generosity cannot ever truly be captured in one "thank you." Being the recipient of another person's generosity – whether it is their time, energy, thoughts or positive emotions – amazes me every time it happens, and I will continue to say thank you, forever and sincerely, for as long as I have a voice.

This book, along with anything and everything else I've done, is possible because of so many people who believe in me – stubbornly so – even at times when I doubt myself. You know who you are, and I hope that you also know how deeply grateful I am to each you. I am especially grateful to those of you who gave your time, your thoughts, you tears, your laughter, your frustrations, your hopes and so much more to this study...this book is your book. I hope that I have honored your stories with honesty, integrity and gratitude. A storyteller is only as good as the stories that people trust you to tell. Thank you for trusting me to tell your stories. I look forward to continuing this journey of change with each of you. Tim, thank you for your faith in my ability to write this book well and your push to make it better! Your vision helped me see more and write better!

Eric, you really are the bestest best friend and life partner I could have ever asked for, and I continue to be amazed at how much possibility and promise you see in every idea I have...even (especially) the craziest ones! I so appreciate how quickly you transitioned from "You can't be serious about writing this book by that deadline!" to "Okay, what do we need to do to make this happen?" You have inspired me, kept me sane, pushed me to get on the treadmill when I started to lose it, made me a drink when I did lose it and after all that, you read draft after draft and gave me the feedback that I needed to hear even if I didn't always want to hear it. I love you "more than you know." Thank you for sharing this adventure of life with me and for giving me the gifts of your friendship, love, strength and laughter every day! Ilya, a

Caelan and Miles, I don't know where to start in expressing my gratitude to you, so let me start with the history of bacon. According to etymological scholars, 'bacon' is derived from the Old High German bacho, meaning "buttock", "ham" or "side of bacon", or from the Saxon era in the 1st millennium AD (it was possibly spelled bacoun back then referring to a specific cut of pork belly and pork loin and mostly cut from breeds of pig that had been specifically bred to make what we now call back bacon). The return of the "butt" cannot be a coincidence, can it? You both are truly the most amazing kids I know (in my totally unbiased opinion), and I am grateful for who you are, how much you teach me and how you continue to make life more interesting every single day. Thank you for holding me accountable for my page counts, helping me print drafts, working with me to carve out writing time and generally being infinite sources of inspiration, laughter and the best hugs in the universe. I love you both so much. Love, Mommy

In a year where death visited our friends and family unexpectedly and too often, expressing gratitude has become a daily habit, a prayer to end each day and start the next one. Krista, Henry, Jordan, Sydnee, Tonya, Kevin, Grace, Abosede...you all sustain me more than you know. For my family – I know it's not always easy to be there for an introvert with OCD, and I thank you for hanging in there. Ricarda and Kristy – thank you for being there way in the beginning of this research! For those to whom we have had to say goodbye in recent months, I thank you for the love you gave while you were here and the legacies you left that demand more from all of us.

Debbie, you were 2 when we went through this journey before, and you are 5 now. I cannot believe how fast time flies! You are one of the strongest and smartest people I have had the fortune to meet, and the grace with which you share that strength and intelligence with others is amazing. Thank you for sharing that strength and intelligence with me and our team. Your friendship is a gift I treasure, and yes, I would say that even if I wasn't scared of you…which I am. Jess, thank you for everything you did to get this project going and keeping it on track. I cannot believe that this went from idea to reality so fast, and I so value how much you contributed to shaping the ideas, helping me gather the research and pushing me to think and write big. I wish you much strength and wisdom as you pursue your passions and dreams. To the rest of the Nextions team (past and present), thank you for sharing your talents with us. Every contribution has mattered, and you will always be a part of the work we do.

I am grateful to the researchers, scholars, writers, practitioners and visionaries who have worked and continue to work to find the elusive pathways to equality in our workplaces. I am honored to share this journey with you, and I am hopeful that all of our efforts collectively will slowly but surely catalyze the change we seek.

Finally, my gratitude for you, the readers, is infused with the hope that the stories you encounter in this book will spark insights for your own journeys. Thank you for allowing me to have this conversation with you.

All my best,
Arin

INDEX